THE PRINCETON REVIEW

High School
Global Studies
Review

THE PRINCETON REVIEW

High School Global Studies Review

BY **KAREN LURIE**

RANDOM HOUSE, INC.
New York 1998
www.randomhouse.com

Princeton Review Publishing, L.L.C.
2315 Broadway, 3rd Floor
New York, NY 10024
E-mail: info@review.com

ISBN 0-375-75079-7

Editor: Lesly Atlas
Production Editor: Amy Bryant
Designer: Illeny Maaza
Production Coordinator: Meher Khambata
Illustrations: The Production Department of The Princeton Review

Manufactured in the United States of America on recycled paper.

9 8 7 6 5 4 3 2 1

First Edition

ACKNOWLEDGMENTS

The author would like to thank Lesly Atlas, Amy Bryant, Karma Lurie, Evan Schnittman, Melanie Sponholz, Patricia Acero, Matthew Covey, Adam Hurwitz, and Evelin Sanchez-O'Hara.

Special thanks to Bob Carlina, Charles Cross, and James P. Farkas, the Global Studies teachers who lent their extremely valuable assistance reviewing this project.

To Robert Schakenberg: I give you...the world.

CONTENTS

INTRODUCTION

WHAT THIS BOOK IS

Five thousand years of world history! Well, not exactly. This book is a review of ninth and tenth grade social studies, touching on everything you need to know to do well in the Global Studies course, or on any standardized test on world history. If social studies teachers and test writers think it's important, it's mentioned here.

WHAT THIS BOOK ISN'T

This book does not contain every detail of world history. If it did, you wouldn't be able to lift it right now! There are whole countries, even a whole continent (Australia), that aren't mentioned in it, plus a complete lack of information about the United States of America and Canada. That's because those places aren't covered in the Global Studies course. If you feel a culture or a person isn't getting its props in this book, don't yell at us; the people who write the syllabi and the tests decide who and what should be covered, so they determined who and what gets mentioned in here. You might as well only review what you need to know, right?

HOW TO USE THIS BOOK

Read through it to see what you know, or at least recognize, and what you don't. If you come across anything that looks totally foreign to you, look it up in your textbooks to get all the details. That includes vocabulary; your textbooks probably have comprehensive glossaries.

MAKING CONNECTIONS

Making connections is what social studies is all about and what history teachers want you to learn to do. For example, if you're reading about World War I in Eastern Europe, think about what was going on in Western Europe at the same time. Or, connect to a region's history. For example, if autocracy existed in a region's past, as in, say, Czarist Russia, Communism might make more sense to the people there than would democracy. Autocratic government would translate better into Communism than it would into democracy—it's just about making connections.

Or, how about this? Karl Marx said that economics is the engine of history; here's how to connect economic need to big changes:

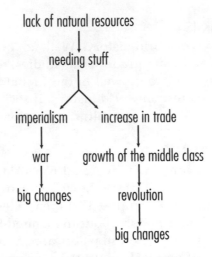

CULTURAL DIFFUSION

The biggest connection that you should be aware of in the Global Studies course is cultural diffusion, which occurs when different cultures share with or influence each other. Cultural Diffusion is promoted by trade, aid, migration, conquest, slavery, war, and even entertainment. There isn't a culture that exists that hasn't been influenced or changed by diffusion. Keep it in mind.

OTHER STUFF YOU NEED TO KNOW

The Global Studies course has eight units. Seven focus on specific regions, and the eighth outlines the major world problems of today. This book is broken down the same way. Throughout the book, there are certain words, phrases, topics, and issues that you need to have crackling in your head, because they are all over the tests.

THE ELEVEN BIG WORLD ISSUES

War and Peace

Population

Hunger and Poverty

Political and Economic Refugees

Environmental Concerns

Economic Growth and Development

Human Rights

World Trade and Finance

Determination of Political and Economic Systems

Energy: Resources and Allocations

Terrorism

THE FIFTEEN BIG GLOBAL CONCEPTS

change: a variation or alteration of an existing situation

choice: determining a preference for a particular idea or system (usually economic)

citizenship: the duties, rights, and privileges of a member of a state or nation

culture: the common habits, art, and institutions of a group of people

diversity: something characterized by many different groups or situations

empathy: the ability to understand other people's problems and points of view

environment: the conditions and circumstances surrounding a group or event

human rights: just and fair claims to natural, traditional, or legal powers and privileges

identity: the set of behavioral or personal characteristics by which an individual is recognizable as a member of a group

interdependence: being mutually influenced or controlled by similar forces

justice: fair and reasonable administration of laws

political systems: specific structures for governing society

power: capability to act decisively in situations

scarcity: limits on quantities of goods and resources causing the need for choices

technology: the practical application of scientific principles for productive uses

Learn them.

HOW THIS BOOK WORKS

The chapters are divided up the way your syllabus probably is, into regions:

- "Africa" means sub-Saharan Africa; the parts of North Africa that are considered part of the Middle East are in the chapter on the Middle East.

- "South and Southeast Asia" means India and surrounding areas, and Vietnam, Indonesia, and the Philippines, and surrounding areas.

- "East Asia" means China, Korea, and Japan.

- "Latin America" means all of South America, Central America, Mexico, and the Caribbean.

- "Middle East" means parts of Asia, Europe, and Africa.

- "Western Europe" means the parts of Europe that aren't in the other chapters, or the parts of Europe that weren't under Soviet rule.

- "Russia and Eastern Europe" means the eastern half of Europe and the lands that were once included in the former Soviet Union.

WHAT'S IN A NAME?

"The West" refers to nations on three continents that share a common cultural tradition that goes back to ancient Greece and Rome, that are mostly Christian, and that have similar cultural biases: Western Europe, the United States and Canada, and Latin America. The term "Western" distinguishes them from the cultures of Asia, Africa, and the Middle East.

In September 1995, the U.S. State Department recommended the use of the term "Central Europe." But many of your teachers are still using the terms *Western Europe* and *Eastern Europe*, even though this might reflect a "Cold War mentality." The same could be said of the term *Third World*, which came into common use early in the Cold War. It referred to those nations that refused to align themselves with either the anti-Communist bloc, including, of course, the U.S. (the "First World") or the Communist bloc, including the USSR (the "Second World"). Now that the prevailing view is that there is only one world, *Third World* has been replaced with *developing nations*.

But since these terms aren't necessarily reflected in the classroom, they don't necessarily appear in this book.

Okay, let's get started.

Africa

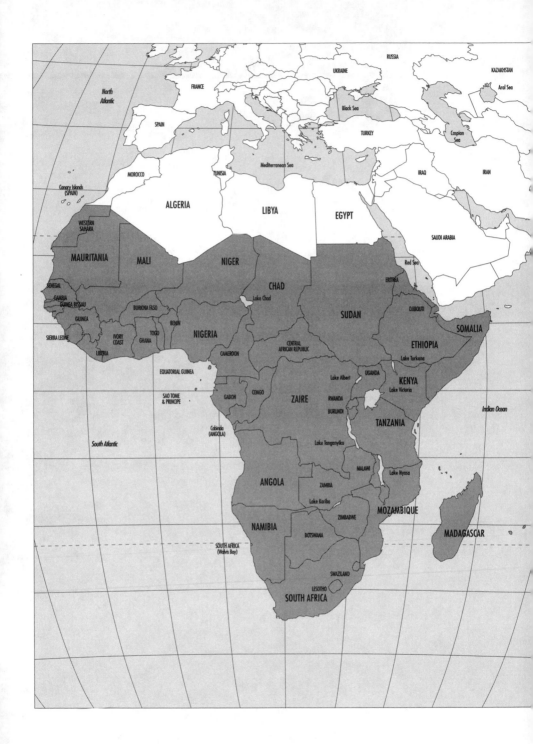

GEOGRAPHY

For many years, Africa was known as the "Dark Continent" because so little was known about it. Let's get to know Africa in the physical sense. It's the second largest continent in the world; only Asia is bigger. In fact, Africa is three times the size of the continental United States. The equator pretty much cuts it in half (Africa is the only continent through which the equator and both tropics—The Tropic of Cancer and the Tropic of Capricorn—pass). It contains 20 percent of the world's land surface, but only 12 percent of the total world population. Africa is surrounded by major bodies of water, including The Indian Ocean, the Atlantic Ocean, the Mediterranean Sea and the Red Sea; so there are water connections to the north, east and west. This is important because this is how the ancient people were able to trade with other cultures. The Indian Ocean enabled trade with India, Southeast Asia, and China, the Mediterranean enabled trade with Europe, and the Red Sea enabled trade with Arabia, as well as a route for cultural diffusion, especially in terms of the religion of Islam. In the northeast is the Suez Canal, which is a major route for the transport of crude oil between the Persian Gulf nations and Europe. Africa's central location between two major oceans allowed it to exchange its human and physical resources with people and cultures on other continents, and influenced its role in the world. We're primarily concerned in this chapter with sub-Saharan Africa, because the Middle East gets a chapter of its own.

Okay, let's talk land. In the middle of the continent there's the tropical rainforest of West and Equatorial Africa; above and below that is the savanna of the Sudan and Central and Southern Africa, then above and below that is the steppe (flat, treeless plain). Then there are the deserts: the Sahara, the Namib (on the southwestern coast), the Kalahari (the south-central section), and then the Mediterranean zone. Tropical rainforests are hot and rainy year-round, and they discouraged European settlement. Savannas are hot and rainy in summer and hot and dry in winter, full of coarse grass and sparse tree growth. About 50 percent of the African continent is savanna, which didn't attract Europeans either, but it does support the well-known wildlife of the continent. Nearly 45 percent of the continent is desert or dry steppe; of course, deserts are hot and dry all year round, and that didn't attract the Europeans either. However, the Mediterranean zone did, as did the highlands because of the good soil (but we'll get to mountains in a minute).

DESERT

The Sahara is the largest desert in the world; in fact, it's larger than the whole continental United States. It takes up one third of Africa. The Sahara was not always a vast wasteland. Before climate changes during the Ice Age, it was a watered grassland with vegetation and animals. The Sahara is inhabited by nomads (people who move around searching for grazing land for their animals) and seminomadic peoples and those who settled in oases. This desert affected intercontinental and intracontinental trade and commerce; if you couldn't get across it, you couldn't sell your wares on the other side. Camels, animals that can store water in their humps, made crossing the desert possible. Ancient Africans and Middle Eastern peoples owe a lot to those lumpy doe-eyed mammals.

Deserts are also a big deal because of desertification. Desertification is caused by the overuse by farmers of semiarid land next to a desert (the steppe) to make up for low crop yields from poor soil, overgrazing by cattle and goats, and overcutting of trees for firewood. The result? With no grass or tree roots to hold topsoil in place, it blows or washes away, and the desert advances. The hardest hit region is the Sahel, the steppe area south of the Sahara, which includes the countries of Mauritania, Mali, Niger, Chad, Sudan, and Ethiopia. Some of the solutions to the problem of desertification include crop rotation to prevent the soil from wearing out, terracing to prevent rain from washing soil away, and tree belts to stop erosion and hold the soil in place.

Speaking of soil, Africa's isn't great. Too much rain in some areas, like the tropical rainforest, causes leaching, or the washing away of nutrients; too little rain, like in drier areas, and the nutrients decompose. Africa needs water management.

TOPOGRAPHY

There are mountains (the highest is Mt. Kilimanjaro at 19,340 feet), lakes (Chad, Victoria, Tanzania, Malawi), and river systems (Niger, Nile, Zambesi, Congo). The north-south river system of the Nile (which will be revisited in the Middle East chapter) is the world's longest river, and its source is at Lake Victoria, which is the largest lake in Africa. The rivers were not navigable all the way to trade centers, because of falls and rapids, and that affected ancient trade. There are no north-south river systems south of the Sahara, like the Mississippi River in the United States, that might have united the continent. The coastline is smooth, so there are no natural harbors. The Great Rift Valley is a large canyon in Eastern Africa stretching from Ethiopia to Mozambique. This valley acted as a barrier, and forced people in East Africa to move in a north-south direction. Some of the oldest objects made by humans have been found in the Great Rift Valley. The various geographical factors in Africa gave rise to over 2,000 culturally distinct societies and more than 1,000 languages. This is how geographic factors promote cultural diversity.

Africa does have natural resources; in tropical areas there are peanuts, bananas, rubber, tea, coffee, cotton, all stuff that the Europeans wanted. Africa is also rich in minerals, like petroleum, bauxite, uranium, tungsten, cobalt, tin, and zinc.

AGRICULTURE

Barriers to the development of agriculture in sub-Saharan Africa included the scarcity of water, the limited use of natural resources, the lack of proximity of resources to market outlets, and the absence of plows, axes, and drills to help with the soil. Another problem was Tsetse flies, which made susceptible horses and oxen unusable in much of the sub-Sahara regions. Early farmers used trial and error; they adapted crops and animals to suit the environmental conditions and overcome geographical limitations.

As an agricultural region with developing nations, Africa is considered part of the third world. Africa is the source of 80 percent of the world's diamond production, and almost 50 percent of the world's gold. Nigeria is the eighth largest producer of oil and the second largest supplier of petroleum to the United States. Congo is one of the largest producers of zinc, and Zambia is fourth in production of copper. Rubber is grown in substantial quantities in Nigeria, Liberia, and Congo.

SOCIETY

There are all kinds of people and languages in Africa. The Bantu languages of sub-Saharan Africa are the most widely spoken. Swahili, a mixture of Arabic and Bantu, is spoken in East Africa. The Khoisan (click) languages are spoken by the Bushmen and Hottentots. Hausa is a common language in West Africa, as is Arabic in North Africa. Also spoken in Africa are English and French, since those countries did the most colonizing in Africa.

Sub-Saharan Africans consider themselves members of particular ethnic groups, or tribes. An individual belongs to the extended family, which belongs to the clan, which belongs to the tribe. Marriage is seen as a union of two families, not two individuals. Polygamy is permitted, though the more urban-oriented a person is, the more monogamous that person is, unless that person can afford polygamy. Polygamy is limited by bride-wealth which is a gift given by the groom to the bride's family to make up for the loss of her work. They believe bride-wealth brings status to the bride and helps guarantee the marriage will last. Many urban Africans return to the rural areas for ceremonies.

RELIGION

One religion that a lot of sub-Saharan people practice is called animism. Animism is a belief that spirits and forces of nature exist in all living and non-living things. It includes ancestor worship and divine kingships (diviners or medicine men who counsel and heal people). According to this tradition, the land was held in trust by the ancestors and could not be owned.

Animism is what most ancient African people believed in; then came Islam. Islam started in the deserts of the Arabian Peninsula in the seventh century and was spread by cultural diffusion (more details in the Middle East chapter). There were conversions, holy wars or jihads in the nineteenth century, and the formation of theocratic states in West Africa. In this century there have been Progressive and Fundamentalist Islamic movements. Islam is the fastest growing religion in the world. Its diversity and accommodating structures enabled Africans to blend Islamic with non-Islamic practices. Islam also contributed to greater uniformity of laws and the objective dispensing of justice, as well as helping to increase trade and market activity. Studying the Koran led to a new class of educated leaders. Islam was a uniting force.

There is also Coptic Christianity, which was brought to the Sudan or Nubia by Egyptian missionaries and made its way to Axum (an early civilization you'll learn more about shortly) in the fourth century, where it was adopted as the official religion in Ethiopia and Nubia. These and later missionaries demanded reorientation of thought and behavior that was a total change for Africans. People resisted, and independent church movements followed. In the 1400s and 1500s, Portuguese and Spanish explorers were accompanied by missionaries; they did not convert many. By the end of the nine-teenth century, with the establishment of Christian schools, Europe-ans had carved up Africa and Christianity came to be associated with colonial regimes. Millions converted, for both spiritual and practical reasons. Being "saved" sure sounded appealing, and Afri-cans soon learned that training at the mission schools was necessary if they wanted to get involved in economic and governmental activi-ties. They used what they learned at those schools to become nation-alistic leaders during the Independence Era.

THE ARTS

Traditional African Art is both utilitarian and sacred in nature. Art is used for communication with the spiritual world and protection against evil forces. Africans believe masks possess spiritual powers when worn during religious ceremonies. The design of African masks has influenced the style of masks worn by goalies in hockey. Masks also inspired the art of Pablo Picasso and Henri Matisse, twentieth century European artists. In painting and sculpture, the emphasis is on the human head because of the importance given to the inner self. Bright, geometric colors are used, which again influ-enced Picasso. Sculptures are representations, so they don't have to be too realistic, and the material mostly used is wood.

Art helps provide societies with an identity, as does literature, dance and music. African history and literature are based on oral tradition. Each ethnic group has a griot, or storyteller, who passes the group's history on to the next generation. The key theme in the literature is the traditional versus the modern, a struggle the people have been wrangling with for a long time. African dance is generally symbolic and has strong ties to traditional religions. African music is polyrhythmic, meaning "many rhythms." See, Western music usually has a maximum of two rhythms at the same time. African music can have as many as five. Drums are very important in the music and in communicating messages between villages

A TIMELINE OF AFRICAN HISTORY

3000 B.C.–A.D. 1600	Rise of African Kingdoms and Empires
1400s	Arrival of Europeans on West African Coast
1500–1800	Peak of African Slave Trade
1870–1945	European Domination in Africa
1950s–1990	African Independence

EARLY HISTORY

There were many geographical obstacles to human, plant and animal migrations that encouraged migration within the continent and discouraged extracontinental cultural contact. But Africa is still the birthplace of man. Recent archaeological discoveries in Ethiopia, Kenya, and Tanzania suggest that modern man originated in Africa and first developed basic technology there. Evidence indicates that there were human-like creatures in Africa as many as 5 million years ago, and that humans may have developed there 1.75 million years ago.

EARLY CIVILIZATIONS

Let's look at some of the early civilizations, starting in East Africa. The Kush developed as early as 2000 B.C. The Iron Age began here in about 500 B.C.; it may have been brought to Kush from a Middle Eastern people known as the Assyrians. Kush developed along the Nile at the same time that Ancient Egypt did, and it conquered Egypt in 750 B.C., which gave it control over an empire stretching from the Mediterranean to present-day Ethiopia. After the decline of Kush around A.D. 200, power shifted to nearby Axum, which originated in the coastal region of modern-day Ethiopia in about 300 B.C.; they were Semitic, had their own language, and they converted to Christianity in A.D. 324. Today's Ethiopians trace their Christian heritage to Axum.

The Kongo reigned in Central Africa in the late fourteenth century; the kingdom disintegrated when the Portuguese arrived in 1482 looking for slaves. The Zimbabwe (a Bantu word meaning "great stone house") reigned in southern Africa, perhaps as early as the sixth century; we don't really know what happened to them, but some of the buildings of this early kingdom still stand in the present-day nation of the same name. In West Africa, along the Niger River, there was Ghana, which developed in 300 A.D., and had a profitable trade in gold and salt between A.D. 400 and 1200. Ghana collapsed and was absorbed by Mali, which developed between 1200 and 1450. After civil wars weakened Mali, it was replaced by Songhai, which lasted until it was conquered by Morocco in 1590. The university at the capital of Timbuktu was a great center of Islamic learning, and the Songhai controlled sub-Saharan trade routes and traded gold and salt with North Africa, Europe, and the Middle East. North Africans had contact with Greeks, Semites, Romans, and Indonesians, so there was cultural diffusion all around.

SLAVERY

Slavery has existed since the development of civilization, but its importance in the development of Africa is immeasurable. The first African slaves to be transported by slave ships to Europe were taken by the Portuguese in the fifteenth century, but when the Caribbean and North America were discovered later in that century, the need for slaves became greater. It is estimated that 50 million Africans died as a result of the slave trade, mostly from disease aboard slave ships, and that 15 million Africans were brought to the Americas as slaves. It was the largest forced migration in world history.

Getting slaves was the Europeans' primary interest in Africa; they had tried to enslave the Native Americans they found in the "New World," but that was commercially unsuccessful because the Native Americans didn't survive the labor. Cultural diffusion was a result of the triangular trade that was established, which worked as follows: Cheap European goods were shipped to Africa and traded for slaves; slaves were shipped to the Americas, and traded for sugar and tobacco, which went back to Europe and were sold for considerable profit. The money the Europeans made this way later made the Industrial Revolution possible.

The effects of the slave trade were numerous. There was depopulation, increased tribal warfare, insecurity and fear among Africans. There was economic disruption and decay, and trans-Saharan trade was destroyed; it lost its importance, and the kingdoms in the interior of West Africa declined. And of course, there's the racism that continues everywhere around the world to this day, stemming from the belief that somehow these people are inferior to others, so it was "okay" to enslave them.

THE ERA OF COLONIZATION

The Industrial Revolution changed things for everyone. Dramatic technical breakthroughs in the West, especially in the nineteenth century, facilitated the exploration of Africa and made conquest safer and quicker. The development of guns allowed Europeans to conquer Africa within a 35-year period. By 1914, all of Africa except Ethiopia and Liberia (named after the people liberated from U.S. slavery who arrived there in the 1800s) was under European control.

The racist legacy of the slave trade, combined with technological superiority in the West, brought about false doctrines of racial inequality, which in turn rationalized all the conquest and subjugation that was going on. The "White Man's Burden" was the racist belief that it was the duty of Europeans to expose Africans to Christianity and Western culture, though their true objectives were power and profit. Africans met these encroachments with conventional and guerrilla warfare, passive movements, or subservience, acting as mercenaries under European leadership.

Some European chartered companies included the British West Africa Company, the Dutch East Indies Company, and the French East India Company. Great Britain and France took most of the continent, but Spain, Portugal, Belgium, Italy and Germany also took some. This scramble for Africa began after King Leopold of Belgium announced he was taking control of the vast Congo Free State in Central Africa in 1879. In 1885, at the Berlin Conference, European nations reached an agreement on how Africa should be divided. These decisions had nothing to do with the ethnic groups of the people already living there; the "borders" they made were random. In partitioning the continent, Europeans arbitrarily drew new national boundaries that cut across historical, ethnic, and cultural lines. Boundary disputes are still a major obstacle to the achievement of unity in Africa today.

Types of Colonial Rule

The British practiced indirect rule: Tribes were used as intermediaries to pass on the rules of the colonial regime. The French had a policy of assimilation, where everyone "became" French. The Portuguese used a similar technique. The Belgians used paternalism, treating the Africans like children. The Germans varied their approach, sometimes forcing labor, and other times using indirect rule. The colonial powers established a system of mercantilism, which required the colonies to buy and sell only to them, thus enabling them to export more than they imported and build up economic profit. Since Africans were encouraged to raise cash crops and were forced to buy more expensive finished products from the "mother" countries, most African nations did not accumulate any capital reserves for themselves. Keep this in mind.

The Effects of Colonial Rule

Besides the lack of capital, there were many other effects of European rule, both good and bad. Preventative medicine and improved nutrition were introduced (which is good), which led to a lower infant mortality rate (also good) and a population explosion (which isn't so good). There was a dramatic increase in agricultural production with new seeds and fertilizers (which is good), which led to an overemphasis on export-related crops, stagnation in food crop production, and the importation of staples that used to be domestically grown (not good). There was a transition from subsistence farming to commercial agriculture (good), which led to the exploitation of raw materials (not good). There was improved transportation and communication, including railroads, which pretty much destroyed the notion of communal land ownership, and opened up remote regions to economic development (good), but which led to forced labor and abuse of human rights, and weakened family and group ties by the acceleration of labor migration (not good). There was a transition from the barter system to a currency system, which stimulated market development, but which created greater disparities of wealth, and heightened social tension. There was greater educational opportunity and a greater choice of careers, but the available Eurocentric education was unrelated to the developmental needs of Africans and downgraded the indigenous culture of the area. There were also new judicial systems established, including uniform codes, the separation of religious and secular laws, and the abandonment or modification of customary legal procedures.

Overall, the colonial era made Africa less self-sufficient, but ultimately contributed to unity by forging different ethnic and political units into larger entities. It also gave the people something to rebel against.

THE END OF IMPERIALISM

World War II (1939–1945) marked the beginning of the end of the colonial era in Africa. Many Africans fought in that war to defeat the Nazis and Fascists, and the war itself weakened racist arguments.

The war also weakened the Europeans, who were too busy recovering from it to be able to deal with their colonies. Also, Asian countries like India and Pakistan had achieved independence. The United Nations helped Africa to achieve independence with the 1941 Atlantic Charter, signed by President Franklin Roosevelt and Great Britain's Prime Minister Winston Churchill on August 14, advocating self-determination. African nationalism shifted the political power from Europeans to young, Western-educated, urban-oriented Africans.

The first country to achieve independence from Great Britain was the Gold Coast, which became Ghana in 1957 under the leadership of Kwame Nkrumah. The Ivory Coast achieved independence from France in 1960 under Felix Houphouet-Boigny. Between 1960 and 1970 there were over thirty revolutions and independence movements throughout the continent. By 1977 there were more than 40 independent nations in Africa. Colonialism officially ended with Namibia's independence in 1990.

Of course, there were problems. The inability of some governments to gain or maintain legitimacy in the eyes of its citizens led to coups d'état (revolts by military leaders to overthrow the government) and the imposition of authoritarian and xenophobic (fear and hatred of foreigners) military rule, like Idi Amin's Uganda in 1971. There were also debts and famines to deal with, not to mention conflicts within tribes. In some African nations, both World Wars led to the erosion of participatory democracy, as well as corruption and nepotism, because authoritarian single-party rule prevented the development of democratic states.

European and American ethnocentrism stimulated Africans to search for their roots and strive for a cultural identity. There was a transition from extended family to nuclear family, a weakening of lineage and kinship bonds, and a transition to monogamy. Also, the role of women was changing, and urbanization brought many changes as well. With the new-found independence came a clash between African Nationalism (patriotism within each nation) and Pan-Africanism (the quest to unite all of Africa, which really started in 1960). In 1963, the Organization of African Unity was formed to promote Pan-Africanism; one founder was Julius K. Nyerere, president of Tanganyika or Tanzania, from 1961 when it achieved independence, to 1985 (more about Tanzania later).

Let's look at some examples of how some countries in Africa attained their independence:

Kenya—Jomo Kenyatta of Kenya was the leader of the nationalist movement, and he became president of the Kenya African Union in 1947. A group called the Mau Mau, created in 1952, used terrorist and guerrilla activities to free Kenya from the British. In 1956 the British began gradual reforms, and finally granted independence to Kenya in 1963. In 1964 it became a republic in the British Commonwealth of Nations with Kenyatta as president. He ruled democratically until his death in 1978. There are still many problems in Kenya, such as human rights violations and overpopulation.

Nigeria—One out of six Africans is Nigerian. Nigeria has many different groups making up its population; the Hausa and Fulani in the North, the Ibo in the southeast, and the Yoruba in the southwest. The British expanded into the area in the mid-nineteenth century; by 1914 Nigeria was a British colony. Nationalism in the country arose after World War I. The British relaxed their rule and in 1954 a constitution was drawn up creating a federal union ensuring the power of the three major regions: east, west, and north. Independence was granted in 1960. Because of the different regions, there have been civil wars, and since 1970, frequent military coups.

South Africa—Conflict in South Africa dates back to the earliest Dutch settlers in the 1600s. In 1815, Holland agreed to give up control of its South African colony to the British, who were interested in it for naval reasons. Unwilling to be governed by foreigners, though, the Dutch farmers, or Boers (Dutch for farmer; also called Afrikaners) moved farther north, away from the British-controlled areas near the coast. Eventually the discovery of gold and diamonds in the inland Boer-controlled areas led to the Boer War (1899-1902); the British wanted to control the gold mines in the interior, where the Afrikaners had settled, and they went to war, which the British won. In 1910, the British united all of the colonies in the area into the Union of South Africa. In 1948, the Afrikaners, who outnumbered the British, gained control of the government. They established apartheid, which literally means *apartness*. Blacks comprised 68 percent of the population, yet they were denied citizenship and access to public facilities. Separate homelands (called *bantustans*) were supposedly set aside for them, but most of the nation's territory was reserved for the white minority, which amounted to less than a fifth of the population.

The African National Congress (ANC) was formed in 1912; it was the first group to advocate fundamental rights for black Africans.

The ANC was declared illegal in 1960, and its leader, Nelson Mandela, was imprisoned. There were demonstrations and riots, like the Soweto riots in 1976. Black activist Steven Biko was killed in 1977 during a police interrogation in jail. There was international response in the form of trade sanctions; South Africa lost its voting privileges in the United Nations in 1974. In 1986 the United States congress passed sanctions against South Africa. In 1989, F.W. de Klerk became president of South Africa, and in 1990 he lifted the ANC ban and released Mandela from jail after twenty-eight years. There were negotiations between Mandela and De Klerk to end apartheid in 1992, in 1993 they both received the Nobel Peace Prize, and in April 1994 South Africa's first multiracial election resulted in Mandela's presidency. Economic, ethnic, and political problems remain to be solved in his coalition government.

NEOCOLONIALISM

Since the mercantilist system left the African nations with little capital reserves, when they became independent, the nations had to borrow from the superpowers and former colonial nations. This is called neocolonialism. Africa relies on imported manufactured goods, and the bulk of its trade is with Europe. Money problems also result from the emphasis on urban development at the expense of the rural, the lack of housing, and the growth of the urban middle class. Also, ethnic rivalries prevent people from working together for progress. In some cases, loan money was wasted on stuff like statues designed to promote national pride, and in other cases, the money was just stolen by corrupt leaders.

MIXED ECONOMIES

Conflicting ideological and economic goals led to the creation of mixed socialist/capitalist economies, where the major stuff is nationalized, and the smaller stuff and agriculture remain in private hands. No African nations have been successful in creating pure socialist or capitalist systems. Some countries with mixed economies are Kenya, Nigeria, Angola, Zambia, and Uganda. Multinational corporations serve local needs in the countries. There has been success in industrial and petroleum output, but agricultural production still lags, and food must be imported.

TANZANIA

Let's look at Tanzania as an example of the economic struggle of an African nation. Julius K. Nyerere founded the Tanganyika African National Union in 1954, and introduced a socialist system called ujamaa (meaning family, sharing). In 1964, Tanganyika and Zanzibar merged to form Tanzania. In 1967, a program was created to nationalize industries and plantations and create cooperative farms out of villages. In the 1970s, the rising cost of petroleum products hurt them, and there were problems with ujamaa. The country suffered droughts in 1980 and 1984, and it had to appeal for international aid. Nyerere resigned in 1985.

CASH CROPS

Only five products—cocoa, coffee, cotton, peanuts, and items from palm trees—account for 80 percent of Africa's agricultural output. The problem with relying on cash crops is that it makes one vulnerable when international prices fluctuate. Price drops, drought, and crop failure are all problems of cash crop economies. Also, countries don't raise enough food for themselves, because they're too busy raising it for others. Dependence on cash crops has continued, in part, because of the structure of international tariffs. Western Europe and North America often impose high tariffs on processed or finished goods coming in from other nations to protect their own native industries, and impose low tariffs on raw materials. This pattern has discouraged African nations from developing their own industries to process their own raw materials, so they receive only a small share of the profits made from their raw materials.

There is a lack of industry in Africa due to unstable political situations, outdated transportation systems, lack of capital, and a shortage of skilled workers and technology. There are also limited energy resources, except for water, but Africa doesn't have the money to develop hydroelectric power.

OVERPOPULATION AND URBANIZATION

Africa is overpopulated in some areas. There's a lack of access to health and education services, and there's been an improvement in life-expectancy rates, which leads to a high population growth rate. Traditional beliefs call for large families, so the birth rate is still high, and sometimes families have children so they can help in the fields and to provide social security by caring for elders, especially since better medical care has decreased the death rate. People are migrating to urban areas to find employment, but the migration exceeds the number of jobs. Urbanization can also lead to the breakdown of ethnicity, causing crises in personal identity and alienation. There are big differences between the "haves" (the rising middle class) and the "have-nots" (the unemployed rural immigrants), and this leads to frustration and unrest.

FOOD

Over 70 percent of Africans are still engaged in agriculture, and rely on subsistence farming. Not everyone can be fed, so people use their time finding food instead of for more productive pursuits. Desertification (which was discussed earlier), deforestation (most Africans still use wood as a source of fuel) and soil erosion also cause problems in growing food, plus there are weak government incentives for domestic producers. There is also the lack of water, and the cost of drilling and irrigation technology is high. Events like the Live Aid concerts and Ethiopia's reforestation project help, but, at times, attempts to improve the situation were interrupted by civil wars, like those in Ethiopia, Sudan, Mozambique, Chad, and Somalia. These wars resulted in a decrease in food production, which contributed to famine. Rival factions in Africa and tribal ethnic power struggles often use food and its distribution as weapons against each other.

Much of Africa is stuck in the cycle of poverty: Low income leads to low savings, which leads to low capital investment, which leads to low productivity, which leads back to low income.

FOREIGN RELATIONS

African countries make up about one third of the United Nations, so they can make a difference. For example, South Africa relinquished the occupation of Namibia as a result of the African countries of the UN voting as a bloc. In fact, they are the most powerful voting bloc, with about fifty members.

Outside of the United Nations, most of Africa's other external alliances have to do with money. They include the 1975 Lome Convention between the European Economic Community (EEC) and forty-six African, Pacific, and Caribbean countries, the Commonwealth of Nations (former British colonies), the Council for Mutual Economic Assistance (CMEA), and the World Bank and the International Monetary Fund (IMF). The Organization of Petroleum Exporting Countries (OPEC) also has four African states: Algeria, Gabon, Libya, and Nigeria.

The United States has helped with food aid, military assistance (there are military bases in Kenya, Somalia, and Liberia), the Peace Corps (since the 1960s), and multinational corporations. Black Africans have had difficulty reconciling American ideals of human rights with the racism that still goes on in the United States, but the divestment and sanctions against South Africa have helped the United States' reputation.

NONALIGNMENT?

Africa has a status of *nonalignment*, meaning it is not politically aligned with any other nation, power, or continent. However, persistent economic crises have forced many African countries to maintain close diplomatic links with former colonial nations and compromise the nonalignment status. Since independence, nations' leaders have designed their foreign policies to prevent Africa from becoming a theater of the Cold War. But deep international divisions with certain countries have led to direct involvement, sometimes making them battlefields for the now-ended Cold War. Let's look at some examples:

THE CONGO CRISIS OF THE SIXTIES

The Belgian Congo became independent in June of 1960. The Province of Katanga, under the leadership of Moise Tshombe, seceded and declared its independence. Belgium sent troops, and the prime minister of the Congo, Patrice Lumumba, sent for Soviet aid. The Soviets sent weapons, transport equipment, technicians and advisers. This Soviet influence scared some Congolese and most Western nations, who encouraged the president of the Congo to dismiss Lumumba. An army leader, Joseph Mobutu, ordered the Soviets to leave the country, and in 1961, Lumumba was assassinated. Meanwhile, the Katanga rebellion continued, with Tshombe using European and South African forces to resist a UN peacekeeping force. An agreement to end the secessionist movement was finally reached, and the UN troops left in 1964. Tshombe was elected president, but in 1965 he was overthrown in a military coup led by Mobutu. In 1971 Mobutu took command and changed the country's name to Zaire, which it was called until 1997, when Mobutu was overthrown by Laurent Kabila, and the name was changed to the Democratic Republic of Congo.

FRENCH MILITARY INVOLVEMENT IN CHAD

Chad gained its independence in 1960 and Francois Tombalbaye became president. Chad had a sparse population, and was mainly Christian in the south and Muslim in the north (Tombalbaye was a southerner). Rebellion broke out in the north and east in 1965 and soon turned into civil war. In 1975 a military coup overthrew the government, but another southerner took control. The conflict continued, and France got involved and supported the south. The north asked Libya for help, and Libya sent troops. In 1981, foreign troops were withdrawn, and in 1982, civil war broke out again. Again, Libya entered for the north, and France and Zaire entered for the south. In 1984, France and Libya agreed to leave, but Libya didn't leave, thereby violating that agreement. In 1987, the government launched an attack against northern and Libyan forces, and got back control of everything except a small strip of land where Libya has an air base. Then, in 1990, a Libyan-supported group overthrew that government, and their leader became president.

ETHIOPIA

Ethiopia had always maintained its independence, except for a short time during World War II when Italy occupied it. Emperor Haile Selassie ruled Ethiopia from 1930 to 1974 (Jamaican Rastafarians see Selassie I as their spiritual leader and Africa as their spiritual home). The United States gave the emperor aid and assistance, partly because of the country's strategic location on the Red Sea. In 1974 Selassie was overthrown. The army began making socialist reforms, and land was taken from rich and given to peasant associations. In 1976, there was a military agreement with the Soviet Union, and U.S. military advisors were expelled. Ethiopia and Somalia have had border disputes since Somalia became independent in 1960, which is why Somalia turned over a military base to the United States (more on Somalia later).

ANGOLA

Angola became independent in 1975. Three rival groups fought for control of the country and there was civil war. The Popular Movement for the Liberation of Angola (MPLA) was supported by the Soviets and Cuba; the National Front for the Liberation of Angola (FNLA) was supported by the United States, France, and Zaire; the National Union for the Total Independence of Angola (UNITA) was supported by Portugal, China, South Africa, and white Angolans. By 1976, the MPLA had won, and established a state with Soviet backing and Cuban support troops. However, the United States continued to support the UNITA rebels. In 1991, terms of an agreement worked out by President Mobutu of Zaire got the last Cuban troops to leave Angola. Later that year, UNITA signed a treaty with the government to end the sixteen-year civil war. UNITA rejected the election results in 1992, and fighting started again. In 1993, the United States recognized the government of Angola for the first time since 1975.

RWANDA

The lingering tension between two groups, the Hutus and the Tutsis, exploded in 1994 when the Hutu president died in a mysterious plane crash. The Hutus blamed the Tutsis, and the resulting fighting is said to have caused 500,000 deaths. Refugees seeking to escape to Zaire met with food shortages, cholera and dysentery.

SOMALIA

The Somali Republic became independent in 1960. There was a coup in 1969, and the country came under the rule of General Mohammed Siyad Barrah. In 1991, Barrah fled the country, and there was fighting between rival clans to gain control. There was also drought and famine to contend with, and people were not getting relief supplies. In November of 1992, the Bush administration volunteered troops for the UN force there to protect relief workers, and the UN authorized U.S. forces to use any means necessary to get relief to the needy. This pressure resulted in the signing of a peace treaty by the two most powerful clan leaders in December 1992. Early in 1993, the agreement was broken, and fighting resumed. In June 1993, Pakistani members of the UN peacekeeping forces were killed and General Mohammed Farah Aidid, one of the most powerful clan leaders in the capital of Mogadishu, was blamed. Attacks were carried out against Aidid's weapons caches and his supporters' holdings. Aidid was targeted for capture, but not caught. In October, members of the peacekeeping forces were killed, including eighteen Americans. An American was captured and interrogated by Aidid's forces, and video excerpts from those interrogations were broadcast worldwide. More American forces were ordered to Somalia, but it was announced that all American forces would be withdrawn by 1994.

MODERN AFRICA

Today on the continent of Africa, rural areas hang on to traditional values, and most Africans still rely on the land. Clashes with traditional ideas come from increased education, communication (like television), industrialization, and Western ideas of democracy.

South and Southeast Asia

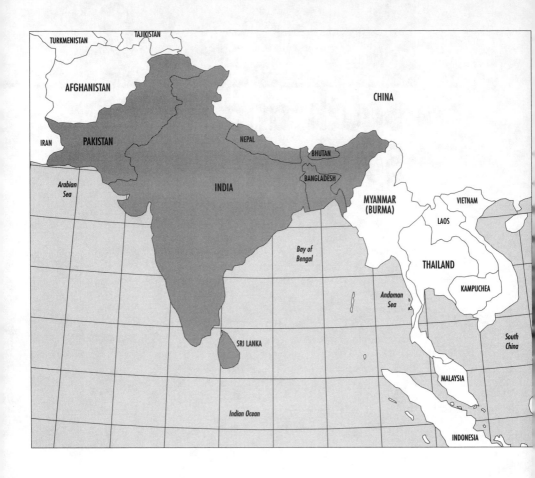

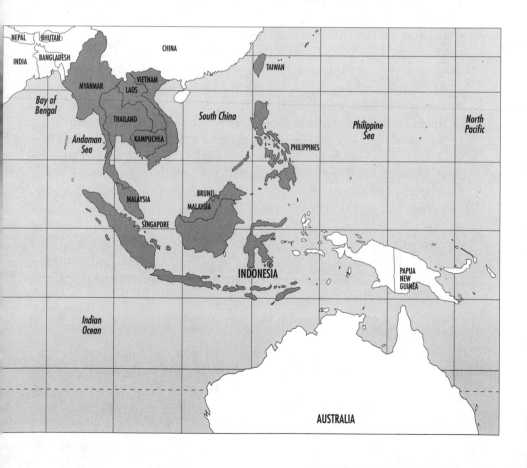

GEOGRAPHY

Let's start with south asia. India is on a subcontinent, which is a large area of land separated from the rest of the continent by a natural barrier. In India's case, the Himalayan and Hindu Kush mountains separate it from the rest of Asia, causing a certain amount of isolation. India is bigger in size and population than all of Western Europe. It is slightly less than half the size of the United States, yet its population is three times that of the United States. The other nations on the subcontinent are Pakistan, Bangladesh, Sri Lanka, Nepal, and Bhutan (where television is banned!). India is the largest nation on the subcontinent, forming a peninsula with the Bay of Bengal to the east, the Arabian Sea to the west, and the Indian Ocean to the south. India is the second oldest continuous civilization on earth (China is the oldest).

Southeast Asia lies between India and China. There are two main areas: Indochina, which is a peninsula that juts out into the Indian Ocean and the South China Sea; and the several archipelagos to the south and east of that peninsula. Indochina is made up of Myanmar (or Burma), Thailand, Cambodia (Kampuchea), Laos, Vietnam, part of Malaysia, and Singapore at the southernmost tip. The island nations (there are over 20,000 of them!) include the rest of Malaysia, Brunei, Indonesia, and the Philippines. Their location exposed them to the cultures of India and China. The two surrounding oceans, the Indian and the Pacific, brought people from almost everywhere, which is why the cultures of Southeast Asia are referred to as a "patchwork quilt." There are many native ethnic groups: Khmers in Cambodia, Chams in Vietnam, and Malays in Indonesia, Malaysia, and the Philippines. There are also Europeans, Indians, and a lot of Chinese in the urban areas, who are referred to as hua-chiao, or "overseas Chinese." Southeast Asia's land portions total about half the area of the United States. Indonesia is the fourth largest nation in the world. The ten Southeast Asian nations contain more people than all of North America.

TOPOGRAPHY

The Himalayan mountains served as a barrier for India. They are the highest in the world (the famous Mt. Everest is there). All of the rivers flow out of the northern mountain ranges. Rivers include the Indus in the west, and the Ganges, which flows from the Himalayas to its ten mouths on the Bay of Bengal. The greatest population density in India is along the Ganges River and on the Ganges plain. The Deccan Plateau is in central India, bordered by mountain ranges called the Ghats on the east and west coasts. These mountains separated the people of northern and southern India.

The Mekong River is the longest in Southeast Asia. It originates in Tibet and flows to the South China Sea. The Irrawaddy and Salween Rivers start in Tibet, and flow through Burma. People settled in the river valleys, which is where civilizations tend to develop. Hundreds of volcanoes lie along the arc of the island nations. In fact, Indonesia has more volcanoes than does any other part of the world.

CLIMATE

About 80 percent of India's rainfall comes during a five-month period, when the monsoons come. Monsoons are seasonal winds that sweep across the Arabian Sea and the Bay of Bengal in the spring, picking up water. As they head inland and run into the mountains, the winds drop their rains. The season lasts from June to October. In the winter, December to March, they reverse direction and head back to sea, bringing cool, dry air to India. People in this area are prisoners of the climate.

Pretty much all of Southeast Asia is close to the Equator, which means a tropical climate, like the Caribbean, and lots of rainforests. Southeast Asia is one of the wettest regions on earth. As in India, monsoons can make the difference between a good and a bad harvest.

RESOURCES

India's resources include iron ore, steel, and manganese. The scarcity of natural gas and petroleum has brought about interdependence with the Middle East. India produces about 40 percent of the world's total tea, and 25 percent of the world's total rice, as well as sugar cane, wheat, cotton, and jute. Malaysia has one third of the world's supply of tin, and deposits of bauxite. Indonesia and Thailand also have tin. There's oil in Indonesia, Burma, Brunei and Malaysia. Plantations in Malaysia produce most of the world's rubber. Of course, there are spices, the stuff the Europeans wanted. Rice is the major crop grown in Southeast Asia, and well over half the population farms.

SOCIETY

Because of India's topography, many diverse cultures developed, and there are fifteen major languages (including English) and over 800 dialects. Sixteen languages are recognized, including Hindi in the north, Tamil in the south, Bengali in Bangladesh, Urdu in Pakistan, and Sinhalese in Sri Lanka. The topography of Southeast Asia resulted in a population concentration in rural areas and a dependence on agriculture. That, combined with the fact that the area was a crossroads for trade and migration, led to many diverse cultures and languages. French is spoken in Cambodia, Laos, Vietnam; Spanish and English in the Philippines; English in Myanmar, Malaysia, and Singapore; and Dutch in Indonesia. Of course there are native languages as well, such as Thai, Vietnamese, Burmese, Lao, Malay, Pilipino, and Tagalog. There are more than 100 languages and dialects. In Malaysia, Chinese make up 32 percent of the population; in Singapore (formerly part of Malaysia), Chinese make up 77 percent of the population.

Indians call their country Bharat. India is the second most populated nation on earth; China is first. There are more than 1 million births each month. Most Indians live in a type of extended family called the joint family. The joint family includes married brothers; they all hold property in common, and the younger brothers assume responsibility for educating the older brothers' kids. It's a patriarchal society, and marriage is seen as a union between two families, with the wife usually moving in with the husband's family. This is called patrilocal marriage. Parents often arrange marriages, which is called endogamy, and their choices are determined by the caste system (which we're about to get to). The village is central to the social structure of India. They follow the Jajmani system: a jajman, or landowner, and members of a caste group inherit the service relationship and mutual obligations that their immediate ancestors had. Also, it's common for sons to assume the occupations held by their fathers. All of these traditions lead to a self-sufficient society. In Southeast Asia, the social life centers around the village and the agricultural production of rice; the fact that there are many islands limits travel.

The Caste System

Okay, you can't talk about India without discussing the caste system. It's a system of social stratification, or a ranking of people. It's all based on Hindu beliefs. There are four main varna, or occupational groupings: The Brahmans are a religious class of priests, the Kshatriyas are the warrior class, the Vaisyas are the landowners, merchants, and herders, and the Sudras are the laboring class of servants and peasants. There are also the Harijans, which is a group outside the caste system known as the "untouchables;" they are literally outcasts. This is not considered one of the varna. The Indian constitution banned discrimination on the basis of caste in 1950, but the caste system still influences everything. The untouchables still drink from certain wells and take jobs that the members of no other caste would consider.

There are thousands of subcastes, or jati, within the four varna. The link between varna and occupation is disappearing, and you're not necessarily stuck where you are. A jati lower in ranking may rise in status by adopting more pure ideals, such as vegetarianism. This is called sanskritization. There have been changes in Indian society, such as the extension of the British system of education, including the right of the untouchables to attend school, and constitutional government giving rights to untouchables and women. Urbanization and industrialization also break down the caste system, but it's still really the core of society.

Hinduism

You can't talk about the caste system without discussing Hinduism. It started developing 5,000 years ago, and it's the world's oldest religion. Eighty-three percent of India's population is Hindu. No one person really founded Hinduism; it evolved over a long time, picking up things along the way, and developing into a flexible, tolerant religion that allows for individual differences in beliefs. There's no one sacred book like the Bible or the Koran, but instead there are the Vedas, collections of prayers and verses, written somewhere between 1500 B.C. and 800 B.C. There are also the Upanishads, philosophical descriptions of the origins of the universe, which were written around 500 B.C. Hindus believe in one supreme force called Brahma, who is in all things. Hindu gods are manifestations of Brahma: There's Brahma, the creator; Vishnu, the preserver of life, who is worshipped in the form of Rama or Krishna; and Shiva, the destroyer and recreator of new life, sometimes worshipped as an ascetic doing yoga, or the form of Kali or Durga.

Hindus believe in reincarnation, or samsara, and that people's actions in this life determine reward or punishment in the next life. A person's present caste is reward or punishment for karma, or deeds committed in a previous life. Acceptable Hindu behavior means following the dharma, or the rules and obligations of the caste you're born into. Because of the belief in reincarnation, Hindus practice cremation (you don't need your body anymore anyway, right?). This cycle of life—birth, death, rebirth—continues until you achieve moksha, the highest state of being, perfect internal peace, the release of the soul. Each human occupies a place on the wheel of life, or the mandala, determined by the law of karma. See, it's not just a religion, it's a social system and a way of life. By the way, working with leather is considered a polluting activity, because Hindus revere cows.

Buddhism

India is also the birthplace of Buddhism. Buddhism was founded by a prince named Siddhartha Gautama, who was born and lived in Nepal from 563 to 483 B.C. He rejected his wealth to search for the meaning of human suffering, and he became the Buddha, or Enlightened One, after meditating under a sacred bodhi tree. There is no supreme being in Buddhism. Buddhists believe in the Four Noble Truths: All life is suffering; suffering is caused by desire; desire can be eliminated; and there is a path, or way, to end desire. A Buddhist follows the Noble Eight-Fold Path, which includes "right" speech, action, intentions, livelihood, effort, concentration, and mindfulness. This path helps you to move toward nirvana, the state of perfect peace and harmony. The goal of one's life is reaching nirvana, which may take many lifetimes, so they also believe in karma and reincarnation. Created in opposition to the Hindu caste system, Buddhism dictates that anyone can achieve nirvana without moving through castes. Buddhism spread to China, Korea, Japan, and Southeast Asia; it could easily be adapted to fit their cultures, unlike Hinduism, which needed the correct social structure. The population of Sri Lanka is mostly Buddhist.

There are a few other religions in India. Jainism is practiced by less than 1 percent of the Indian population, and was also created in opposition to Hinduism. Adherents of Jainism believe in nonviolence, that all of nature is alive so nothing should ever be killed, and thus, vegetarianism. It was founded by Mahavira in about 500 B.C. Sikhism is practiced by 2 percent of the population; it was founded by Nanak, around 1500. Adherents of Sikhism believe in monotheism and reincarnation, and they reject the caste system. Sikh males don't cut their hair, and they are mostly members of the warrior class.

Islam (see Middle East for more details) is practiced by 11 percent of the population. Pakistan and Bangladesh, after Indonesia, are the second and third largest Muslim nations in the world. There were waves of Muslim invaders from the eighth to the sixteenth centuries, and the Mughal dynasty brought Islam to India. Christianity, brought by European missionaries during the age of imperialism, is also found in India, as are Jews and Parsees; together they make up no more than 3 percent of the south asia population.

Arab traders brought Islam to Southeast Asia in the 1200s, and the majority of people in Malaysia and Indonesia adopted it. Today, Indonesia is the most populous Muslim nation in the world. In Cambodia, Hinduism influenced the architecture of Angkor Wat, while Buddhism affected the styles of modern temples and dance forms. Because of contact with Arab traders, Islamic culture found its way into Indonesia and Malaysia. Roman Catholicism is practiced in the Philippines, due to 400 years of colonial rule by Spain; the Philippines is the only Christian state in Asia. Animism, or nature worship, is native to Southeast Asia. Most of the people on the mainland are Buddhists. Buddhism spread there when an Indian ruler named Ashoka embraced it and sent missionaries to Southeast Asia and China. There are variations on Buddhism in different parts of Southeast Asia. In Theravada Buddhism, practiced in Cambodia, Laos, and Thailand, one can be released from secular, or worldly, suffering through meditation. Many young men are expected to live part of their lives as monks. In Mahayana Buddhism, practiced in Vietnam and northern Asia, salvation is open to everyone, not just monks, through the achievement of perfect faith. They believe in bodhissatvas, or people who achieved buddhahood but have given up that status to return to earth and help humans.

THE ARTS

In India, all of the arts reveal the strong influence of its three major religions. Hindu temples, like those at Ellora, include carvings that tell important Hindu stories, which can be understood even by those who cannot read. One of the most famous architectural creations is the Taj Mahal in Agra, which was built in the 1600s by the Muslim ruler Shah Jahan as a tomb for his wife.

Religion shows up in literature, too. The *Mahabharata* is an epic poem about the influence of the Hindu deity Krishna. It contains the *Bhagavad-Gita*, a poem prescribing correct Hindu conduct; it describes conflicts between related families and kingdoms. Another famous Hindu poem, the *Ramayana*, also expresses values; written between 400 B.C. and 100 B.C., it's the story of Prince Rama, an incarnation of Vishnu, and his wife Sita. These poems are well known all over the area. Indian music is centered around its melody and a countless variation of notes called ragas. The sitar is an important Indian instrument. Listen to The Beatles (especially George Harrison) to hear the sitar in action. Today, India produces more movies than any other nation in the world. Adventure films and films with religious overtones are the most popular.

AND NOW, SOME TIMELINES

History of India

3000 B.C.–1500 B.C.	Harappan Cilvilization
320 B.C.–A.D. 535	Maurya and Gupta Empires
1526–1857	Mogul Empire
1756–1947	British Rule in India
1947–present	Independence

History of Southeast Asia

800s–1500s	Early Southeast Asian Empires
1500s–1900s	European Imperialism
1945–present	Independence and Nationhood

EARLY CIVILIZATIONS

The earliest people to settle in south asia and India were the Dravidians. Between 1500 B.C. and 500 B.C., the Dravidians were conquered by the Aryans, who came from Central Asia. The blending of Dravidian and Aryan cultures led to Hinduism and the Sanskrit language. Between 3000 and 1500 B.C., the Harappan civilization developed along the Indus River. They built dams and had a well-organized central government. The Maurya Empire (321–185 B.C.)

was a dynasty, which is a hereditary ruling family. This was a well-run empire, with Ashoka the Great as its best-known ruler. Ashoka converted to Buddhism, and during his reign, many Buddhist beliefs were incorporated into Hinduism. The Maurya Empire crumbled after the death of Ashoka. During the Gupta Empire (A.D. 320–535), Hinduism dominated Indian life. There was a lot of progress in the arts and sciences, including the creation of a numeral system with the concept of zero, discoveries in astronomy, and the practice of surgery. The Gupta era became known as the Golden Age of Hindu.

Waves of invasions by the Huns broke the Gupta Empire into small kingdoms, but Hinduism remained strong. Starting in the eighth century, a succession of Islamic invaders brought the Muslim religion to India. By the 1500s, the Mongols founded the great Mongul Empire (1526–1760). From their capital at Delhi, they ruled the country for over 300 years, stimulating a new cultural flowering. British imperial expansion in the 1700s gradually eroded Mongul control.

Before the British got to India, it had a self-sufficient economy based on subsistence farming and the production of hand-woven textiles. Between the eleventh and fifteenth centuries, India was part of the Muslim trading network, which was heavy into the spice trade. Its ports grew, people wanted its raw materials, and Europeans began trading there in the sixteenth century.

In the first century A.D., Indian merchants set up trading centers in Southeast Asia, and brought the Hindu and Buddhist religions with them. The Funan Empire, starting around A.D. 100, was located in Cambodia and southeast Vietnam. This empire controlled trade routes with India and China. The Khmer Empire, a great Hindu-influenced empire from 800 to the 1430s, was in what is now western Cambodia. The Srivilaya Empire, a Buddhist dynasty from the 800s to the 1200s, ruled on the Indonesian island of Sumatra.

THE BRITISH ASSUME POWER

The British East India Company received permission from the Monguls to trade in India as early as 1613. The company had its own private army. The British had a pretty easy time taking over: religious differences (Hindus versus Muslims) in the country kept it from being unified; the Hindu acceptance of karma and dharma prevented the people from resisting; and the caste system was already maintaining social order at local levels. By 1756, the British forced any rivals, particularly the French, from the subcontinent.

COLONIAL RULE

The British used a system of divide and conquer. They undermined efforts by Indian princes to unify, and of course, they had better weapons. They armed Indian soldiers known as *sepoys* to protect British holdings. In 1857, the sepoys revolted when the British disregarded their religious beliefs. The British government suppressed the Sepoy Mutiny (called the "Anglo-Indian War of 1857" by Indians) and took control of India from the East India Company in 1858. British governors took about two-thirds of India directly and closely supervised local Indian princes in the rest. In 1876, England's Queen Victoria was proclaimed Empress of India; the "Crown Colony" of India included Pakistan and Bangladesh.

Any changes were introduced to solidify colonial rule, not to transform the society being ruled. The colonial government improved health conditions, expanded transportation and communication, widened educational opportunities, and treated Indian culture as inferior. There was a shift to world market priorities, which disrupted the supply of locally needed goods and services. Improved health and sanitary conditions increased the population, but didn't expand economic opportunity, because the British took the jobs. Some of these changes, however, did help Indians acquire the background for eventual political and economic independence.

India under British rule exported raw materials and imported manufactured goods. This is the economic system known as mercantilism. The opening of the Suez canal in 1869 made it easier for the British to ship cotton from India to British textile mills. They returned machine-made cloth to sell in India. This selling of imported cloth undermined local production of hand-woven cloth, which put a lot of Indians out of work. The British also placed taxes on Indian-manufactured goods.

But there were also improvements associated with British imperialism. There was an increased amount of farmland due to irrigation, revolutionized transportation through the construction of railroads which could move goods and people cheaply, and the arrival of the Industrial Revolution to India through the construction of steel and Jute mills near Calcutta and textile mills near Bombay. The British also established Western educational institutions and modern medical care, and set up a modern banking system to handle business transactions within India.

MEANWHILE, IN SOUTHEAST ASIA...

The Southeast Asian islands were known as the "Spice Islands" in Europe, or the famous "Indies" that Columbus sailed off to look for. The first Europeans to arrive in Southeast Asia were the Portuguese, drawn there in 1511 by the spice trade, and taking control of the Strait of Malacca. The Spanish landed at Cebu Island, part of the Philippines, in 1521. Eventually, all of Southeast Asia came under European domination except Siam (now Thailand), which remained independent by acting as a buffer state, separating the territories of Britain and France.

Britain took Burma, Malaya, Singapore, Sarawak, Brunei, Northern Borneo, and Southern New Guinea. France took Indochina (present-day Laos, Cambodia, and Vietnam). Germany took Northern New Guinea. The Netherlands took the East Indies (present-day Indonesia). Portugal took Malacca and Timor. Spain took the Philippine Islands. Europeans would import raw materials from the colonies, turn them into manufactured goods in factories at home, then export them to the world as finished products. This prevented economic development in the colonies; it didn't improve the standard of living, either, because cash crops left little time for people living in the colonies to grow their own food.

INDIA UNIFIES

Two centuries of British rule unified India and created a sense of identity. Indians resented being banned from authority, and were wounded by Christian criticism of the Hindu and Muslim religions. In 1885, urban intellectuals educated in Europe from India's middle class formed the Indian National Congress, which became known as the Congress Party. Religious divisions between Hindus and Muslims led to the creation of the nationalist Muslim League in 1906, under the Aga Khan. During World War I, many Indians served with the British, hoping it would loosen colonial bonds, but all it did is make them wonder who they were fighting for. During the 1919 Amritsar Massacre, British troops fired on unarmed Indians attending a political rally. In 1921, the Montagu-Chelmsford Reforms provided for a limited amount of self-government for Indians. In 1935, the Government of India Act let Indian provinces have more control over their own affairs.

GANDHI

Mohandas K. Gandhi, known as Mahatma, or the great soul, organized a mass political movement for independence. He called for broad-based reform, and improved status for women and "untouchables," by employing the following methods: passive resistance (nonviolent noncooperation), civil disobedience, economic boycott (refusal to buy British-made cloth), and hunger strikes. He taught that the people were Indians first, and Hindus or Muslims second.

THE PARTITION

World War II had weakened British control of everything, including the Crown Colony of India, and in 1947, British leaders agreed to Indian demands for independence. To avoid civil war between Hindus and Muslims, the British partitioned the subcontinent into the Hindu nation of India and the Muslim nation of Pakistan. This set off a mass migration, forcing resettlement of millions; Muslim minorities from India and Hindu minorities from Pakistan tried to resettle.

Differences in the religious beliefs of Hindus and Muslims include: Muslims worship only one god, while Hindus worship many; Muslims eat all meats other than pork, while many Hindus are vegetarians, and all Hindus refuse to eat beef (Hindus regard the cow as sacred); Muslims believe in the idea of social equality, while Hindus developed a caste system.

The partition brought about poverty, famine, civil strife, and unresolved territorial claims; thousands were killed in bloody rioting. Gandhi tried to restore peace, but a Hindu fanatic assassinated him in 1948.

POST-GANDHI INDIA

Jawahawlal Nehru, India's first prime minister, steered India through the infancy of its independent nationhood, from 1947 to 1964. The new Indian government was modeled after British rule, retaining democratic institutions. India is currently the world's largest parliamentary democracy. The Indian Constitution of 1950 and its amendments called for total enfranchisement for all over twenty-one, and banned discrimination against people outside the caste system, like the untouchables. India's huge population and economic and political power made it a leader among third world countries.

In 1966, Nehru's daughter, Indira Gandhi, became prime minister, and she ruled with an iron fist. She was turned out of office in 1977 for her suspension of civil liberties, but her successors couldn't achieve their goals, so she was returned to power in 1981. She governed till her assassination in 1984 by two of her Sikh bodyguards, who wanted a separate Sikh state in the Punjab region. Her son Rajiv assumed the office of prime minister and ruled India till 1989, when corruption toppled that government.

The first two prime ministers to follow were V.P. Singh (who only lasted eleven months due to caste and religious upheavals) and Chandra Shekhar, who succeeded him. Rajiv Gandhi was assassinated in 1991, and P.V. Rao became prime minister after Shekhar's government collapsed. Rao's government collapsed after the 1996 elections, in which the Congress Party, which had ruled India since independence, didn't capture the majority of seats in parliament. Who did? The Hindu Nationalist Bharatiya Janata Party (BJP). But, it was unable to assemble a majority in parliament. So, a coalition including the Congress Party formed a new government.

MODERN INDIAN SOCIETY

In Indian society, the village and the caste system remain central to the social structure. There are population issues in India and Pakistan, brought about by huge growth rates and the advantages of large families to farmers, plus the decreased death rates. Increased urbanization affects traditional values. There is better health care and medicine, and attempts to lower the birth rate, such as birth control, monetary incentives for sterilization, and the Hindu Marriage Act, which decrees the minimum age a person can get married is eighteen for men and fifteen for women. The diversity of languages and religions in south asia has made communication and unification difficult; identity in South Asia still is based more on cultural groupings than on national or political loyalty.

INDIA'S AGRICULTURE

Agriculture is still the mainstay of India's economy. Improved irrigation made possible double cropping, which is the planting of two crops a year on the same land. The Green Revolution, an attempt to apply modern technology to persistent problems in agriculture, doubled and tripled India's agricultural output since 1947. Some negative aspects of the Green Revolution included the resistance of the farmers, higher financial costs for machinery, the need for a nationwide infrastructure (including storage facilities, highways, and dams), and the fact that the food tastes different from traditional crops. India no longer depends on trade and foreign assistance for adequate food, but its population has more than doubled, too. So, India still faces the challenge of maintaining self-sufficiency in food production. A significant portion of Indians still live in poverty.

INDIA'S ECONOMY

After independence, a mixed economy was established in India to meet the views of disparate leaders; Gandhi emphasized the village and cottage industries, wealthy industrialists favored free enterprise, and Nehru wanted socialism. Socialist five-year plans were an attempt by the government to increase self-reliance while decreasing foreign dependency.

The single largest obstacle to full economic development in India is its population. Its Gross National Product (the total monetary value of goods and services produced in a year) is one of the highest in the world. But India's per capita GNP (GNP divided by population) ranks among the world's lowest. More than 80 percent of Indian people live in villages. India has to borrow money, and a trade imbalance (where the value of imports exceeds that of exports) exists. India is dependent on foreign capital, which the continuing violence between religious groups sometimes discourages. In 1991 and 1993 India tried to boost its economy by selling off some state-controlled companies, cutting interest rates, and raising the ceiling on executive pay to reduce "brain drain," the migration of skilled and educated people to other nations to gain better jobs and more money.

To encourage industrialization, India set up a reserve bank to control the supply of money in the economy. Economic planning and large, government-owned industries have negatively affected India's ability to compete in world markets. The economy has not kept up with nations in which there is more free enterprise, like Taiwan and South Korea. As a result, the Indian government is allowing more private ownership of industries and encouraging more foreign investment.

Today, India is a democratic republic, like the United States. Its technological progress was demonstrated in 1974 when Indian scientists exploded a nuclear device. The entry of a developing nation into the "nuclear club" signified a major shift in global power.

PAKISTAN AND BANGLADESH

Pakistan has been governed by a succession of military regimes, except for the civilian governments of President Zulfikar Ali Bhutto (1971–1977) and his daughter Benazir Bhutto (1989–1990), who was the first woman ever to lead a Muslim nation. In 1990, Pakistan's president dismissed the government of Bhutto, accusing it of corruption and nepotism; Bhutto said they didn't like her democratic reforms. Mian Nawaz Sharif was the next prime minister, and he did not foster good relations with the United States. Antigovernment demonstrations increased, there were new elections in 1993, and Bhutto returned to power.

In 1971, with military assistance from India, the area called East Pakistan became the independent nation of Bangladesh; three years later, West Pakistan (now Pakistan) agreed to recognize Bangladesh. Tensions over Kashmir, a mostly-Muslim disputed area, remained high. The first prime minister of Bangladesh, Sheik Mujibur Rahman, couldn't deal with it, and was assassinated. There were several coups, including one led by Lt. General Hussain Mohammed Ershad, who then ruled Bangladesh as a military dictator from 1982–1990. He resigned due to protests. There were elections in 1991; Begum Khaleda Zia was elected, and her Bangladesh Nationalist Party (BNP) was victorious.

MEANWHILE, IN SOUTHEAST ASIA...

Prior to World War II, all of Southeast Asia was under foreign control except Thailand (in fact, Thailand is the only Southeast Asian land that was never colonized; its name means "land of the free"). World War II helped end colonialism. While the war raged in Europe, Japan, a country hated as much as the European imperialist countries were, seized much of Southeast Asia. The European powers couldn't hold on in the face of local nationalism; they were drained from the war, and also wanted to comply with the UN charter. The British, weakened by war, freed its colonies in a largely nonviolent transition of political power. Without longstanding traditions of democratic rule, many of these countries adopted military regimes and Communist dictatorships. Let's look at some.

INDONESIA

In 1927, the Indonesian Nationalist Party was formed under the leadership of Achmed Sukarno to achieve independence. The Dutch had reestablished control of Indonesia after the Japanese lost World War II. Sukarno declared independence from the Dutch, and war broke out in 1946 between Indonesia and the Netherlands. In 1949, the Netherlands granted Indonesia independence. Sukarno, whose government had to unite 300 ethnic groups that spoke over 250 languages, remained in office till 1967, when General Suharto took control after an attempted Communist coup d'état. Indonesia has been able to remain politically and economically stable; it is an oil producer, and a member of OPEC.

THE FRENCH-INDOCHINA WAR (1946–1954)

In Indochina, the independence movement was spearheaded by the Viet Minh, a Communist-dominated movement led by Ho Chi Minh, which was formed during World War II. They fought the Japanese occupation with help from the United States and won. The Japanese occupation forces surrendered in 1945, and Ho Chi Minh proclaimed independence, but France wasn't ready to give up. The Viet Minh responded with guerrilla warfare. Great Britain and the United States supported the French, and China and the Soviets supported Ho Chi Minh. The French were defeated at the Battle of Dien Bien Phu in 1954. The Geneva Conference of 1954 created the independent countries of Cambodia, Laos, and Vietnam out of Indochina.

VIETNAM

When Vietnam was created, it was divided into the Communist north and the non-Communist south. This division was supposed to be temporary until general elections were held in 1956, but those elections were never held. The government under Ho Chi Minh took over the north, and the non-Communist government, which was supported by the United States took over the south. In 1960, the Communists in the south formed the National Liberation Front in South Vietnam, known as the Viet Cong, and they conducted a systematic campaign of armed resistance against the government in the south. The United States sent military forces as part of its plan to stop Communism. The Viet Cong and the North got help from China and the Soviets. In 1964, North Vietnamese boats reportedly attacked two U.S. ships in the Gulf of Tonkin; the U.S. Congress adopted the Gulf of Tonkin Resolution, in which President Lyndon Johnson was authorized to take all necessary means to stop the North's aggression. The United States expanded its role in the Vietnam "conflict" as a result. Direct U.S. involvement ended with the Paris Peace Treaty of 1973, in which representatives from the North, South, the United States, and the National Liberation Front got together to end the longest war in U.S. history by calling for the withdrawal of foreign forces and a prisoner-of-war exchange. After the United States withdrew, North and South Vietnam continued fighting, resulting in the April 30, 1975 Communist victory, when North Vietnamese forces overran the south and united the country. The capital of this newly-unified nation was Hanoi; Saigon, which had been the capital of South Vietnam, had its named changed to Ho Chi Minh City. Hundreds of thousands of Vietnamese fled as "boat people."

CAMBODIA

Cambodia had been involved in the Vietnam War as a hideaway from the Viet Cong and Northern troops. After the 1975 victory of the Communists in Vietnam, fighting resumed in Cambodia under the authoritarian rule of Pol Pot, the leader of the genocidal Khmer Rouge, which changed its name to Kampuchea, although no one really calls it that. Under the repressive regime of the Khmer Rouge, it is estimated that over one million Cambodians died in its efforts to restructure society; there were even more who became refugees. (See the movie *The Killing Fields* for the details.) This totalitarian government forced hundreds of thousands of city-dwellers into the country where they often died in work camps. Border clashes with Vietnam led to invasion by the Vietnamese in 1978. With Soviet help, Vietnam conquered Cambodia, Pol Pot was overthrown in 1979, and Vietnam installed a new government. The invasion was countered by a border assault from China, which sided with Cambodia. Vietnamese forces occupied Cambodia until a negotiated settlement ended the war in 1990; guerrilla warfare persists. A coalition government was established to bring everyone together. There was a UN cease-fire in 1991, and UN-sponsored elections, which produced a 120-member National Assembly. The Assembly drew up a new constitution, and Norodom Sihanouk returned as king in an elaborate ceremony in 1993, and a UN-sponsored national election brought to power a coalition government. The Khmer Rouge, however, refused to give up their arms and were excluded from the government. They have resumed their war against that government. Cambodia has the world's highest rate of widows and orphans.

PHILIPPINES

The United States had acquired the Philippines from Spain in 1898 after the Spanish-American War (thus becoming involved in the politics of Southeast Asia), and gave the islands their independence in 1946. In fact, the Philippines was the first Southeast Asian country to gain independence after World War II. Ferdinand Marcos ruled from 1965 to 1986. Martial law was established in 1972, and lasted till 1981. Marcos was very unpopular, and he made himself quite rich. In 1983, opposition leader Beningno Aquino was assassinated. This resulted in widespread demonstrations, which drove Marcos out. In 1986, rebels overthrew the dictatorship of Marcos, who fled into exile (and eventually died in Hawaii in 1989), and democracy was restored under Corazon Aquino. But Aquino faced ongoing Communist insurgency, attempted military coups, and inflation, not to mention a devastating earthquake in 1990. She was president until 1992, when she was succeeded by former defense secretary Fidel V. Ramos.

SOUTHEAST ASIA TODAY

By 1963, when the British left Malaysia and Singapore, nearly every nation was independent, but technically, the colonial period didn't end until 1983, when England gave up its protectorate in Brunei. Many Southeast Asian countries suffer from political repression and economic hardship. Others, like Singapore and Brunei, are quite prosperous. The Sultan of Brunei spent US$450 million to build his palace, the world's largest. The non-Communist nations in the region—Brunei, Malaysia, Thailand, the Philippines, Indonesia, Singapore—formed the Association of Southeast Asian Nations (ASEAN), headquartered in Jakarta, Indonesia in 1967, to protect their interests.

Southeast Asian Economies

Southeast Asian economies are based on agriculture. More than 80 percent of the population work at some type of farming, especially subsistence farming and cash crops, such as rice, rubber, and hardwoods. Rubber trees were introduced into Southeast Asia from Brazil by the Europeans. War-torn economies are hard to manage, and the political turmoil and refugees don't help either. The capitalist countries of Southeast Asia are Singapore, Malaysia, and the Philippines. Indonesia, Cambodia, and Vietnam have centralized control.

The Europeans kept tight control of industry and held the highest-paying economic jobs in the Southeast Asian countries they colonized. So, few Southeast Asians learned the technical skills necessary to manage industry; today, their stuff is still shipped out raw instead of finished. There is generally a low standard of living, except in Singapore (one of the "four tigers;" see the East Asia chapter), which is a processing nation; it imports raw materials and exports manufactured goods, and enjoys prosperity and an 85 percent literacy rate. Crime is limited, perhaps because punishment is so severe.

Foreign Relations
India is the leader of the nonaligned third world countries bloc in the UN. It's an advocate of the nonproliferation of nuclear weapons. India has been practicing nonalignment since Nehru took charge in 1947, but it has accepted help from both the Soviets and the United States. Its friendship with the Soviet Union lasted from the mid 1950s to 1979. The relationship between India and the Soviets strengthened when India adopted central planning for its industries; relations with the United States suffered when the United States supported Pakistan during the India-Pakistan War of 1971 (the war that resulted in the creation of Bangladesh).

There have been many border disputes between India and China. China strained its relations with India when India invaded Tibet in 1950. In 1959, China violently put down the Tibetan revolt, forcing the Dalai Lama (the religious ruler of Tibet) to flee to India for his safety. Also, China took territory bordering India in 1962 and supported Pakistan in the 1971 Bangladesh War. The change in Chinese leadership under Deng Xiaoping helped improve relations with India. Relations are better now with the United States too, especially since there is no more Soviet Union.

The biggest problem facing Indians and Sri Lankans is secessionist movements. In India's Punjab state, the Sikhs want their own nation called Khalistan. Also, there is growing unrest by the Muslim majority in the northern state of Kashmir. Pakistan also challenges India's claims, especially since Pakistan is Muslim. This has caused riots and violence. In Sri Lanka, the Tamil people (who are of Indian origin) want their own state, and Indian troops helped keep peace from 1987 to 1989. There have been cease-fire agreements, which have broken down.

There have been three wars between India and Pakistan so far, brought on by the partition. Pakistan's need for national security has been best served by agreements and alliances with the Western powers; Pakistan was alarmed when Russia invaded Afghanistan.

Southeast Asia has experienced direct involvement in international power struggles, which can be seen clearly in the Vietnam War. Vietnam has since had economic problems; war has drained its treasury, the collapse of the Soviet Union cut the amount of aid it receives, and its productivity has been hurt by centralized planning and its refusal to make changes. In 1990, Vietnam established contacts with the United States; they want peace, they need financial aid, and the United States is willing to help because the United States wants to find MIA/POWs. In 1993 and 1994, U.S. business people and politicians visited Vietnam, trying to normalize relations.

Other Problems in Southeast Asia

In Myanmar, local tribal groups, called Karens, refuse to obey the national government in Yangon (Rangoon). Indonesia has had disagreements with Malaysia about human rights violations. Chinese and Vietnamese antagonism surfaced in 1979 with a short border war. Thailand worried about the spread of Communism from Vietnam, and is also dealing with refugees from Cambodia. It was unstable politically in the early 1990s, had a civilian-led government installed for the first time in sixty years, and recently has seen a huge spread of AIDS among its urban population. Singapore, with its heavy Chinese population, is trying to maintain good relations with Indonesia and Malaysia.

East Asia

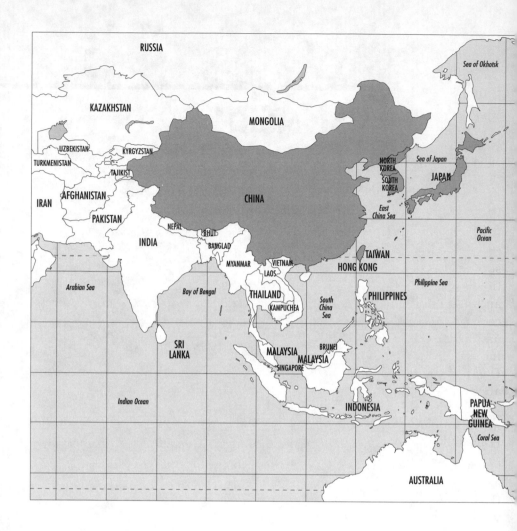

CHINA

GEOGRAPHY
China is the largest country in Asia, and the third largest country in the world; only Russia and Canada cover more territory. It is also the world's most populous nation.

TOPOGRAPHY
This is a big place. The Gobi Desert extends from Mongolia (the world's largest landlocked nation) into northern China. It isolated the Chinese, but didn't necessarily stop all invaders. The Pacific Ocean is to the east, the Himalayas and Tien Shan mountains are to the west, and jungles and the Himalayan Mountains are to the south. These natural boundaries kept China isolated from other nations; keep in mind that two-thirds of its area consists of mountains and deserts. This affected the distribution of people; nearly 96 percent of the population of China lives in the eastern part of that nation, which is known as China Proper. Other mountain ranges include the Altai, Kunlan Shan, and the Altun Shan. Tibet (where the Dalai Lama is from) is on a high plateau between the Kunlan Shan and the Himalayas, and it has the highest elevation of any nation on earth. The Qinling Mountains, in central-eastern China, separate the north and the south, and serve as a cultural dividing line. The Himalayas separate China from India.

Most of China's rivers start in the western mountains, head east and empty into the Pacific. There are the Chang (Yangtze), the Xi (Hsi), and the Huang (Yellow; flooding has left fertile deposits of yellow soil, or loess, on plains surrounding it). The Grand Canal, started almost 1,300 years ago, links the Huang and the Chang. China has irregular coastlines, which means good harbors.

CLIMATE AND CROPS
Southern China is affected by monsoons (see the South and Southeast Asia chapter for more details on those). They cause crop failures and food shortages when they don't arrive on time and can create unexpected flooding. Here there are hot humid summers and heavy rains, and the farmers grow tea and rice. Northeastern China gets little rain; those mountains in the center block monsoons. Here there are hot summers and cold winters, and the farmers produce wheat, sorghum, millet, and soybeans. Manchuria, in northeast China, has

lowland plains and lots of mineral resources. Manchuria is especially rich in iron ore, which brought about lots of invasions, especially from Japan. Inner Mongolia and Xinjiang (Sinkiang), in north-
central and western China, are largely desert and dry steppe. Tibet,
in the southwest, is a vast, cold plateau with high elevation. China
also has coal, iron ore, and uranium.

Only 11 percent of China's land is suitable for farming, and peasants must overproduce to feed all those people. Most of the arable
land lies in the basin between the Chang, Huang and Xi rivers. Here
about 80 percent of China's population farms; the farming is labor-
intensive, without machinery.

SOCIETY

China's unique culture was affected very little by outside influences. This geographic isolation led to ethnocentrism, or the thought
that its kingdom was the center of the world. The Chinese even
called it the "Middle Kingdom," kind of like they were the middle of
everything. You can see this attitude as Chinese culture spread to
Korea, Vietnam, and Japan; they adapted elements of Chinese culture, not the other way around. The early Chinese thought of China
not as a nation with distinct physical borders, but as a civilization.
Many philosophies developed there.

Confucianism

The teachings of Confucius (or Kung Fu-tzu, 551–479 B.C.) became
the basis for Chinese society during the Han Dynasty (you'll see
more about the different dynasties soon). Confucius taught anyone
regardless of their finances. By the T'ang Dynasty (618–907), Confucianism dominated political life in China. In Confucianism, there are
five key human relationships: ruler and subject, father and son,
husband and wife, elder brother and younger brother, friend and
friend. Notice that four out of five of those relationships are between
superiors and inferiors. Also notice that the only relationship role
assigned to women was wife; sister-sister and mother-daughter
were not considered important relationships.

In Confucianism, there is a basic natural order to the universe,
which was reflected in those human relationships, and the emperor
had a pivotal role in the social hierarchy. Confucianism is not a
religion; the teachings were confined to ethics and morality, not a
god or gods. It was the foundation of Chinese civilization, influenc-

ing the social organization, the political structure, and the educational system. It was the basis of the civil service examination used to recruit able administrators, so it provided the emperor with a trained corps of administrators schooled in Confucian ideas. Confucianists believed in the Mandate of Heaven, which you will learn about soon.

There were four social classes: The scholar-gentry, who were the only ones who could serve in government and used their power to protect the interests of their social class; peasants, who were the largest portion of society, mostly subsistence farmers who farmed a part of a landowner's property in exchange for a small share of the crop; artisans, who were skilled tradesmen, like blacksmiths; and merchants, who were the lowest class, even though they were often the wealthiest. The nobility were above the class system, and soldiers and chien-min (barbers and entertainers) were below it.

Family was the most important aspect of society; notice that three out of five of those relationships mentioned above pertain to family. Families were patriarchal and patrilocal (check the Africa chapter if you forgot what those words mean). People believed in the superiority of male over female and old over young. Wives moved in with their husband's family, and mothers-in-law, finally superior to someone, would often mistreat young wives. To be without family was to be without position, and the family was the basic economic unit. Marriages were arranged, and were part of the social and economic standing of the families, not the individuals involved. Love and devotion to one's family and respect and obedience to one's parents were major beliefs. So was ancestor worship, which reduced the mobility of Chinese families; you had to stay near the graves and spirits of your ancestors to worship them. They believed that spirits watched over them, and were responsible for prosperity or the lack thereof.

The head of the family had to punish infractions to "save face," and the oldest living male was responsible for everything. Sons learned the trade of their fathers. It was considered shameful for a woman not to produce a son; in fact, female children were often abandoned to die during times of famine. The feet of upper-class females were bound, thereby grossly disfigured, because small feet were so important that they were necessary for making a good marriage arrangement. These strong family beliefs provided a lifelong "belonging," or security in a nation of conflict.

Taoism

Lao-tzu (the "old master") introduced Taoism in the sixth century B.C. Taoism reflects an order through a sense of nature and man's part in it. It emphasizes self-knowledge and contemplation. While Confucianism emphasized social conformity, Taoism emphasized personal freedom. It stressed ridding oneself of the burden of unnatural laws and customs. You ponder the Tao, or the source of life, to find harmony with Nature and the universe. Nature is a marriage of opposites: yin-yang, female-male. Teachers saw no conflict with a person practicing Confucianism within a family and Taoism in private meditation; in fact, a balance was considered a good thing. Taoism became a religion with a priesthood, ceremonies, and rituals. Some Taoists practiced magic and alchemy (turning metal into gold).

Legalism

Legalism developed at the same time as the other two philosophies. It maintained that peace and order were possible through a centralized, tightly governed state. Legalists believed that human nature was just plain evil and that people needed laws. You could get people to obey through harsh punishment, strong central government, and unquestioned authority. There were only two occupations allowed under legalism: farmer and soldier.

Buddhism

The introduction of Buddhism came from India; it was brought to China in the first century A.D. (see South and Southeast Asia for the details on Buddhism). All of east Asia has a long history of cultural interchange and development. Like Taoism, Buddhism teaches the denial of worldly goods and a life of meditation. The first converts to Buddhism were members of the upper class, and as usual, the Chinese put their own stamp on it: in the Chinese version, nirvana was not a place empty of human thought, but was a continuation of life on earth, just without the usual suffering. After the fall of the Han dynasty, many Chinese accepted Buddhism. Monasteries gained power and became the centers of education. And no, there was no contradiction in being a Buddhist-Confucianist-Taoist-Legalist; in fact, it all kind of fit together. Buddhism offered optimism and hope, Confucianism offered harmony and strong family relationships, Taoism offered ceremonies and rituals, and legalism offered control.

TECHNOLOGICAL DEVELOPMENT

Some of China's technological developments include making silk, tea, porcelain, paper, block printing, gunpowder, and the mariner's compass. Most of these were diffused to Europe between 200 B.C. and A.D. 1800, by one of two routes: The Old Silk Road, which ran from China to Central Asia to the Middle East to Europe; or the southern sea route, which ran from China to India to the Middle East to Europe.

China was one of the world's leading civilizations in terms of technological development. The Chinese writing system contains ideographs, or symbols used for expressing ideas. There are fifty thousand Chinese symbols, and they spread to Korea, Japan, and Vietnam. As you now know, Buddhism was adapted to Chinese civilization, then spread to Korea, Japan, and Vietnam. Confucian tradition also influenced Korea, Japan, and Vietnam. So it's like cultural developments would pass through China, and then move on.

THE ARTS

Traditional Chinese artists were big on ceramics, like the vases of the Ming Dynasty (1368–1644). Paintings were done on paper scrolls. The subjects of the paintings were landscapes, birds and flowers, and portraits. Calligraphy was always part of the painting. Taoist painters tried to suggest their feelings about nature rather than trying to duplicate reality. After the Communists took over, art was used as propaganda to speed up the transformation of society, and during the Cultural Revolution all art glorified goals of Mao Zedong (we'll get to all of this soon). Since Mao's death, this has relaxed somewhat.

A TIMELINE OF CHINESE HISTORY

Rule by Imperial Dynasty	2000 B.C.–A.D. 1911
Shang Dynasty	1500–1122 B.C.
Chou Dynasty	1122–256 B.C.
Period of Disunity	256–221 B.C.
Ch'in Dynasty	221–206 B.C.
Han Dynasty	206 B.C.–A.D. 220
Period of Disunity in the North, Six Dynasties in the South	220–589
Sui Dynasty	589–618
T'ang Dynasty	618–907
Period of Disunity	907–960
Sung Dynasty	960–1279
Yuan (Mongol) Dynasty	1279–1368
Ming Dynasty	1368–1644
Ch'ing (Manchu) Dynasty	1644–1911
Period of European and Japanese Imperialism	1839–1945
Republic of China	1912–1949
People's Republic of China	1949–present

THE MANDATE OF HEAVEN

The earliest Chinese civilizations developed in river valleys. During nearly 400 years of its history, the Chinese came to view history as a series of dynastic cycles rather than as a movement forward in time.

A part of Confucianism called the Mandate of Heaven, introduced by a Confucian philosopher named Mencius in the 300s B.C., explains the operation of this dynastic cycle.

The Mandate of Heaven was the belief in the divine right of an emperor or empress to rule; as long as rulers kept political control, they were thought to hold this Mandate, but if rulers became corrupt or incompetent, or if the subjects were able to rebel successfully, that meant that the Mandate was lost. So, anyone who overthrew a ruler could claim the Mandate. The emperor was considered the "son of heaven." Whenever there was a flood or drought, it was considered a sign from heaven, and rebellion would break out.

The periods of disunity between dynasties were times when the Mandate seemed to be withheld. Sometimes these periods allowed new ideas in, like Buddhism being accepted between the Han and the Sui dynasties. Any dynasties that were brief were probably "conquest dynasties," when someone conquered but couldn't control, and these were usually followed by long dynasties, like the Sui and T'ang. The Mandate could also be extended to foreign rulers; for example, the Yuan Dynasty originated in Mongolia, and the Ch'ing in Manchuria, and both accepted Chinese culture and governed traditionally. But for the most part, foreigners were considered barbarians who were expected to render a tribute, a payment or gift showing submission to the ruling dynasty.

Speaking of the Yuan, this dynasty created an empire in the 1200s that spread across Asia to the Danube River in the west. It encouraged East-West trade and tolerated Christianity and the spread of Islam. Marco Polo established direct European trade with China during the Yuan Dynasty (more in the chapter on Western Europe) and there was cultural diffusion in both directions as a result.

IMPERIALISM

In the 1800s, the Western Europeans wanted to get into China to convert everyone there to Christianity, and establish trade. They thought they could do in China what they did in India and Africa. But the Chinese were not very interested in Christianity, and they restricted trade. Remember, they thought foreigners were barbarians, and expected them to recognize China as superior and give gifts (that's the tributary system). They weren't interested in the Europeans' stuff, and they thought they were doing the Europeans a favor by dealing with them at all. China disagreed with the Western powers on matters of international relations and justice.

But, despite inventing gunpowder, China had failed to develop the modern armaments that the Europeans had (see the Industrial Revolution, Western Europe). The economic, political and military strength of European imperialism challenged China's ethnocentrism, cultural values, and dynastic rule. Imperialism eroded the social class system described earlier.

The Opium War (1839–1842)

The British didn't like being restricted in China. In opium, Europeans finally found something to tip the balance of trade in their favor. Opium, a mind-altering drug made from a poppy plant grown in British India, was something that many Chinese wanted to buy. British merchants introduced the opium trade, and lots of Chinese, including those in the upper ranks, got hooked. The Chinese government tried to stop it, and a war broke out. The British troops won; they were, after all, technologically superior. The Treaty of Nanking, in 1842, forced China to pay for the opium, open five ports of trade, give Hong Kong to the British, and be more open to trade (they were restricted from using tariffs). Britain took control of parts of the country, including Hong Kong and those five ports. This whole thing had a big effect on Chinese populations, causing drug addiction and upsetting the economy.

Following Britain's example, France, Portugal, Russia, Germany, and Japan also carved China up into "spheres of influence," or areas of economic control where only one imperialist power was allowed to dominate, with exclusive rights to trade. Christian missionaries were allowed to set up churches.

Other Wars

In 1894, China and Japan went to war over Korea, and Japan won. China was forced to cede Taiwan and the Pescadores, and Chinese influence in Korea ended. China was being whittled away, and with its inferior technology, there wasn't much it could do to stop it. One Chinese response to foreign imperialism was the grafting of Western technical learning onto the "Chinese essence." The United States, getting into the picture, feared the European imperial powers would exclude Americans from trading with the Chinese, so in 1899 the U.S. government established the "Open Door Policy" that proposed equal trade in China for all nations.

The Boxer Rebellion

Many Chinese bitterly resented the decline of their empire and all the foreigners taking over. Many joined secret societies that plotted against the Manchu government, which they blamed for China's decline. In the 1900s, there was a large-scale revolt against foreign domination. A group known as "boxers" (nothing to do with underwear, folks; it comes from the "Society of Harmonious Fists") were originally opposed to the Ch'ing dynasty, but were manipulated by the government into becoming a primarily anti-Western force. The Boxers supported Manchu rule and hoped to restore China's traditional ways and independence from foreign dominance. They attacked both imperialists and the Chinese who associated with them, assaulting foreign delegations in Beijing. A multinational army made up of troops supplied by Britain, France, Japan, and the United States crushed the Boxer Rebellion in fifty-five days. The victors forced China to pay war damages and grant even more concessions to foreigners.

Change in the Air

After the Boxer Rebellion and the repeated failure of the Ch'ing dynasty to protect China from all this interference and control, nationalist forces overthrew the last emperor and proclaimed the Republic of China in 1911 to 1912. Right after the overthrow, there was a period of disunity. The Nationalists included Dr. Sun Yat-sen, who formed a new political party, the Kuomintang (Nationalist Party), whose program was the Three Principles of the People: nationalism, democracy, and livelihood. They wanted the redistribution of land to the peasants, and the end of tenant farming, among other things.

The Nationalist Revolution was supported by the wealthy landowners and the expanding merchant class who had been enriched by contact with Europeans. They faced opposition from the local warlords, who liked the land thing the way it was, and the Communists, who were growing in number. Sun, elected President of China in 1911, ended thousands of years of rule by dynasties. He is known as the "father of the Chinese Republic," and when he died in 1925, his son-in-law, Chiang Kai-shek, took control of the Nationalists. In 1927, Chiang, fearing the Communists, turned on them, executing and imprisoning them, and the Nationalists were the official government of China, though there would be intermittent fighting with the Communists until 1949.

MAO ZEDONG

So Chiang handled the warlords, and tried to purge the Communists. A certain Communist named Mao Zedong escaped to southeastern China and built up his Red Army with fellow Communists. In 1934, Chiang surrounded and blockaded the Communists, and the Communists broke out of the Nationalist encirclement and began the Long March, a 6,000-mile trek into the northwestern part of China. During the march, Mao emerged as leader of the Communist Party. Out of about 100,000 participants, fewer than 20,000 survived.

THE APPEAL OF COMMUNISM

Look at the history of dynasties in China; the Chinese people had no tradition of democracy. Democracy is not necessarily the first thing that comes to your mind if it's not in your history. The Communists had predicted an end of imperialism worldwide, and called for a government made up of peasants, the proletariat (workers), and scholars. This idea appealed to almost all Chinese people. Also, the Russian (Bolshevik) Revolution of 1917 looked pretty good. The Chinese thought they would finally be able to compete with the West; Communism was the opposite of the old Confucian order, and Mao was a charismatic leader. The Chinese adopted Maoism hoping to industrialize while sharing the benefits of economic development equally among the proletariat and the peasantry. (For more details on Communism, check out the Russia and Eastern Europe chapter).

The traditional Chinese economy resisted Western technology from the Industrial Revolution; they linked it with Western imperialism, and thought it would undermine Chinese social values. The scholar-gentry class controlled most of the land and rented it to a vast number of peasant tenant-farmers. Crop failures, flooding, high taxes, and indebtedness to landlords caused peasant rebellions throughout history, sometimes overthrowing dynasties. In the mid-1900s, during the civil war between the Nationalists and the Communists, many peasants turned to Communism because it promised ambitious land reforms.

AN INTERRUPTION IN THE CIVIL WAR

In 1931, the Japanese invaded the Chinese province of Manchuria and installed a puppet government. Then in 1937, Japan invaded the Chinese mainland, and World War II in Asia had begun. Japan took the eastern third of China, and did huge damage, causing death, destruction, and displacement.

World War II temporarily halted the civil strife in China, because both nationalists and Communists joined together to battle Japan, a battle which lasted from 1937 to 1945. But when the Japanese surrendered, the Chinese civil war resumed. In 1947 there was a battle for control of Manchuria, and the Communists won, pushing the Nationalists southward. The Communists were in better shape because they were better equipped; not all of them fought in World War II, so they were fresh. The Communists also had a broad base of peasant support; the Nationalists didn't do anything for the peasants. The Communists finally drove Chiang and the Nationalists off the mainland and onto Taiwan. In 1949, Mao proclaimed the birth of the People's Republic of China. Chiang named his island-government on Taiwan, Nationalist China.

RECOGNITION AND FOREIGN RELATIONS

The United States didn't recognize the People's Republic of China; instead it recognized Taiwan under Chiang Kai-shek. China had an alliance with the Soviets and received a lot of foreign aid from them. Chinese troops fought U.S. troops and other UN forces during the Korean War. The Korean War broke out in 1950 when North Korean troops invaded South Korea (more on that later). UN forces rushed in to help South Korea. The fighting got close to the boundary between North Korea and China. Mao feared an invasion of Manchuria, and sent in Chinese forces, and the fighting raged till 1953 when an armistice was finally signed establishing the Korean border along the 38th parallel. As a result, the United States recognized Nationalist China (Taiwan) as the legitimate government of China, and resisted all attempts of Communist China to get into the UN. Mao didn't like this. It wasn't until 1971 that the United States ended its objection to seating the People's Republic in the UN, arguing that both parts of China should be seated. But Communist China was seated and Nationalist China was expelled.

Communists resented the continuing U.S. support for the Nationalist Party rule on the island of Taiwan. By 1969, ideological disputes between the USSR and Chinese Communists led to the withdrawal of Soviet aid, and border clashes erupted. There were many reasons for this, and they still go on. The Russian leader Khrushchev attacked Stalin, and Mao loved Stalin; Khrushchev wanted peaceful coexistence, and Mao wanted to spread Communism; the Soviet Union thought it was the leader of the world Communist movement, and Mao disputed that; the Soviets helped India when it clashed with China over territory; there were border disputes in central Asia and northeastern China that China claimed, and China objected to Russia's invasion of Afghanistan. Russia's Gorbachev took a trip to China in 1989 to normalize the relationship between Russia and China, but his visit was upstaged by the events at Tiananmen Square (which we'll get to). Russia and China signed a treaty of friendship in 1997, effectively ending their feud and allowing a scaling back of Russian forces along the Chinese border.

THE PEOPLE'S REPUBLIC OF CHINA

The People's Republic had a strong, centralized, authoritarian government, and offered a sense of unity and stability after years of unrest. It was a totally new society. With the help of the Soviets, Mao reshaped Chinese society with Stalinist political and economic principles. Mao adopted Stalinist Communism, hoping to achieve industrialization and share the benefits of economic development equally among the proletariat (industrial workers) and the peasantry (farmers). Communism saw the end of the scholar-gentry; land was redistributed, and the ideal of the scholar-gentry was replaced with the ideal of the model farmer working on a communal farm. All industry and commerce was nationalized, and trade with the West was restricted. Mao challenged Confucian values, and targeted Confucianism for destruction during his Cultural Revolution. Children were rewarded for loyalty to the state instead of to the family. Mao also improved the position of women, didn't force arranged marriage, and improved health and sanitation. He wanted to remove all foreign imperialists, take back industry, and ban Christianity. Mao's goal was to reestablish China's world prominence, advance its economic development, and improve the quality of life of the majority. From the founding of the People's Republic until his death in 1976, Mao's vision of the Chinese Revolution dominated developments in China.

Mao's first Five-year Plan (1953–1957) sought to turn China into a command economy, or an economic system in which the government controls and directs all aspects of production. He abolished privately-owned farms and made them cooperative; farmers worked the land together but had small private plots near their homes. Output did increase, but the government's share was not enough to feed China's growing population.

The Great Leap Forward

The Great Leap Forward (1958–1962) was the second five-year plan. Mao reorganized cooperatives into communes, where as many as 20,000 people might collectively work the land. Because of this system, families no longer lived together but in dormitories. This policy weakened the traditional Chinese family and undermined ancestor worship because land could not be passed on from generation to generation anymore. Each commune member was paid a wage to do work assigned by the commune leaders. Communal labor produced steel and built roads, dams, and factories. The population was mobilized into "production teams." To please Mao, Communist officials reported huge increases in food production at a time when, in fact, millions were starving.

The peasants resented all of this. Add to that the crop failures; this was supposed to increase grain production by 100 percent in one year, but it decreased by 20 percent in two years. Also consider the withdrawal of Soviet aid, and you'll get the failure of the Great Leap Forward. It was canceled and private plots were again given to farmers.

The Cultural Revolution (1966–1976)

Mao blamed the failure of the Great Leap Forward on Chinese bureaucrats. He started schools on those communes and in cities, where students read a book called *Thoughts of Chairman Mao*, also known as the Little Red Book. But there were splits within the Party. Some people didn't like Mao's efforts to break with the Soviet Union, and others didn't like his plans for agricultural and industrial reform. So, fearing his revolution might be in danger, Mao launched the Cultural Revolution of 1966. Mao shut down schools and universities all over China, and urged 11 million Communist-trained students to join the Red Guards, who organized demonstrations in support of Mao. They upheld the ideal of rule by the peasants and workers by attacking writers, intellectuals, and other "anti-party" figures. Thousands of professionals, including teachers, white-collar workers, and government officials, were imprisoned or sent to do manual work in fields or factories. Ideological purity was considered more important than technical expertise, and this became known as the "Red vs. Expert" controversy. Workers were all paid the same salary regardless of their individual productivity and responsibilities. Mao ended this in 1969, but it disrupted Chinese life until his death in 1976. During the last decade of Mao's rule, economic development was limited by the removal of technically-qualified personnel and the elimination of higher pay for more productive work.

Mao Dies

After Mao died, there was a power struggle between his widow, Jiang Qing, who wanted to renew the Cultural Revolution, and moderate leaders under premier Zhou Enlai. Jiang Qing and her strongest allies were known as the Gang of Four. They tried to take power, but were arrested, tried in 1980, and found guilty. The real ruler after Mao's death was Deng Xiaoping. Deng was imprisoned during the Cultural Revolution, and once in power, Deng wanted to remove the cult of Mao and discredit Mao's policies. Deng promised to make China a modern nation by the year 2000; he died in 1997.

DENG XIAOPING'S RULE

Deng opened China to foreign trade and allowed greater contact with the West. He also introduced the Four Modernizations: the modernization and mechanization of agriculture, the improvement of military forces, the upgrading and expansion of industry, and the development of science and industry. Deng's policies opened China to Western culture and encouraged individual expression.

Under Deng, farming and management of small business was put back in the hands of the individual or family rather than large organizations. The Four Modernizations attempted to increase productivity through limited private ownership and trade in the West. Material incentives were introduced by offering higher wages and bonuses for workers who produced more. Responsibility for state factories went to the factory manager rather than to the bureaucracy, and individuals could keep the profits above what it contracted to the state. The responsibility system was established, in which farmers agreed to sell a portion of their crops to the government at set prices. They could then sell their surplus crops privately and keep the profits.

Deng ended China's economic isolation and welcomed foreign investment through joint-venture companies in which ownership and profits were shared by the Chinese government and foreign investors. He allowed Chinese students to study abroad. All of this spurred agricultural production, and the standard of living improved.

PING-PONG BRIDGES THE GAP

Relations between the United States and China improved in 1971 when an American ping-pong team visited there; it was the first time in over twenty years that Americans were invited to China. President Richard Nixon then visited the People's Republic in 1972. The Communist government of mainland China replaced the Nationalist government of Taiwan as the legitimate representative of China to the UN. In 1979, the People's Republic and the United States established full diplomatic relations, and greater commercial ties. In 1984, China and Great Britain agreed to the return of Hong Kong to mainland China in 1997, with Hong Kong's economy being based on private enterprise until at least 2047, and China in charge of its defense and foreign affairs.

CHINA TODAY

Today, China has trade and diplomatic ties with Japan. But Taiwan is still a problem. The United States still maintains an unofficial representation there through an American Institute. Both Taiwan and China consider Taiwan a part of China; the dispute is over who should control it. China has conducted military maneuvers to intimidate Taiwan. Taiwan doesn't want to unify with China, but Taiwan-China relations are getting better.

China now has a mixed economy rather than a strict command economy. Production of consumer goods has also been stressed. Foreign companies have been encouraged to locate in Special Economic Zones (SEZ) located in coastal southeastern China, where almost none of the restrictions placed on Chinese businesses apply; so, there are capitalist enclaves in China. There are major foreign investments from Great Britain, the United States, Germany, France, and Japan. Western music and television are allowed in China now.

Tiananmen Square

Some Communists foresaw danger in all of this loosening-up, and their fears were backed up by the 1989 student rebellion in Beijing's Tiananmen Square, where students demanded political freedom as part of the modernization process. Deng's troops crushed this pro-democracy demonstration, causing thousands of deaths and injuries. As a result, several foreign investors pulled out of China and have only recently returned, albeit cautiously; the United States temporarily restricted trade and financial aid to China. Now China enjoys Most Favored Nation status in the United States, but there are big human rights issues there. The United States wants China to stop exporting stuff made by prison inmates who were used as forced labor, to come to some agreement regarding political prisoners, and to follow the UN Universal Declaration of Human Rights.

China is also strained by its huge population (over 1 billion). The population taxes China's resources and limits its economic progress. They've started a program called the "one-child family" that offers financial incentives to couples willing to limit their families. It's worked in urban areas, but not so much in rural areas, because kids are needed as a source of labor there.

TAIWAN

Taiwan is one of several Asian nations that have recently made big and impressive advances in their standard of living. It is considered one of the "four tigers," the others being Hong Kong, Singapore, and South Korea. Like these nations, Taiwan's success is based on its ability to manufacture low-priced but high-quality goods, like clothing, electronics, and processed foods, for export and sale on the world market. For the ultimate proof of Taiwan's economic success, one need only learn that they have 200 times as many televisions and cars as they had twenty years ago.

KOREA

GEOGRAPHY

The Korean peninsula, shaped like a large thumb, is bordered by the Yellow Sea, the Sea of Japan, and the Korea Strait. It's got a pretty strategic location. It was one of China's tribute states, Russia was interested in its ports, and Japan used it as a launching point for invasions of the Asian continent. Known as "land of the morning calm," Korea is half the size of California, and the peninsula contains two countries, the Democratic Republic of Korea, or North Korea, where there are more natural resources, and the Republic of Korea, or South Korea, where there is more arable land. This division was made after World War II.

SOCIETY

The Korean people probably came from Siberia, Manchuria, and northeastern China, and migrated in prehistoric times. All these different peoples intermingled, resulting in the Korean people, a homogeneous people with a single language. The Korean written script is called hangul, and it originated in the fifteenth century. It's a very scientific language, and its simplicity accounts for Korea's high literacy rate. Koreans were strongly influenced by Chinese culture, Confucian philosophy, and Buddhism. Korea was a cultural bridge between China and Japan; Koreans would adopt something Chinese, make it their own, and then pass it on to Japan.

RELIGION
Korea's oldest religious belief is Shamanism, a form of animism. The shaman was a person who was believed to act as an intermediary with the spiritual world. The shaman was called upon to perform a kut, a ritual to get rid of evil spirits. Today, South Korea's major religions are Buddhism and Christianity. There's no religion in Communist North Korea.

EARLY HISTORY
Korea was politically united by the kingdom of Silla in A.D. 668. There were advances in the arts and literature, and movable metal type was invented. In 935, Silla was replaced by Koryo, which was subjected to Mongol invasions in the thirteenth century. In 1392, Koryo was replaced by the Chosen Kingdom, or the Yi dynasty, which controlled the area until 1910.

THE HERMIT KINGDOM
There were Japanese and Manchu invasions in the late sixteenth and seventeenth centuries, so Korea responded by closing itself to the outside world for almost 250 years, becoming known as the "Hermit Kingdom." In 1876, the Japanese forced Korea to open with a treaty; the United States and Europe soon followed. China was threatened by this; after all, Korea was a tributary state. The Sino-Japanese War (1894–1895) was China's attempt to reassert its influence in Korea. Japan won that war, which resulted in no more Chinese influence in Korea. Then there was the Russo-Japanese War (1904–1905), which was the result of conflicting interests of Japan and Russia in Manchuria and Korea. Both of these wars devastated Korea.

By 1910, Japan had annexed Korea. They developed transportation and opened mines. Rice was exported to Japan while Koreans starved, and children were taught in the Japanese language. The Mansei Uprising was a nationalist rebellion in 1919, and was brutally put down by the Japanese with torture, beatings, and arrests. After that, Japan was even more repressive with Korea until the end of World War II. Then, the Soviet Union accepted surrender from the Japanese north of the 38th parallel, and the United States accepted surrender south of the 38th parallel. Elections were supposed to be held, but were resisted by the Soviet Union, and in 1948 a Communist regime was declared in the north, and a republic in the south.

THE KOREAN WAR

In 1950, North Korea, under Kim Il Sung, launched an unprovoked attack on the south, and Seoul fell in three days. The UN General Assembly sent troops to help the south under General Douglas MacArthur (more about him later). They forced the North Koreans northward, toward China, but the Chinese entered the war and drove the UN soldiers to retreat. In 1953, an armistice was signed in Panmunjom. A demilitarized zone, or DMZ, separates the two Koreas now. Millions became refugees, there is hardly any contact between the north and the south, and unification is a controversial issue.

NORTH KOREA

U.S. troops still patrol the border between the two Koreas. In 1993, North Korea threatened to withdraw from a ten-year-old nuclear nonproliferation treaty. They wouldn't let their facilities be inspected; the suspicion is that they might have at least two weapons. The United States wanted to stop this, and called for a UN resolution threatening sanctions against North Korea. China came up with a plan that encouraged North Korea to allow inspection of their facilities instead. Everyone, even South Korea, supported China's plan. In mid-1994, the death of Kim Il Sung ("Great Leader") was a big deal, and his son Kim Jong Il ("Dear Leader") was designated as his successor. Also in 1994, North Korea agreed to dismantle its nuclear program in exchange for over $4 billion in energy aid from the United States, South Korea, and Japan. The economy of North Korea isn't doing well, especially since 1990, which was when aid from the USSR stopped (because the USSR itself stopped). Private cars and phones are forbidden there.

SOUTH KOREA

South Korea has a military defense treaty with the United States. In 1987, South Korea's constitution was amended to provide for the direct election of a president, and Roh Tae Woo was elected in 1988, followed by Kim Young Sam in 1992. In recent decades, South Korea's economy has grown quite a bit. Along with Hong Kong, Singapore and Taiwan, it's one of the "four tigers." South Korea's success, like Japan's, is mostly due to a highly educated and skilled labor force, and governmental policies that encourage the manufacturing of goods for export. South Korea has been able to produce steel more cheaply than either Japan or the United States. Many Americans have purchased South Korean cars and electronics. In a thirty-year period, South Koreans have increased their average income by six times.

JAPAN

GEOGRAPHY
Japan is an archipelago, or a large group of islands, with four main islands and more than 3,000 smaller ones. It's roughly the same size as California, but contains over four times as many people. It is the most densely populated nation in the world.

The four main islands are: Honshu, which is the largest, and contains most of the population and the best farmland; Kyushu; Shikoku, where Japanese civilization developed; and Hokkaido, which was settled in the nineteenth century by the Japanese, has rough terrain, and is considered the frontier. Though Korea and the East China Sea served as a bridge to China, Japan's distance from the Asian continent served to provide it with both political and cultural independence. Its insular physical geography allowed it to observe and selectively borrow from other cultures without being overwhelmed by them.

TOPOGRAPHY
Mountains cover about 85 percent of Japan. This results in a small percentage of land being suitable for farming, so the Japanese use terrace farming by building step-like levels of gardens up hillsides. Japan has about 200 volcanoes, the most famous of which is the inactive Mt. Fuji. There are also earthquakes. Japan has many short, fast rivers which are not good for transportation, but are good for irrigation and hydro-electric power. The coastline is irregular, with many good harbors for trade, and it was easy for Japan to turn the sea into a valuable resource. It's one of the leading fishing nations in the world, and fish is a big part of the Japanese diet (especially raw

fish!). More than 75 percent of the Japanese population lives in cities along the coast.

The Japanese people got their sense of identity from secure boundaries and their nation's remoteness. Its topography has influenced the economic development of Japan as a nonagricultural island nation. It also helped it ward off invasions; Mongol invasions failed twice in the thirteenth century.

CLIMATE

Japan is in a temperate zone, like the United States, and it has four seasons. There are hot humid summers, and cold winds out of Siberia produce cold winters in the north; southern winters are milder, and the monsoons sweep off the Pacific in the summer and drop a lot of rain onto the southern islands. No part of Japan receives less than forty inches of rain; many areas get much more, which is very good for growing rice. In September and October there are dangerous typhoons, which are tropical wind storms like hurricanes.

RESOURCES

Japan lacks many mineral resources, and it must import 90 percent of its oil from the Middle East. Because of this scarcity, it became an imperial power in the late 1800s and the first half of the 1900s, taking over mineral-rich Manchuria and other territories. Needing stuff led Japan into many military conflicts, including World War II; in fact, it's a general rule that needing stuff is what usually leads to wars. Today, Japan's leading export is technology, which it trades for raw materials.

SOCIETY

The people of Japan gradually migrated there from northern Asia, Korea, China, and Southeast Asia. They intermingled and became what we know as the Japanese, an ethnically homogeneous group who think of themselves as racially pure, and seldom accept foreigners as full members of society.

Japan's homogeneous population is expected to stabilize, or cease to grow, by 2030. Over 99 percent of the people are ethnic Japanese. Only Japanese is spoken there, and over 80 percent of the people belong to the Shinto/Buddhism religion. Minorities in Japan include the Ainu, the original inhabitants of Japan, who were driven up to Hokkaido and integrated into rural life there. There are also Koreans, who came during World War II, and were discriminated against; they were not allowed to become citizens until 1985. The Burakumin, descendants of people who did "unclean" jobs like butchering, used to be outcasts, but now live in segregated slums and are discriminated against.

The traditional Japanese family was influenced by Confucianism; it was patriarchal, parents arranged marriages, women had a lower status than did men, and the oldest male in the household looked out for everyone. If an individual threatened the family's good name, he was expelled; one could disown a child by removing his name from a register with the local authorities, and it was as if the child were dead. Open displays of love between husband and wife were considered "unmanly" according to the warrior code (which will be discussed soon). In fact, everything was looked at in terms of how it would reflect on the family.

After World War II, the second-class status of women in Japan began to change. The Japanese adopted a Western approach to love and marriage (meaning you can choose whom you want to marry yourself), and women got the right to vote. Japanese women have rarely occupied leading roles in business or government, but that may be changing, as in 1993, for the first time, a woman was selected to preside over the Japanese Diet (legislature).

RELIGION

The native religion of Japan is a form of animism called Shinto, "the way of the Gods." It has no founder or sacred scriptures. Shinto means the way of the kami, or spirits. The belief is that all things, living or not, possess a kami, or divine spirit (even Mt. Fuji!). The imperial family's kami comes from the Sun Goddess. Shinto teaches no moral precepts, no ethical code, just that you should be thankful for and reverent to nature. Physical, not moral, purity is the most important thing. There's no god involved, so Shinto can coexist with other religions; in fact, Shinto has blended with Buddhism through most of Japan's history.

Mahayana Buddhism was introduced to Japan in A.D. 552 by the Koreans. At first just upper classes converted; after all, Buddhism is kind of a complicated and pessimistic religion, which would only appeal to those who were living comfortably already. But soon, people blended pieces of it with Shinto to form a branch of Buddhism known as Tendai. Two popular Buddhist sects grew out of

Tendai. They are Jodo, which offers enlightenment to all people through faith and the intervention of a deity known as the Infinite Light, and Zen, which calls for strict discipline, meditation, and humility as the paths to satori, or nirvana.

THE ARTS

Sensitivity to and pride in the environment are reflected in Japanese culture. Chinese scroll art was the model for Japanese painters. As a result of the influence of Zen, nature is a popular subject. The Zen emphasis on ritual and precision led to highly stylized tea ceremonies (called chanoyu), flower arranging (called ikebana), and landscape gardening. In literature, there is haiku (the old 5-7-5) poetry, and Noh and Kabuki drama.

Let's talk about Godzilla. In 1954, the first Godzilla movie, *Godzilla, King of the Monsters,* hit the screens. Godzilla was a mutated lizard, and what caused him to mutate? Radiation. Remember, Japan is the only country ever to experience a nuclear bomb, much less two. When Japan was occupied after World War II, it wasn't allowed to build up its military. As time and the Cold War went on, Japan was able to build a self-defense military, and Godzilla changed from an evil destructive monster to a kind of protector of Japanese kids, like in 1969's *Godzilla's Revenge.* Think all of this is a coincidence?

A TIMELINE OF JAPANESE HISTORY

660 B.C.–A.D. 1185	Imperial Period
1185–1600	Feudal Period
1868–1912	Meiji Restoration
1945–1952	U.S. Occupation of Japan
1953–present	Parliamentary Democracy

EARLY HISTORY

Archeological discoveries indicate that Stone Age people lived in Japan as long as 200,000 years ago. From 300 B.C. to A.D. 300, a new wave of migrants called Yayol brought wet-rice cultivation, and bronze and iron working. Early sources of Japanese history are contained in the chronicles of Chinese and Korean visitors as early as the third century A.D.

The Tomb Period (A.D. 300–650) was marked by a society organized around clan governments or chieftains. Yamato clan leaders were the first historical emperors of Japan, and they abolished private ownership of land so that everything belonged to the imperial government. By 660 B.C. a single emperor, claiming descent from the Sun Goddess, emerged to unite the Japanese under his rule. To justify this, the myths, legends and traditions of the Japanese were first written down in the eighth century in the Kojiki (Record of Ancient Matters) in 712, and in the Nihongi (Chronicles of Japan) in 720. They said that rulers of the Yamato were descended from Amaterasu, the sun goddess, who was descended from Izanagi and Izanami, the creators of Japan.

Chinese Influence

The greatest flowering of Chinese culture in Japan occurred during the Nara period (710–794). But no matter what, the Japanese never lost their own sense of identity. The Japanese integrated the Chinese system of characters with their own phonetic writing system; they accepted many Buddhist and Confucian beliefs, which existed alongside Shinto. While Chinese history is divided by dynasties, in Japan it is divided by the family who actually held the power at a given time and who used the emperor to legitimize its authority. There was no civil service, like in China, but Japanese officials were chosen because of their connections and families. There was no Mandate of Heaven, but the Japanese emperor was considered divine.

Japan reduced contact with China in the Heian classical period (794–1185); they believed they had advanced enough to develop alone. This is when Japanese art and literature blossomed; the world's first novel, *The Tale of Genji*, which described court life, was written by Lady Murusaki in A.D.1000. During this time the literacy rate increased, and Japan really developed a feeling of its own uniqueness. So, the Japanese had learned much from abroad, and then they changed what they imported to suit their own needs and tastes.

THE RISE OF FEUDALISM (1185–1600)

The imperial system, where rule was by an emperor, gradually weakened as noble families gained power in the 800s during the Heian period. The emperor became primarily a religious and ceremonial figure and had no real power. In the late 1100s, feudalism emerged. It was a social, political and economic system based on personal loyalties, class distinctions, and the granting of land rights.

Under feudalism, political power rested in the hands of military warlords. The Shogun was the military governor general; he was appointed by the emperor, assumed the political power of the emperor, and ruled with the support of the noble class of landowners. The Daimyo was the landholder class, who swore allegiance to the shogun, but were powerful in their own right. The Samurai was the warrior class, who swore allegiance to the shogun or the daimyo, and in return for military support, were granted land and estates. The code of conduct, or bushido, was a blend of military discipline, Confucian ethics, and Zen Buddhist influences; it made up the rules of ideal warrior behavior. The Bushido stressed simplicity, courage, honor, unquestioning obedience to one's lord, and indifference to death. In fact, to avoid surrender or capture, or to atone for disloyal behavior, a samurai was expected to commit hara-kiri, a ritual suicide involving disembowelment. Warriors with no overlord to serve were called ronin and could be hired by other nobles.

Peasants and Artisans were the next class down from the samurai, and they worked the farms and made weapons, respectively. They got protection from the samurai in return for their services. The next class down was the merchants, who were wealthier than the other classes, but had low social status. So, the Japanese ordered society a lot like the Chinese did, with one important difference: in China, the scholar-gentry was the highest class, and in Japan, the warriors were the highest class. This helped to shape the history of these two countries, so keep it in mind. Feudalism limited the influence of Confucianism in Japan; Confucianism put family first, but in Japan, the lord was first.

Samurai bands and the weather saved Japan from Mongol invasions in thirteenth century. In 1270, Kublai Khan demanded the Japanese pay tribute, the shogun refused, and the Mongols sent troops. But a typhoon helped the Japanese by destroying much of the Mongol fleet. The Mongols abandoned the invasion, and the Japanese thought typhoons were divine winds or kamikaze (gods' winds). The same thing happened again when the Mongols came in 1281.

The Tokugawa Period

Feudalism caused political power to be shifted to local authorities, and a strong bureaucratic military government was established in

1600 during the Tokugawa period, with a new capital at Edo, or Tokyo. The system of sankin-kotai (alternate attendance) dictated that each of the daimyo was required to spend every other year in Edo, and his family was required to reside in Edo at all times as hostages. The class system really became a caste system. Europeans arrived in Japan in the 1500s, but the Japanese feared being conquered, so in the early 1600s, the shoguns banned almost all contact with the outside world. The Tokugawas persecuted Christians, crushed Christianity, and expelled all foreigners. The Japanese couldn't go abroad, and any Japanese in other countries couldn't return.

This self-imposed isolation lasted 250 years. The bad news was that they were cut off from the Industrial Revolution, but the good news was that there was no colonial exploitation going on. This long peace stimulated the growth of cities and the rise of a commercial economy based on the production of rice. The Japanese expanded literacy among a skilled class of urban workers.

THE MEIJI RESTORATION (1869–1912)

The end of isolation came with Commodore Matthew Perry (not the guy on "Friends"), who was sent to Japan by the United States in 1853 to seek protection for shipwrecked sailors and to institute trade negotiations; he brought with him a letter from President Millard Fillmore demanding they open up. The Japanese had never seen a steam ship before, and they knew they couldn't defend themselves against American technology. Fearing U.S. military action, the shogun opened Japan's doors to trade in 1854, and soon after, Europeans began sniffing around. The daimyo didn't like the shogun's new dealings with foreigners, so they broke his power and brought back imperial rule under Emperor Meiji (Meiji is Japanese for "enlightened rule").

With the overthrow of the shogun came the end of feudalism and the beginning of modernization. The decline of the samurai began as the rise of industry and Western education blurred class lines. The arrival of Western powers was perceived as a threat to Japan's national survival; the Japanese feared their country would be carved up into spheres of influence like China had been unless something was done to prevent it. The answer was in reforms that would allow Japan to avoid falling victim to the Western imperialists who divided China in the late 1800s.

MODERNIZATION

Japan was the first non-Western nation to modernize, and it did so pretty quickly. Students were sent abroad to learn Western technology and bring it back. They instituted a broad-based program of public education, built a modern army based on the draft (now anyone could be in the military), constructed a fleet of steam-powered iron ships, adopted a written constitution in 1889, and implemented a parliamentary government with the emperor as its head. Also, construction of the nation's first railroad was begun. A few families formed large-scale business enterprises known as zaibatsu, which helped Japan industrialize. Again, the Japanese were borrowing technology to modernize, but they didn't Westernize; Westernization and modernization are not necessarily synonymous. Even today, Japan and the United States have similar technological and economic development, but cultural diversity as well.

By 1912, Japan had a highly centralized bureaucratic government, a constitution establishing an elected parliament, a well-developed transport and communication system, a highly educated population free of feudal class restrictions, a rapidly growing industrial sector based on the latest technology, and a powerful army and navy. And remember, because of advances during the Tokugawa shogunate, Japan already had a high literacy rate, a high degree of urbanization, and a large pool of skilled labor.

IMPERIALIST JAPAN

Japan's efforts to establish itself as an industrial power resulted in the quest for raw materials; it needed these to be industrially successful. In the late nineteenth and early twentieth centuries, scarcity of raw materials was a determining factor in Japan's international relations as well as in its strategy of economic development. Remember, the need for stuff leads to war, and sure enough, in the Sino-Japanese War (1894–1895), Japan gained Formosa (now Taiwan), the Pescadores Islands, and part of Manchuria. In the Russo-Japanese War (1904–1905), Japan seized the southern half of Sakhalin Island and Russia's port and rail rights in Manchuria. In 1910, Japan annexed Korea. In World War I (1914–1918), Japan joined the Allied Powers, who rewarded it by giving it former German possessions in the Pacific.

Meanwhile, in 1915, Japan secretly presented China with the Twenty-One Demands, which called for political, economic, and military concessions. But China made these demands public. The United States objected, as did many Japanese people who didn't like their government's imperialist policies, so Japan dropped it. The "Greater East Asia Co-Prosperity Sphere" was Japan's effort to persuade all East Asian nations that economic cooperation with Japan was best for everyone. It relied on the exploitation of labor supplies and resources. It was pretty much like the mercantilist policies Britain used in its colonies: Japan would provide manufactured stuff, and the other nations would provide raw materials. In fact, Japan's aggressions against its weaker neighbors were modeled after the imperialist actions of the Western powers in late nineteenth and early twentieth centuries.

In 1931, Japan, still wanting raw materials, invaded Manchuria (the Manchurian Incident) and set up a puppet state called Manchukuo. The League of Nations objected, so Japan withdrew from the League of Nations. The second Sino-Japanese War, starting in 1937, was a full-scale war against China to control the Asian mainland, and thus, World War II in Asia had begun. Japan had conquered China's coastal areas, major cities, and railroad lines. Japan made plans to extend its control to the Philippines, Dutch East Indies (now Indonesia), and the mainland of Southeast Asia. This is when it began to establish its empire in the Pacific known as the "Greater East Asia Co-Prosperity Sphere." In 1940, a year after war had broken out in Europe, Japan joined with Germany and Italy, forming the Axis Powers (or the Tripartite Pact, or the Rome-Berlin-Tokyo Axis). They also seized French Indochina and eventually conquered a significant portion of Southeast Asia. Although the shogunate had been abolished in 1868, the military still made the decisions in Japan.

THE DAY THAT SHALL LIVE IN INFAMY
The United States didn't enter the war right away, but it felt that Japanese aggression in the Pacific threatened U.S. interests there. So, the United States joined the Allies in cutting off Japan's oil supply. Japan responded by attacking Pearl Harbor, a U.S. naval base in Hawaii, on December 7, 1941. Japan was hoping to knock U.S. forces out of the Pacific and negotiate a favorable peace treaty. Instead, the United States declared war against Japan. Japan expected the United States to cave in quickly, but the war in the Pacific went on for four years. Japanese forces had expanded their control over a region

stretching from Japan to Australia to the south and borders of India to the west. The American victory at the Battle of Midway in 1942 was the turning point, and the United States started island hopping (conquering important islands and skipping others, and leaving Japanese forces cut off from supplies). This island hopping drove the Japanese from the Pacific. By 1945, they retreated to their own shores.

THE BOMB

After the Allies won the war in Europe, they focused on the Pacific. President Harry Truman hoped to save the lives of thousands of U.S. troops by ending the war quickly, so he authorized dropping atomic bombs on the Japanese cities of Hiroshima and Nagasaki. On August 14, 1945, Japan surrendered unconditionally. The United States and forty-two other non-Communist nations signed a peace treaty with Japan, and the United States and Japan also signed a bilateral (two-nation) defense agreement.

For the first time, Japan was conquered and about to be occupied. Japan is the only nation ever to experience nuclear attack, and this resulted in worldwide empathy. The Japanese oppose and protest nuclear weapons. The United States-Japanese Mutual Security pact was revised in 1960 to include a clause stating that the United States couldn't bring nuclear weapons into Japan without that government's knowledge. Japan has developed the peaceful use of nuclear power, as in power plants, but some Japanese citizens don't like that either.

THE U.S. OCCUPATION OF JAPAN (1945–1952)

Japan was in ruins after the war. Millions died or were homeless. U.S. forces under General Douglas MacArthur occupied Japan after the war. The Americans helped the Japanese write a new constitution that went into effect in 1947. The terms: Japanese territory was restricted to the four main islands, Japan renounced its right to wage war and dismantled its military, though the Cold War led to the establishment of Japan's limited self-defense forces, and now Japan maintains self-defense forces for defense of Japanese islands. (In 1990, during the Persian Gulf Crisis, Saudi Arabia asked Japan to help and deploy troops, but Japan didn't, because it didn't want to establish an overseas military presence.) Emperor Hirohito publicly gave up all claims to divinity but was still a symbol of the nation (Hirohito died in 1989; he was Japan's longest reigning monarch, and now his son Akihito is emperor). The Japanese bicameral (two-house) legislature, the Diet, assumed all lawmaking powers. The constitution gave women more rights, too. They can vote, choose their own husbands, and seek divorce. Now nearly 40 percent of the workforce is female, but they still make less money and have lower-level jobs.

Those guilty of "war crimes" were tried, but many crimes were concealed, even from the Japanese, until 1996, when the Japanese government admitted publicly to the following war crimes: the mistreatment/torture of combatants and noncombatants; the use of slave labor; the use of prisoners of war for medical experiments; forced prostitution of women.

The U.S. occupation of Japan led to the diffusion of American ideas and practices into Japanese culture, and reforms that produced lasting change. The Japanese Constitution is one of the most democratic in the world. The authority of the head of the family was abolished, and compulsory education was extended for three more years. The Liberal-Democrats have been the dominating political party in Japan for the most part. They are conservative, and favor business and economic expansion. Their opposition comes from the Socialists, the Democratic Socialists, and the Communists, who tend to be in urban areas, disagree over United States-Japanese relations, and are supported by trade unions. Japan's present prime minister, Tomiichi Marayama, is a Socialist.

The Treaty of Mutual Cooperation and Security between the United States and Japan stated that Japan would be protected by the U.S. "nuclear umbrella;" in other words, the U.S. agreed to take the major responsibility for defending Japan. After 1952, when the U.S. occupation ended, Japan joined the UN. The United States and Japan are allies by treaty, and there are U.S. military bases there. The Soviet Union blocked Japan's admission to the UN from 1952 to 1956, because of a dispute over the southern portion of the Kurile Islands and the uneasiness they felt over the Japan-U.S. alliance. Japan was finally admitted in 1956.

ECONOMIC RECOVERY

MacArthur redistributed the land more fairly, and tried to break up the large business monopolies of the zaibatsu. But they could help Japan rebuild, so the effort to break them up was dropped. The United States sped Japan's recovery through direct aid and orders for supplies during the Korean War (1950–1953), which stimulated Japanese growth. After the U.S. occupation, through a combination of selective borrowing and innovation, rapid industrial expansion occurred. Japan needed technology to overcome the problems posed by its physical environment, particularly the lack of natural resources. Today, it keeps turning to advanced technology to improve its position in the world market.

THE JAPANESE WORKPLACE

Ninety-seven percent of the Japanese people are employed in the manufacturing, mining, or service industries. The Japanese tradition of *wa*, or obedience to superiors and team spirit, along with its commitment to high-quality production, helped it grow. Japanese firms expect loyalty; people are hardly ever fired, and there are quality-control circles to seek worker suggestions on how to improve production. Japanese people don't like emotional confrontations or losing face (pride). Decisions are reached by consensus, which takes a long time, but the cities are so overcrowded that only harmony in relationships would make such close proximity bearable.

JAPAN TODAY

Education has unmatched importance in Japan and there is major pressure on students. School is compulsory through junior high, and some schools have entrance exams for kindergarten, so there is fierce competition. The school day, week, and year are longer in Japan than in the United States. Japan has almost universal literacy, and its schools train more engineers than any other Western nation, including the United States.

By limiting its defense spending to about 1 percent of its Gross National Product, Japan has lower military expenditures than the United States, so more money is available for investment and expansion. Japanese people save a lot, don't buy a lot on credit, and the government helps with loans, tax breaks, and high tariffs on foreign stuff. The minimal regulation coming from the government favors large corporations and zaibatsu (like Mitsubishi), and it keeps the value of the yen down.

Japan's economy has experienced tremendous growth since the 1950s, with a heavy emphasis on electronics and other technology-related products. Today, Japan's Gross Domestic Product is second only to the United States. It is the world's leading shipbuilding nation. Today Japan is the third largest economic power in world, and plays an important role in international affairs. It's a leading producer of cars, ships, electronic goods, and it bought a lot of well-known businesses and a lot of real estate in the United States .

Japan's economic problems revolve around the scarcity of raw materials and oil; it's entirely dependent on imported petroleum. Its prosperity depends on world trading conditions and on Japan's capacity to maintain and expand its exports. Also, most Japanese workers don't work for large corporations, so they don't get those benefits. Housing and food costs are high, and purchasing power is low. There's also a big aging population with inadequate pensions and health-care facilities. And there's pollution, a need for better roads, and traffic problems. Tokyo's commuters wear masks to keep airborne chemicals out of their lungs. Today more than 75 percent of Japan's population lives in cities, and there's a major overcrowding problem. At the rush hour in Tokyo, commuters are jammed into subway cars by people wearing white gloves, called *pushers*.

JAPAN AND THE UNITED STATES
Japan is a processing nation, a country that imports natural resources and exports manufactured goods. In fact, it exports far more goods to the United States than it allows the United States to send into Japan, which is a trade imbalance. So interdependence is the name of the game. Japan needs to build a surplus in its export account to pay for raw materials, specifically oil imports. America needs to increase its exports to Japan. This trade imbalance has contributed to the U.S. trade deficit, which results from more money leaving the United States than coming in.

Due to U.S. government pressure, the Japanese allowed the yen to increase in value so that American products would be more price-competitive in Japan, but so far the Japanese have been loyal to their own stuff. So, the United States placed high tariffs on Japanese goods, and then Japan placed quotas on the number of cars it ships to the United States. The trade imbalance continues to be a key issue in the 1990s.

RELATIONSHIPS WITH OTHER ASIAN NATIONS
After World War II, many Asian nations couldn't shake the image of Japan as a militaristic and imperialist invader, and some still felt exploited through economic trade. To create good will, Japan paid

war reparations to anyone who suffered from their aggression. Now, Japan is an important economic factor in China and Southeast Asia, increasing competition with other Asian nations, and contributing to the Asian Development Bank. In 1972, the People's Republic of China and Japan signed an agreement where Japan recognized them and cut off diplomatic ties with Taiwan. Asian nations, such as South Korea, Taiwan, Singapore, and China, compete with Japan by producing textiles, electronics, and cars, but Japan still rules.

4

Latin America

Caribbean Sea

North
Atlantic
Ocean

VENEZUELA

GUYANA

COLOMBIA

SURINAME

FRENCH GUIANA (FRANCE)

ECUADOR

PERU

BRAZIL

South
Pacific
Ocean

BOLIVIA

CHILE

PARAGUAY

URUGUAY

ARGENTINA

South
Atlantic

FALKLAND
ISLANDS
(U.K.)

SOUTH
GEORGIA
ISLAND
(U.K.)

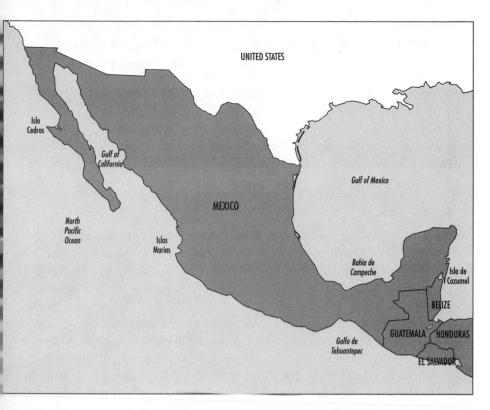

UNITED STATES

Isla
Cedros

Gulf of
California

North
Pacific
Ocean

Islas
Marias

MEXICO

Gulf of Mexico

Bahia de
Campeche

Isla de
I Cozumel

BELIZE

Golfo de
Tehuantepec

GUATEMALA   HONDURAS

EL SALVADOR

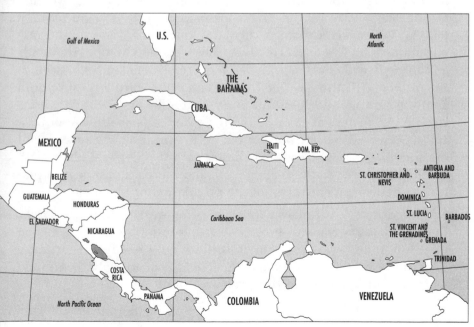

Gulf of Mexico

U.S.

North
Atlantic

THE
BAHAMAS

CUBA

HAITI

DOM. REP.

JAMAICA

MEXICO

BELIZE

GUATEMALA

HONDURAS

EL SALVADOR

NICARAGUA

Caribbean Sea

ST. CHRISTOPHER AND
NEVIS

ANTIGUA AND
BARBUDA

DOMINICA

ST. LUCIA

BARBADOS

ST. VINCENT AND
THE GRENADINES

GRENADA

TRINIDAD

COSTA
RICA

North Pacific Ocean

PANAMA

COLOMBIA

VENEZUELA

GEOGRAPHY

Latin America includes Mexico, Central America, the Caribbean Islands, and South America. It has a diverse landscape, with many physical barriers that have thwarted unity. This has created regionalism, or loyalty to a specific area. The Caribbean includes twenty-four nations and dependent lands. Brazil is larger than the continental United States, is the fifth largest nation in the world, and takes up half the South American continent. It is the Western Hemisphere's second largest nation in terms of territory, population, and economy.

TOPOGRAPHY

Because of its latitudinal extension, there are lots of different landscapes in Latin America. Let's start with the mountains. The Andes are on the western coast of South America; this is the highest mountain range in the Western Hemisphere, and the second highest in world (only the Himalayas are higher). The Andes cut South America into east and west. There are the highlands in Mexico and Central America, and rugged terrain all around them. The Atacama desert in Chile is the driest place on earth. As far as rivers, there's the Amazon, which is the longest river in Latin America and the second longest in world (the Nile is the longest). The Amazon begins in the Andes Mountains in Peru and empties into the Atlantic Ocean. The Amazon Basin covers almost half of Brazil and parts of Bolivia, Venezuela, Colombia, Ecuador, and Peru. It's a vital transportation link. The Orinoco River starts in the Guiana Highlands and forms a wide delta across much of Venezuela, and it also empties into the Atlantic. The Rio De La Plata is the third largest river in South America, and it flows through Argentina and Uruguay. It's a commercial waterway, and unlike the others, it's shallow and difficult to navigate. South America has few natural harbors because of the smooth coastlines. In Mexico, there are the Sierra Madres, both Occidental (west) and Oriental (east), and there's a vast central plateau in between where most of the population of Mexico lives.

One major problem in Latin America is deforestation. In the 1980s, Brazil ordered a massive program of deforestation in the Amazon rainforest in order to open it up to settlers, but these forests produce a lot of the Earth's oxygen, and this could lead to global warming, which is bad (more about this problem later).

CLIMATE

Around the Equator, the tropical rain forests make up lots of the east coast of Central America, and the northeastern and northwestern coasts of South America. The tropical lowlands are too hot and humid for dense human settlements, unlike the mountains or highlands. Tropical Savannas with warm temperatures are found in north and central South America and several Caribbean Islands. Desert and dry lands occupy much of Mexico, the Pacific coast of South America, and the southern part of Argentina.

RESOURCES

Latin America's topography is bad for farming, but even so, its nations are still agricultural. Latin America produces one half of the world's coffee and bananas and one third of the world's sugar and cocoa. Overdependence on a single cash crop has made these countries vulnerable to poor weather or world price fluctuations. There's oil in Mexico, Venezuela (the leading producer in Latin America), and Colombia. Bolivia is the second largest tin producer in the world. Chile is the world's largest exporter of copper. Mexico is the number one producer of silver in the world. Ecuador is number one in banana production.

SOCIETY

There are many languages spoken in Latin America. Spanish and Portuguese are the most common, but Creole is spoken in Haiti; English in Barbados, Belize, Jamaica, and Puerto Rico; Dutch in Curacao and Aruba; French in Martinique and Guadeloupe; and there are also some areas where Native American languages are spoken. There are things that tie the people of Latin America together: the Iberian influence, the Romance languages, the predominance of Roman Catholicism, a similar colonization experience, and most of the nations are in the OAS (the Organization of American States). These are things that help define Latin America as a region despite the regionalism.

The racial and ethnic composition of many Latin American countries has resulted in more blending and blurring of racial lines than in North America. Latin American people are a mix of Native American, European, African, and Asian, so the population is heterogeneous, especially in Brazil, Mexico, and Venezuela, where urbanization blurs racial lines even more. But there is more homogeneity in Argentina, Uruguay and Costa Rica, where the people are primarily of European heritage. In parts of the Andean region and in Guatemala, many Bolivians, Peruvians, Ecuadorians, and Guatemalans would be classified as Native American. There have been big population increases in Latin America, caused by high birth rates, the Roman Catholic tradition that disallows abortion and birth control, improvements in public health, and a decline in the death rate.

The families in Latin America tend to be patriarchal, and there is the idea of *machismo*, which glorifies masculinity; men demand obedience from their wives and children. People marry in the Roman Catholic Church, and parents frown upon marriages between couples from different social classes. Affluent couples keep two surnames to show their family status. Godparents, or *padrinos*, are considered a central part of family, and take part in social occasions.

RELIGION

First there was the native religion of animism, the belief that all objects possess spirits. If the spirits are taken together, they often represent one Supreme Being; the Inca worshipped a Supreme Being called Viracocha the Creator. Then the Conquistadors came over to convert everyone. The strength of the Spanish church was reinforced by the Counter Reformation (the movement to stop the spread of Protestantism), and missionaries were sent to convert Indians. Roman Catholic priests used this belief in a Supreme Being to convert them to Christian monotheism. Some turned native sacred shrines into Christian holy places; others looked down on the native faith and just destroyed their stuff. This was a major violation of human rights and broke the native people's morale. Some still practice their beliefs in remote areas.

The church became a major influence: it got land, built schools and hospitals, and served as a government agency. It opposed some glaring abuses of Native American human rights, but it still operated as an instrument of the colonial power and justified their enslavement.

THE ARTS

South American art is a blend of the Pre-Columbian, Spanish, Portuguese, and African. Mexican painting is represented by the murals of Jose Clemente Orozco, David Alfaro Siqueiros, and Diego Rivera. Rivera's wife, Frida Kahlo, painted hundreds of self-portraits. There was an outpouring of literature in the 1900s. Two Chilean poets, Gabriela Mistral and Pablo Neruda, won Nobel Prizes in Literature. Gabriel Garcia Marquez also won a Nobel Prize (for his novel *One Hundred Years of Solitude*). Others include Guatemalan author Miguel Angel Asturias and Uruguayan prose writer Enrique Rodo. Latin American music draws upon melodies and instruments used in European, African, and Indian music. Popular dance rhythms include the rumba, tango, mambo, samba, cha-cha, and bossa nova. Some leading composers include Brazilian Hector Villa-Lobos and Mexican Carlos Chavez. Check out some Stan Getz for the Latin influence in American jazz. From the Caribbean, there are calypso and reggae, and a blend of Afro-Cuban jazz and traditional Puerto Rican music called salsa is also popular.

A TIMELINE OF LATIN AMERICAN HISTORY

50,000–10,000	Migrations from Asia
15000 B.C.–A.D. 1530	Pre-Columbian Civilizations
1492–1546	European Exploration and Conquest
1520–1808	Era of European Colonialism
1808–1825	Independence Movements
1825–1910	Rule by Caudillos
1823–present	U.S. Involvement

EARLY HISTORY

It is believed that the first people came to North and South America during the Ice Age over a land bridge across the Bering Strait near Alaska. They were nomadic hunters from Asia, and they established Native American civilizations.

Pre-Columbian refers to the time before Christopher Columbus arrived and "discovered" America. There were pre-Columbian peoples in Mexico, Central America, the Caribbean, South America; the heritage has survived to this day, but it was not a big component of political systems. Pre-Columbian civilizations were just as brilliant as other early civilizations, but there were hindrances: the horse, mule, camel and other work animals were not found in America when these civilizations prospered, and the wheel and iron tools and weapons were not in use.

Olmec Culture developed in Mexico along the Gulf from 1500 B.C. to 600 B.C. They were capable of developing raised land platforms to plant in swamp areas. They were accomplished artists and traders who built what are believed to be some of the first ceremonial centers in Meso (Middle) America. We don't know what happened to them.

The Mayan Civilization (300–900)

The Mayans were a complex agricultural society centered in present-day southern Mexico and northern Central America. They practiced polytheism, and their rituals revolved around agricultural seasons. Some of their accomplishments include systems of writing and math, including the concept of zero; a more accurate calendar than the Europeans had at the time; astronomical observatories; elaborate art; stone sculptures; wall paintings; flat-topped pyramids; and great cities that served as administrative and ceremonial centers. The Mayans developed in what is now the Yucatan Peninsula of Mexico and Central America. They were ruled by nobles and a priestly class; warriors, farmers, merchants and slaves made up the vast majority of this highly rigid, stratified social structure. Rival city-states engaged in major wars, devastating Mayan life. By 900 they moved north to the Yucatan Peninsula and south to the Guatemalan highlands.

The Aztec Empire (1200–1535)

The Aztecs were a warrior group big on rigid social structure. They borrowed stuff from conquered peoples, like astronomy and math and the calendar. They were skilled engineers and architects. They forced conquered people to pay tribute to prevent war; tributes included the supplying of slaves for sacrifice. They used prisoners for human sacrifice to the Aztec gods. The Aztec capital was Tenochtitlan, which was near where present-day Mexico City is. The Aztecs were ruled by a warrior king, who was supported by a warrior class and a priestly class who controlled religious ceremonies. Like all meso-Americans, they practiced polytheism. Not surprisingly, particularly important was the god of war, Huitzilopochtli, who could only be worshipped properly through human sacrifice and the offering of blood. The Aztecs were still expanding in the 1500s, but they couldn't conquer all of their enemies in central Mexico. They were the center of Meso-American civilization before the Spaniards arrived. Corn, beans and squash were their main staples, and they were a literate people who spoke a language called Na'nhautl.

The Inca "Inland" Empire (1200–1535)
The Incan empire took up much of the Andean region of South America, stretching from southern Colombia through Ecuador, Bolivia, and Peru, into northern Chile and northwestern Argentina. There were several million Incan people in the Andes Mountains. The term *Inca* refers to the ruler of the empire and his extended family, which numbered in the thousands. The Incan emperor, who was thought to be a descendent of the sun god Inti, strictly controlled everything through a network of officials and priests. Some of their accomplishments include an extensive road network; a system of measurement and record keeping; medical knowledge of surgery and diseases; and building and engineering. This highly regimented state had eliminated the problem of scarcity of food and housing with a farming system. Cuzco, in the highlands of Peru, was their capital. The official language was Quechua, but subjects were allowed to speak their own languages too. There were no written language or records; instead they used a quipu, which was a main string with small colored strings attached and tied into knots to record knowledge. In the 1530s the Spanish, led by Pizarro, destroyed their civilization and conquered everything and everyone.

These were advanced civilizations. The Spanish destroyed much of the writings, so they are known mostly through their monuments, but there is still some pottery, jewelry, dance, music, and handicrafts.

THE EXPLORERS, 1492–1542
Spain's conquistadores (literally "conquerors") sought adventure and riches and wanted to spread Roman Catholicism. Some of the explorers who "discovered" the Caribbean, Mexico, and Central America include Columbus, Cortez (in 1521, the Aztecs fell to him), Balboa, and Coronado. In South America, there was Cabral, Vespucci, Magellan, S. Cabot and Pizarro (who conquered the Incas in 1535). The conquerors had guns, cannons, horses, all of which were unknown in the Americas, so it was easy to take over; they also brought with them European diseases that wiped out native em-

pires. Any native people who survived all this were enslaved. Europeans renamed everything they saw. For example, because Columbus mistakenly thought he had found the Indies of Asia, he named the people he found "Indians," a name still used today.

Your parents were probably taught that Columbus discovered America in 1492. Today, many people question whether "discover" is the right word. It's true that his voyages made Europeans aware that this land existed. But the Aztecs, Incas, and other native peoples had been living there for thousands of years. They certainly didn't call their homeland the "New World." Those who came to their land were considered foreign invaders. Also, Columbus wasn't looking for a "New World;" he was in search of the Far East for Queen Isabella of Spain, who was hoping to break the Asian trade monopoly the Italians held (in the 1400s, Italian city-states such as Genoa and Venice controlled the trade routes to Asia). Columbus never realized, even upon his death, that two entire continents and a whole ocean lay between Spain and China. However, Columbus' voyages did change the world forever.

The Europeans claimed sovereignty (sole control) of Latin America, justified by the totally Eurocentric idea that they had "discovered" America. In 1494, the Treaty of Tordesillas dictated that Spain get everything but Brazil, which would go to Portugal. England, France and the Netherlands took some smaller colonies, especially in the Caribbean (in 1667, Surinam was ceded to Holland by the British in exchange for New Amsterdam, which is known today as New York City). There were so many diverse cultures in Latin America, it was hard for the people to unify and stop colonial rule. Spanish colonial organization penetrated wherever wealth could be found and Roman Catholicism could be preached. The Spanish ruled for almost 300 years.

COLONIAL ORGANIZATION

The scarcity of Indian labor led to the importation of slaves from Africa. The colonial society was a hierarchical organization. On top, there were the *peninsulares*, the select group of Spanish officials sent to govern the colonies. Then there were the *criollos*, or creoles, people born in the colonies of Spanish parents, who were looked down upon, and barred from high positions. They were educated and wealthy, and their treatment fostered feelings of bitterness; they later became leaders of revolutions. Then there were the *mestizos*, those with Caucasian and Native American ancestry, and they were followed by the mulattos, those with Caucasian and African ancestry. Then there were the African slaves, and then the Native Americans. Native Americans and African slaves had little or no freedom, and worked on estates (*haciendas* were large, self-sufficient plantations) or in mines.

The colonial economy stemmed from a mercantilist system aided by a monopolistic relationship between colonial power and colony; the colonies provided raw materials and markets for the mother country. Spain maintained a monopoly over colonial trade and exploited the colonies. The Encomienda System involved the large-scale cultivation of cash crops such as coffee, sugar, and tobacco, and land was concentrated in the hands of a few. This system gave certain Spanish settlers grants of land and control of the labor of specific groups of native peoples. Viceroys, colonial representatives of the king or queen of the mother country, ruled in the colonies, and the people had no voice. The viceroyalties of New Spain, Peru, New Granada, and La Plata were the four major territorial units of the Spanish colonial empire by 1800.

PORTUGUESE AMERICA

Credit for the discovery of Brazil is given to Pedro Cabral, who claimed it in 1500. The primary interests of the Portuguese were in Africa and Asia at first, until the 1600s when Portugal lost its Asian colonies, and gold and diamonds were discovered in Brazil. Class lines were more economic than racial; there weren't as many settlers, and they were mostly men, so there was a great deal of intermarriage. The Tupi-Guarani, an Amerindian grouping of tribes who spoke dialects of the Tupian language, inhabited the Brazilian coastline when the Portuguese arrived to trade and settle in the 1500s. They were subsistence farmers, and were fierce, but contact with Europeans proved fatal due to disease, warfare, and the attempted enslavement for labor. The Portuguese penetrated deeply beyond the boundary set by the Treaty of Tordesillas. There was less domination by the mother country, and intermarriage caused the population to increase. Agriculture was the chief activity for Brazilians. The Roman Catholic Church was less important than in Spanish America, but was still cohesive. African slaves were able to retain some of their religious beliefs, and these blended with Christian and Native American concepts and emerged as Candomble, an

Africanized ritualistic and formalized cult that existed beneath the facade of the Roman Catholic Church.

OTHER EUROPEAN COUNTRIES

Other countries wanted in on the raw materials. In the 1580s, the Dutch tried to get northeastern Brazil, and they were there until the 1640s when Portugal reestablished its independence from Spain, which enabled them to drive out the Dutch. The Dutch did hold on to Dutch Guyana, present-day Suriname, and retained the Netherlands Antilles (the islands of Curacao, Aruba, Bonaire, St. Eustatius, Saba, and part of St. Martin). The French tried to get into Brazil, but were defeated by the Portuguese in the mid-1500s. The French settled Cayenne in French Guiana in 1604, settled Martinique and Guadeloupe in 1635, and Haiti was ceded by Spain to France in 1697. The western region of Hispaniola was the most prosperous French colony in the Americas. The British took Jamaica, Barbados, and Trinidad&Tobago (these became the British West Indies) in the late 1600s, and English settlements in present-day Guyana began in the 1600s (Guyana is the only English-speaking country in South America). African slaves were brought to work the sugar plantations all over the Caribbean.

INDEPENDENCE MOVEMENTS

As you can see, the Latin American colonies had reasons to feel resentment. They were also very far away from the seat of power, and they saw the effects of the successful American and French Revolutions. Also, Napoleon's armies invaded Spain and Portugal in 1806 and 1807, resulting in the capture and exile of the Spanish royal family to France and the placement of Joseph Bonaparte on the Spanish throne. Wars fought against Napoleon diverted Spanish and Portuguese attention from Latin America, and all of this broke the bond that tied Spanish America to Spain. Also, trade with the English, French, Dutch, and Americans decreased Latin America's loyalty to and dependence on Spain. All of this led to a period of Latin American revolutions from 1808 to 1826, inspired by the spread of democratic and revolutionary ideals of the European Enlightenment, and the unjust conditions in which they lived.

The Latin American independence movements were a major crisis for the church. It grew rich through gifts, grants of land, and church taxes, all the time becoming more conservative and supporting the ruling elite. A religious order called the Jesuits interfered with the Spanish colonists' exploitation of the Native American population by educating them, which led to their expulsion from Portuguese America in 1759 and Spanish America in 1767. So, the clergy had long been split over social policy; some supported the crown, and others, especially the native-born, supported the people. Liberation theology is the controversial idea that the church has a responsibility to bring about secular, or worldly change, and some priests do speak out against human rights violations.

Haiti became the first independent country in Latin America. Haiti's independence movement was sparked by the French Revolution. In 1791, slaves in this French colony on the western half of the Caribbean Island of Hispaniola revolted under the leadership of Toussaint L'Ouverture, a former slave. He led the African slaves who worked on the sugar plantations to fight against the French. He was captured and jailed in France, and died in 1803. Haiti gained its independence a year later, becoming the first black republic.

THE LIBERATOR
Simon Bolivar, "The Liberator," was an educated and wealthy criollo, influenced by the ideas of the Enlightenment, and he fought for an independent and unified Latin America. In 1819, he organized an army and led a successful revolt against the Spanish. Between 1810 and 1821 the Liberator was involved in wars to free the future nations of Venezuela, Colombia, Ecuador, Bolivia, and Peru. He was later named the president of the Republic of Gran Colombia (present-day Venezuela, Colombia, Ecuador and Panama), which was established in 1819. In 1830, first Venezuela and then Ecuador formally seceded, and the remaining part of Gran Colombia became the Republic of New Granada. Bolivar's southern counterpart was Jose de San Martin, a professional soldier whose rebel army won independence for his native Argentina in 1816. He joined forces with Chilean general Bernardo O'Higgins, and together they crossed the Andes and drove the Spanish from Chile, which declared independence in 1818. San Martin also freed parts of Peru in the 1820s.

MEXICO
Miguel Hidalgo and Jose Morelos were two Catholic priests who helped Mexico gain its independence in the early 1800s. They were criollos, but they led Indians and mestizos in revolution. Hidalgo issued the Grito de Dolores, which raised the cry of rebellion. The

Spanish executed them, but the revolution continued. Mexico declared its independence in 1821 when Agustin de Iturbide, a creole military officer, negotiated with Vincente Guerrero, an insurgent leader, to form the Plan of Iguala. The plan called for independence under a monarchy. Iturbide forced the Spanish out and briefly ruled as Mexico's emperor.

THE FEDERATION OF CENTRAL AMERICA

The Federation of Central America was created when five provinces—Guatemala, El Salvador, Honduras, Nicaragua, and Costa Rica—declared their independence in 1821 and joined the Mexican empire under Iturbide. They drafted a constitution and adopted a republican form of government, but experienced political difficulties, and in 1823 the five provinces left the federation and became independent states. The federation ceased to exist by the 1840s.

BRAZIL

Brazil experienced a more peaceful transition, and it was granted independence in 1822. Napoleon's invasion of Portugal had led to the royal family heading to Brazil, where King Joao VI became king of Portugal, Brazil and the Algarve in 1816. He had to return to Portugal in 1821, but he left his son Pedro I as regent of Brazil. Pedro was ordered to return in 1822, but he refused. Later that year, independence for Brazil was granted with Pedro as emperor.

THE CARIBBEAN

The Caribbean has progressed more slowly; France, the Netherlands, and Britain still retain possessions there. Cuba and Puerto Rico remained possessions of Spain until the Spanish-American War in 1898. They were dominated by sugar plantation owners, and slaves were the main source of labor. The cooperation of Spanish and creole landowners prevented independence movements. In fact, many British-held islands didn't get their independence until the post-World War II period. The French-speaking islands were made overseas departments, which gave them French citizenship and representation, but no real power.

OBSTACLES TO CHANGE

The overthrow of colonial rule ended mercantilism, but the land and wealth remained in the hands of a few criollos. The gap between rich and poor grew wider, and Indians, blacks, mestizos, and mulattos had few rights. The aristocracy, the military and the church opposed liberal changes that might have benefited the majority. All three of those groups would have benefited from the maintenance of the status quo, since they had all of the privileges.

It was hard to institute a republican form of government in some of these newly independent countries; there wasn't a solid sense of citizenship, and there were numerous coups d'état. The long tradition of absolute rule had left the people illiterate and ill-prepared to create democracies. Military dictators called caudillos emerged, using repressive law-and-order tactics, and favoring the upper class. Constitutions were written, elected legislative bodies were provided for, and judicial systems were created. In practice, however, the caudillo acted as a dictator and often ignored the democratic features of the government. This new tradition of dictatorship grew out of the Spanish colonization.

THE MONROE DOCTRINE (1823)
The Monroe Doctrine prevented European powers from intervening in unstable Latin American nations, and stated that any European attempt to extend to this hemisphere would be considered dangerous to the peace and safety of the United States (the first nation in the Western Hemisphere to throw off colonial rule). It also stated that the United States wouldn't interfere in European affairs. The Monroe Doctrine declared the Western Hemisphere closed to further European colonization. Although the United States didn't have the military force to back this up, it knew that the British navy would protect Latin America because of Britain's commercial interests in the region. Great Britain saw the link between Latin American independence and new markets, so it supported the United States.

DON'T MESS WITH TEXAS
In the 1820s, Texas was a part of Mexico. By the mid-1830s, Texas had a greater population of Americans than it did Mexicans. When Mexico tried to stop further American immigration, the Americans already there revolted and declared Texas an independent nation (called the *Lone Star Republic*) in 1836 (it was granted statehood in 1945). Mexican President Antonio Lopez de Santa Anna led troops into Texas. He was forced to grant the Texans independence after the Texans captured him.

In 1946, U.S. troops were sent to Mexico over a dispute concerning the Mexican Border with Texas. After two years of fighting, the Mexican government conceded in 1948. As part of the peace agreement, Mexico lost California and other territories in what is now known as the U.S. Southwest.

THE SPANISH-AMERICAN WAR

The United States didn't do much to enforce the Monroe Doctrine till the late 1800s and the Spanish-American War (1898), which centered around Cuba. The United States supported Cuban nationalism; it wanted a Cuban government favorable to U.S. investors. Spain was defeated. Cuba became independent, but the United States imposed the Platt Amendment on their constitution, which gave the United States the right to intervene in Cuban affairs, set up naval bases, and protect its interests. The war gave the United States control of Guam, Puerto Rico, and the Philippines. It also marked the beginning of the continuing U.S. intervention in Latin America.

ECONOMIC IMPERIALISM

The legacy of colonialism lived on. Latin American countries may have been politically independent, but they were economically dependent on foreign trade and investment. So economic imperialism replaced mercantilism. Americans and Europeans invested billions in the underdeveloped countries in the late 1800s, which encouraged a large-scale immigration from Europe. Investor nations sent warships to collect loan payments, and the United States and Europe supported caudillos to protect their own interests. This perpetuated Latin America's pattern of economic dependence: first on a colonial power, then on other European countries, then later on the United States.

The Roosevelt Corollary (1904) to the Monroe Doctrine was to keep European warships out of Latin America. It declared that the United States would exercise international police power in Latin American countries to protect foreign investments and ensure loans were paid back; if Latin American nations failed to properly maintain their political and financial affairs, the U.S. would intervene to restore order. This corollary was used several times to justify American intervention in Latin America, especially in the Dominican Republic, Nicaragua, and Haiti, and other presidents continued Roosevelt's aggressive policy. All of this interference caused growing resentment among Latin Americans toward the "colossus of the north." This resentment combined with the need for cooperation is an ongoing conflict.

In 1933, President Franklin Roosevelt instituted the Good Neighbor Policy, which sought to modify the U.S. policy toward Latin America, but it wasn't very successful. The Good Neighbor Policy led to the Alliance for Progress (1961), which was instituted by President John Kennedy to improve political, economic and social conditions in Latin America. It was a ten-year plan which was later abandoned by President Richard Nixon because it wasn't very effective either.

THE PANAMA CANAL

The United States won the right to build a canal in Panama by backing a revolution there; Panama sought independence from Colombia. In 1903, the Hay-Bunau-Varilla Treaty was negotiated with Panama to build the canal, which was built between 1904 and 1914 on the isthmus. It provides easy access to both coasts and to overseas markets. In 1978, Panamanians signed a treaty with the United States to regain control of the canal zone in 2000, but the United States will retain the right to use military force to keep the canal open.

PUERTO RICO

Puerto Rico and the United States have a special relationship. The Jones Act of 1917 allowed the popular election of both houses of the bicameral legislature in Puerto Rico and gave the people a voice in appointing the governor's cabinet. In 1952, under Public Law 600, Puerto Rico became an associated free state with full autonomy in internal matters and its own constitution. Puerto Ricans are citizens of the United States, with a common currency and the right to U.S. defense. In 1967, a plebiscite (vote) resulted in the majority of the people favoring commonwealth status instead of statehood; less than 1 percent voted for independence. The current government is in favor of statehood, but Puerto Rico has economic advantages as a commonwealth that it wouldn't have as a state, for example, not having to pay U.S. income taxes.

TWENTIETH CENTURY REVOLUTIONS

The Great Depression greatly affected Latin America, since the United States had so much invested there. The economic hardship, political corruption, and social injustice all added up to more revolutions.

MEXICO

In the late 1820s, a conservative and centralist caudillo, Antonio Santa Anna, rose to power and dominated Mexican politics. Under dictatorial rule, Mexico fell victim to U.S. expansionism; the successful rebellion led by Americans in Texas in the 1830s and the Mexican War in the 1840s led to the loss of over 40 percent of Mexico's territory. After Santa Anna's exile in 1855, Benito Juarez tried to rule more democratically. In the mid-1870s, Porfirio Diaz, a soldier and protégé of Juarez, was elected president, and he held power until the revolution in 1911. He encouraged foreign investment and transformed Mexico into a politically stable and economically progressive nation, but at the expense of freedom and democracy. He used a repressive police force called the *rurales* to control opposition. Peasants lived under terrible conditions, and the urban labor movement was suppressed. Diaz was supported by the elite hacienda owners, the church, and the military; the big three who wanted to keep their power.

The revolution started in 1911, when demands for land reform and the end of foreign domination drove Diaz from power. The revolutionaries split into factions, and there were six years of civil war. Two Mexican rebels, Emiliano Zapato and Francisco "Pancho" Villa, appealed to Mexican peasants. In 1917, a new Mexican constitution was created, providing for democratic reforms, curbs on the power of the church, and the redistribution of land. About half of the large estates were converted into community lands called *ejidos* following the Revolution, which were worked by peasants but owned by the village. Ejidos account for about 50 percent of Mexico's farm land. Labor movements were allowed to develop and became quite important. These changes were put into effect in the 1920s and 1930s, and Mexico became more nationalistic, with a constitutional government based on a one-party political system (called the PRI).

In 1988, Carlos Salinas de Gotari took office in Mexico and made some painful budgetary reductions in education, health care, and other social services. There were layoffs, and state-owned industries were sold to private investors. In 1993, Mexico joined with the legislatures of Canada and the United States to ratify the North American Free Trade Agreement (NAFTA), creating the Western Hemisphere's largest free trade zone. NAFTA provides for the elimination of tariffs and other trade barriers among the countries involved. In 1994, Salinas hand-picked Ernest Zedillo as the next candidate, and he was elected for a six-year term. Rebellion broke out in the mid-1990s in Chiapas, a poor state in southern Mexico, where descendants of the Maya live in poverty. This is a sign that reforms are still needed in Mexico.

DON'T CRY FOR ME, ARGENTINA
Juan Peron came to power in 1946. He was a populist caudillo (kind of a contradiction in terms) who favored the middle and labor sectors. Perhaps you've heard of his wife Eva Duarte, or Evita, who championed women and the poor. But Peron's programs, like Justicialismo, which sought a balance between society's opposing forces, had a negative impact on the economy, especially agriculture. His social welfare programs resulted in large debt for his nation. The power rested in the military, and in 1955 Peron lost that support. He was overthrown by the military with the support of threatened traditional elite and fled to Spain. Peronism continued to be a political force, and Peron even returned to power for a short time in 1972. When he died, his new wife Isabel became president (the first woman president of a nation in the Western Hemisphere), but she was overthrown by the military because of internal problems. From 1976 to 1983, there was a series of military dictatorships, not to mention terrorism.

In 1982, after Argentina's disastrous invasion of the British-ruled Falkland Islands (which are also called the Malvinas Islands) and its subsequent defeat by Great Britain, Argentina's military had lost credibility, and military dictator General Galtieri was forced to resign. In 1983, Raul Alfonsin, a Radical, was elected president, and he restored civilian rule. But, in 1989, inflation and a huge foreign debt resulted in his resignation and the installation of Carlos Menem, a Peronist, as the new president. He made some drastic reforms, curbed inflation, and restored economic growth.

CUBA
An army sergeant named Fulgencio Batista seized power and became caudillo of Cuba between 1933 and 1959. He didn't do much to help unemployment and starvation, and in the mid-1950s, the revolution began. Some of the causes were the repressive police state, corruption and bribery among government officials, the elite upper class controlling sugar plantations, the unequal distribution of

wealth, the lack of housing, education, medical care, and discrimination. A young lawyer named Fidel Castro organized a guerrilla army that launched a three-year fight against Batista's forces. Castro gained support, promised reforms, and in 1959 he forced Batista out and took control.

Castro tried to establish relations with the United States, but failed. He then turned to the Soviet Union, with its long tradition of dictatorships, and modeled Cuba after it. He also borrowed a ton of money from them. By 1965, Castro's state was officially ruled by the Cuban Communist Party. Cuba supported Communism and guerrilla movements in other countries, like Ethiopia, Angola, Grenada, and Nicaragua, and this forced the United States to take notice. Starting in the 1960s, the United States began to isolate Cuba, politically and economically, with a trade embargo. Castro nationalized American business and industry in Cuba, so the United States refused to recognize the government. In 1961, the United States secretly sponsored an assault by Cuban exiles against Castro which was called the Bay of Pigs invasion. It failed, and United States-Cuban tensions increased. The United States kept up the trade embargo, which continued to hurt the Cuban economy and people.

Since the Soviet Union dissolved in 1991, Cuba has maintained trade agreements with former Soviet republics, but can't rely on them for as much aid as it used to. Castro follows a hard-line Communist policy, but the economy continues to deteriorate. The results of Castro's rule include a totalitarian regime, the denial of basic political rights such as freedom of speech and the press, the violation of human rights, a reorganization to collective farms, nationalization of business and industry, seizure of foreign property with no compensation, the prohibition of discrimination, the end to widespread illiteracy, the expansion of public education, and housing and medical improvements. Castro's policies led many Cubans to flee their homeland, and many came to the United States. In 1994, Cuba and the United States reached an agreement concerning increased Cuban migration. Castro's still there, and so is the United States trade embargo.

NICARAGUA

Let's go back a little. Nicaragua gained its independence in 1838. In the late 1840s, the American government contested British supremacy in Central America, and the United States began its military occupation of Nicaragua in 1912, which lasted until 1933. The national guard, trained by the U.S. military, maintained order and was the instrument for the rise of the Somoza dictatorship, the family that ruled from 1936 to the 1970s. Remember, Castro's dictatorship was supporting other Communist movements, and in the 1970s, he backed guerrillas in Nicaragua called the Sandinistas. The Sandinistas led a popular revolt against the dictatorship of Anastasio Somoza. The United States supported the Somozas because they were anti-Communist, even though they used the military to rule, were corrupt, and concentrated all the wealth in the hands of a few landowners and business people. The 1978 assassination of Pedro Chamorro, an opposition newspaper publisher, sparked an uprising that toppled the Somoza dictatorship. In 1979, the Sandinistas overthrew Somoza and set up a regime under Daniel Ortega, which the U.S. didn't like. The Sandinistas restricted opposition activities and denied basic civil rights, but they improved education, housing, medical care, social and land reforms.

Throughout the 1980s, the Sandinistas faced an armed counter-revolutionary group called the Contras, who were financed by the U.S. government because it was afraid Nicaragua was becoming a Communist stronghold. A costly civil war in Nicaragua led to many casualties, increased emigration, and the deterioration of the economy. The United States also put a trade embargo on Nicaragua. In 1987, a group of neutral Latin America countries known as the Contadora Nations met to end this crisis. Oscar Arias Sanchez, the president of Costa Rica (the only country whose constitution forbids national armies), proposed a plan that called for negotiations and the end of aid for guerrillas. In 1988, the U.S. Congress cut off aid, and an uneasy truce was declared. Elections were held in February 1990, and the democratic Violeta Chamorro (Pedro's wife) defeated Ortega, mostly because of the inflation and unemployment in Nicaragua. Chamorro ended eleven years of Sandinista rule. The Sandinistas peacefully gave up power, but are still influential, especially in the military. There are still problems in Nicaragua, like unemployment, inflation, and a national debt.

EL SALVADOR
In the 1980s, U.S. military and economic aid helped the government of El Salvador resist rebel forces there. From 1979 to 1984, civil war took place in El Salvador between government troops and rebel

guerrilla forces. Jose Napoleon Duarte was elected in 1984, and the fighting and terrorist acts continued, but neither the rebels nor the conservatives liked Duarte's political and economic reforms. El Salvador was also very dependent on the United States. In 1988, right-wing Alfredo Christiani was elected, and there were further problems. Finally, in 1992, the government signed a peace treaty with guerrilla forces that formally ended the civil war. In 1994, the new president, the right-wing Armando Calderon Sol, pledged to continue the peace process.

BRAZIL

Brazil became independent in 1822, but a Portuguese monarch (Pedro I, remember?) continued to rule until a military coup in 1889. Then it became a republic with an elected president. In 1930, the army took over and installed caudillo Getulio Vargas, who ruled on and off for the next 25 years. In the 1950s, Juscelino Kubitschek was elected president and created a new capital, Brasilia, in the country's interior. He also started to improve the highways and universities. The army took over in 1954, and Vargas killed himself. Then there was a succession of military leaders who banned political parties and encouraged economic growth and foreign investments.

An economic boom known as *the Brazil miracle* took place in the 1970s; the upper and middle classes benefited the most from this "miracle." In the late 1980s, Brazil's huge foreign debt and huge inflation rate resulted in the election of Fernando Collor de Mello in 1990. He made some drastic economic reforms to control the spiraling inflation. In 1993 he was impeached because of corruption, and vice president Itamar Franco took over. Fernando Henrique Cardoso was elected in 1994. Some of Brazil's problems include the largest foreign debt in Latin America, inflation, poverty, malnutrition, lack of adequate health care, and crime.

In 1991 Brazil, Argentina, Paraguay, and Uruguay signed a treaty establishing a free-trade zone (much like NAFTA). Also that year, another free-trade pact was signed by Mexico, Venezuela, and Colombia.

HUMAN RIGHTS ABUSES

For many years, a military regime in Guatemala employed death squads to terrorize the country's indigenous population. Thousands of Guatemalans were massacred, and others fled the country. In

1993, a new president was elected who was dedicated to defending the human rights of the citizens.

In the late 1980s and early 1990s in Peru, right-wing death squads were involved in killings of leftist opponents of the Peruvian government. In one incident in 1992, the squads killed nine university students and a professor. Many believe Peru's military was involved in these incidents, but top army officials denied the charges and refused to cooperate with nonmilitary investigations.

EVEN MORE U.S. INTERVENTION

As you can already see, Latin America became a Cold War theater. The fear of the spread of Communism seemed to justify all of the butting in the United States was doing there. During the Cuban Missile Crisis (1962), the United States imposed a blockade that required the Soviet Union to dismantle its weapons in Cuba. Ultimately, the Soviet Union complied and removed missiles after a "quarantine" and a U.S. pledge not to invade Cuba, thus avoiding a nuclear confrontation between the two superpowers. The United States has continued to try to topple the Castro regime, or at least to isolate it. In 1973, the CIA helped overthrow the freely elected Marxist government of Salvador Allende in Chile. A dictatorship was then established under General Augusto Pinochet, who ruled till his 1989 defeat by Patricio Aylwin.

In 1983, U.S. troops invaded Grenada, an island in the Caribbean, aided by members of the Organization of Eastern Caribbean States. It was feared that Grenada would become a base for exporting the Communist revolution in the region. Communism usually appeals to countries that lack economic stability, and this was an example of Castro's policy of exporting the Cuban Revolution elsewhere. (Also, the Cubans were building a 10,000-foot runway. A Grenada air facility would place it within striking distance of Venezuelan oil shipping routes in a time of crisis, thereby creating a "choke-point.") Prime Minister Maurice Bishop was overthrown and killed in a coup d'état in 1984, and Herbert Blaize was elected Prime Minister. In 1989, U.S. troops invaded Panama and overthrew the dictatorship of Manuel Noriega, who was then arrested and brought to the U.S. to stand trial for drug trafficking. Guillermo Endara was installed as president there in 1990.

In Haiti, Father Jean-Bertrand Aristide was elected president in 1990, and was unable to maintain order; later, he was arrested by the military and forced to leave the country. The United Nations responded with a strict embargo, and then military leaders reneged on a deal to allow Aristide back in power. The economy worsened, and many Haitians fled to the U.S. by boat, with many dying en route. In 1994, the UN Security Council okayed the invasion of Haiti by a multinational force. As the U.S. forces started on their way, the invasion was called off when military leaders agreed to step down. Aristide was restored to office in 1994 with help from lots of U.S. troops. The U.S. forces are still in Haiti to maintain Aristide and his supporters in power, as well as those elements favorable to U.S. interests.

ORGANIZATION OF AMERICAN STATES

The OAS was formed in 1948 to promote international cooperation, and provide a peaceful forum for settling regional disputes. It includes 32 member nations from the Americas, including the United States, which has a dominating role, and Canada. The OAS stresses economic development, social justice, and regional integration, and it has a mixed record. The 1961 Bay of Pigs Invasion and the 1965 military occupation of the Dominican Republic by the U.S. were seen by many as violations, but Latin America did support the United States by voting to exclude Cuba from the OAS. Latin America also opposed U.S. intervention in Nicaragua, and the invasions of Grenada and Panama. The OAS continues to provide a legal channel for solving international disputes in Latin America. Although Cuba is excluded from the OAS, it has maintained links with several Latin American countries.

THE LATIN AMERICAN ECONOMY

Today, most Latin American countries have capitalist economies, though some socialist leaders have gained a foothold. Poor tenant farmers still live on the estates or plantations of the landowning elite; in return, they get a little plot of land on which they practice subsistence farming. There have been attempts to break up the large estates and distribute the land more evenly, but they have not been effectively pursued. When Brazil opened up the Amazon rainforest to settlers, the land they cleared lost its fertility within two years, and the resulting deforestation may be devastating worldwide.

Crop diversification has also been attempted as a way of preventing dependence on risky cash crops; they've tried growing staple crops, like wheat and corn. Those who control the land don't really like this, because those crops are not as profitable as cash crops. Here's an example of why overdependence on cash crops is risky: Reduced demand for Colombian coffee depressed the world market price, and the Colombian people resorted to growing coca, which is used to produce cocaine, to increase their incomes. The Colombian government appealed to the U.S. government to increase their coffee importing to stop this illegal activity.

There are industrialized regions in Mexico, Brazil, Argentina, Venezuela, Colombia, Peru, and Chile. But Latin America needs to be more industrial in order to satisfy internal demands for goods and provide manufactured goods for export The main problem is the lack of capital; people are afraid to invest there because of political instability. Money borrowed to foster industrialization creates indebtedness, and when debtor nations fall behind in payments, foreign banks tighten their credit, and the economic problems deepen. And again, sometimes farmers turn to growing coca leaves, marijuana and poppy plants. So Latin America needs to get capital without increasing its foreign debt; this runs counter to their traditional (colonial) role as exporters of raw materials and importers of manufactured goods. Local industries can't compete with the multinational corporations that take as profit the capital that is much needed, instead of reinvesting it. This illustrates the growing interdependence between more-developed and less-developed regions. Cooperative efforts to improve the situation are difficult because of all the diverse nations in Latin America; it's hard for them to unify about anything.

Japan is investing in Latin America, and more industrialized Latin American nations such as Brazil export cars, military equipment, and commercial aircraft to Africa and the Middle East. It helps that there are petroleum resources in Mexico and Venezuela.

LATIN AMERICA TODAY

The occupation of idle land by the poor fuels the current conflict between private property and social justice. Rapid growth has led to squatter settlements known as barridas or favelas, which are inhabited by marginal populations who don't have access to enough productive work or many goods and services. The gap between rich and poor is increasing, and still, the urban elites won't evenly distribute profits, because they're on the side of the landed elite, the military, and the Roman Catholic Church, and against social change. The building of highways, the burning of vegetation to claim land for cattle raising, and increased mining using technology, all destroy Native American peoples. The invasion of lands set aside for tribal reservations by poor rural farmers and miners has led to even more violations of Native Americans' rights.

Besides human rights violations, some of Latin America's current problems include overpopulation, pollution, overcrowding, the drug trade, deforestation, unemployment, marginalized youth, and a debt crisis. They also need to establish fairer systems of taxation; the rich don't pay their fair share, and the nations lose revenue.

There has been some social change. Traditionally, the landed upper class, the military, and the clergy resisted change, and dominated the mestizos, Indians, and blacks. The growth of the new industrial middle class of mestizos led to more democracy, and there are some successful democratic governments, like in Brazil and Venezuela. The clergy is more interested in relieving poverty. The military's influence is declining, and the rise of labor unions has also helped.

The nations of the Caribbean Community and Common Market (CARICOM) are working on policies to liberalize trade among its members. Many countries are turning to the "natural resource" of tourism, especially the Dominican Republic and Jamaica, and even Mexico and Brazil. Sometimes it's the mainstay of the economy in certain countries, which is a mixed blessing.

Television is breaking down some cultural barriers. Change is slow to affect Latin America's male-dominated society. Family is still very important, but the roles of men and women are changing. The double standard has weakened; there are women in the labor force, and some are actually heading families in urban sectors. Suffrage has been accepted, but there are still obstacles to full equality, like that pesky machismo. Personal ties are still more important that economic, political and social organizations. Rural families still value large families as a source of labor, and food supplies can't keep pace. Family planning is hard to carry through because of religious and cultural beliefs.

Argentina and Brazil are both home to immigrants from England, Italy, France, Germany, and the Middle East. In Brazil, a large community of Japanese immigrants has contributed to the development of an agricultural sector in Sao Paulo. There is also emigration. Migrants move from Mexico and Central America to the United States, from Central America to Mexico, from Colombia to Venezuela, from Paraguay to Bolivia, Brazil, and Argentina, and from the Caribbean to the United States. Latin Americans are the fastest-growing immigrant group in the United States.

5

The Middle East

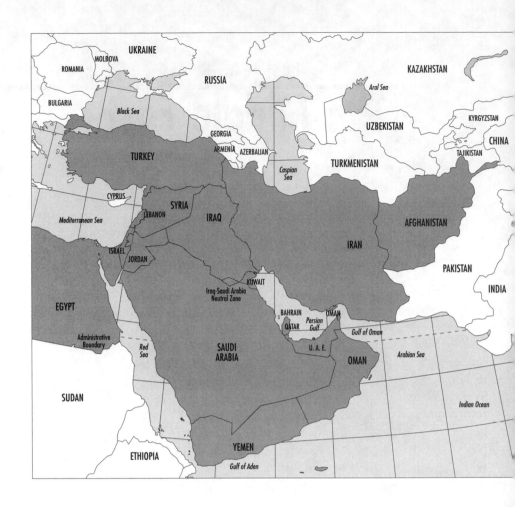

GEOGRAPHY

The area called the Middle East is the junction of three continents: Europe, Africa, and Asia. This quite strategic location earned it the name "the crossroads of the world." It extends from Morocco (home of the oldest educational institution in the world, Karueein University, which was established in 859 A.D.) in the west, to Afghanistan in the east, and from Turkey in the north, to the Arabian Peninsula in the south. Its total area is twice that of the United States.

The African portion is called North Africa, and includes five nations: Morocco, Algeria, Tunisia, Libya, and Egypt. The Asian portion includes what might be called Southwest Asia (see the map in the Africa chapter), or SWASIA, which contains fifteen nations: Turkey, Syria, Lebanon, Israel, Jordan, Saudi Arabia (itself the size of Western Europe), Yemen, Oman, the United Arab Emirates, Bahrain (the only other country besides the United States that doesn't use the metric system), Qatar, Kuwait, Iraq, Iran (where no less than 109 offenses carry the death penalty), and Afghanistan. The European portion of the Middle East is the European part of Turkey—the part that contains the city of Istanbul. The Levant refers to lands touching the eastern Mediterranean Sea, like modern-day Syria, Lebanon, and Israel. The Asian part of Turkey is sometimes referred to as Asia Minor, which is not a political reference, but a geographical one. In fact, the Middle East is sometimes called the Near East. It's interesting to note that these names only make sense when you're looking at a map with Western Europe at the center; they were the ones naming places.

TOPOGRAPHY

Desert, desert, desert. The Middle East is mostly desert, so the nomadic lifestyles of the Bedouins, Arabs and early Israelites put the emphasis on sharing, group values, and conformity. The major deserts are the Sahara in North Africa, which separates it from the rest of Africa, and the Arabian Desert, which includes the Rub' al Khali, or Empty Quarter, and covers most of the Arabian Peninsula. Together, these two deserts account for more than 90 percent of the land surface of these two areas. Other deserts include the Sinai in Egypt, the Nafud in Saudi Arabia, the Negev in Israel, and the Dasht-i-Kavir in Iran.

The emptiness of the landscape may also have had a strong impact on the growth of religious feelings in the Middle East; a person or group's religious devotion can become more intense when they live amid harsh natural conditions. Not only did the world's three major religions, Judaism, Christianity, and Islam, originate in this part of the world, but a central figure from each had a profound religious experience while alone somewhere in the Middle East; respectively, Moses at Mount Sinai, Jesus in the wilderness, and Muhammad in a cave.

The Arabian Peninsula is shaped like a huge boot (not a high-heeled one, like Italy and New Zealand, but a flat one), and contains several nations including the largest, Saudi Arabia. It's surrounded by the Red Sea to the west, the Arabian Sea to the south, and the Persian Gulf to the east. The Suez Canal connects the Red Sea to the Mediterranean Sea, and serves as a vital link between Europe and Asia. In the Northern Tier, there are two large plateaus; the Plateau of Iran covers most of Iran, and Turkey occupies the Plateau of Anatolia. Mountains stretch across North Africa, Turkey, Iran, the Arabian Peninsula, and Afghanistan. The Atlas Mountains are in Morocco, and acted as a barrier to trade and communication with the rest of North Africa and the interior of the continent. The Pontic Mountains are in the north of Turkey, and the Taurus Mountains are in the south and east; they surround the Plateau of Anatolia. The Elburz Mountains in the north of Iran and the Zagros Mountains in the west surround the Plateau of Iran.

The Nile River is the longest river in the world, and it flows through Sudan and Egypt; the ancient river valley civilization of Egypt developed along its banks. The Blue Nile's source is in Central Africa, and the White Nile's source is in East Africa. They converge in the Sudan and flow northward to the Mediterranean Sea. When the Nile overflows its banks, silt (soil rich in minerals) forms. The Jordan River is smaller than the Nile, but it's vital to the people of Lebanon, Syria, Jordan and Israel. The land portion just west of the river is called the West Bank (as well as by its biblical names, Judea and Samaria), and has long been a disputed political boundary. It's a good source of fish, and it flows into the Dead Sea, which happens to be the lowest place on earth. The Tigris and Euphrates rivers, which originate in the Taurus Mountains of Turkey, converge in Iraq.

WHAT'S IN A NAME?

Fertile Crescent. Breadbasket in the Desert. Cradle of Civilization. Mesopotamia. These names all refer to the core of the Middle East, a fertile strip of land along the Tigris and Euphrates rivers. It's shaped like an arch, or crescent, and stretches from the Mediterranean Sea in the west to the Persian Gulf in the east. Melting snows in the nearby mountains have flooded those rivers each spring, and that flooding deposits silt on the surrounding plain. It's unpredictable, but it helped make agriculture possible in this desert region. There are no natural barriers here, and over the centuries, many different peoples have migrated across, settled in, or invaded the area. In ancient times, the Fertile Crescent was called Mesopotamia, or "land between two rivers." Three great river valley civilizations flourished here between 3500 B.C. and 612 B.C. They were Sumer, Babylonia, and Assyria. Ancient Hebrews carved out a home here, too. Judaism, Christianity and Islam all took root here.

CLIMATE

The Middle East is one of the driest areas in the world. Mountains along the coastal areas, such as the Atlas Mountains, prevent moisture-bearing clouds from getting to the interior of the region. Also, the Middle East is near the equator, so there's warm water, hot summers, and hardly any rain; when rain does come, there is sometimes flash-flooding. The scarcity of water in the Middle East has caused most of the population to concentrate in areas where irrigation is possible, like in the Mediterranean area.

RESOURCES

About 70 percent of the world's known oil reserves are found in certain Middle Eastern countries, mostly those in the Persian Gulf. They produce 50 percent of the world's current oil supply. This has fostered global interdependence and created worldwide tensions (more about "oil politics" later). While oil politics is often the way Western nations interrelate with the Middle East, within the region "water politics" is a more dominant factor.

STRATEGIC WATERWAYS

Oil and water do mix, in the way that strategic waterways are looked upon. Industrial nations want to protect their sea routes to the Middle East, so these strategic waterways are very important to these outside powers. One such waterway is the Suez Canal, which allows merchant ships to go directly from the Mediterranean to the Red Sea, and then out into the open waters of the Indian Ocean. A second important waterway is the Persian Gulf, which is surrounded by the oil-producing Gulf States. If any one nation ever gained total military control of the Persian Gulf, it could control much of the world's oil supply. The Bosporus and the Dardanelles are located in western Turkey, and they control the movement of ships between the Black Sea and the Mediterranean. These are also strategic waterways. In the nineteenth century, Russia's desire to control them led to war.

So, water is precious, and only about 7 percent of land can be farmed. Most Middle Eastern land grows wheat, barley, rice, and millet, and some produces grapes, olives, and citrus fruits. Israel exports Jaffa oranges; Iraq is the world's leader in date production; Turkey exports nuts, figs, olives, and tobacco; and Egypt exports cotton. Some nomads raise donkeys, camels, and horses. Sheep and goat raising are prevalent because cattle require too much water and a different type of grazing. Most nations in the Middle East don't produce enough food to feed their people.

SOCIETY

Over 90 percent of the people of the Middle East can be described as Semites or Semitic. Now, let's get this straight. These terms describe a family of languages that includes Arabic and Hebrew, although the term anti-Semitic almost always refers to discrimination against Jews. The terms Semite and Semitic are also used to refer to anyone who speaks one of these Semitic languages and who belongs to an ethnic group that follows certain customs. Now, an Arab is a person who speaks Arabic and who follows traditions associated with an Arab way of life, that is, traditions connected with existence in a desert environment in the Middle East. Although most Muslims in the Middle East are Arabs, the word "Arab" doesn't refer to a particular religious group; Arab doesn't mean Muslim. In fact, a small number of people in Egypt, Israel, and Lebanon consider themselves to be Christian Arabs, and Muslims in Turkey and Iran do not consider themselves to be Arabs.

Most village people in the Middle East cluster around sources of water, and less than 50 percent of the population live in villages. Nomads generally live in small groups bound by kinship. Nomads travel in search of water and pasturelands. Their possessions are determined by what they can transport by camel. Nomads who inhabit the Arabian and Sahara deserts are called Bedouin (the Arabic word for "desert dweller"). Other nomads include the Berbers in northwest Africa and the Kurds in western Iran. There aren't as many nomads today as there used to be.

Over 75 percent of the people in Arab countries are farmers, or *fellahin*, who have traditionally leased the land as tenants from wealthy landowners. But there's been some redistribution of land in Egypt, Syria, and Iraq, so more farmers have become landowners. Sheep herding has been big in the Middle East since biblical times (because of the lack of water, remember?), which is why lamb is such a basic part of the Middle Eastern diet.

City life, like that in Alexandria, Baghdad, Cairo, and Istanbul, developed along key waterways. The Middle East was the hub of commerce in the ancient world, and trade still takes place on a daily basis in busy Middle Eastern marketplaces called *souks*. Prices are determined by negotiation between buyers and sellers. They borrowed the Hindu number system with its concept of zero; the Hindu-Arabic number system facilitated financial activities, and was eventually adopted by the West. The word "check" is Arabic in origin, and they were the first to use checks. "Bazaar" still describes the busy marketplaces of the region. Other English words derived from Arabic include alcohol, algebra, almanac, coffee, cotton, magazine, orange, sherbet, sugar, and syrup.

RELIGION

The Middle East is the birthplace of three major world religions, all three of which are founded on a monotheistic belief in one God. The holy lands in this region make it one of the most hotly disputed and violent areas in the world.

Judaism

Judaism is the world's oldest monotheistic religion, starting some 6,000 years ago. With its rejection of polytheism and insistence on monotheism, social justice and law, Judaism marked a significant change from the religions of other Middle Eastern cultures. The religious literature of Judaism, especially the Ten Commandments and the Torah, influenced Christianity and Islam.

The Torah is the Jewish Holy Scripture, sometimes referred to as the Old Testament. It contains the history of the Hebrews (the ancestors of modern-day Jews), including their enslavement by the Pharaohs of Egypt. A prophet named Moses led the Hebrews out of Egypt to Canaan (now Israel), the Promised Land, around 1300 B.C.

According to the Torah, Moses gave them the Ten Commandments of God (or Yahweh, which would be Jehovah in Modern English), and the Hebrews believed that these laws formed part of a covenant, or solemn agreement, with Yahweh. The Talmud, a repository of knowledge and ethics, has commentaries on the Tanach, which are the Old Testament, the Torah, and other writings. The Hebrews lived in the kingdom of Israel for several hundred years, and built a temple honoring God in the capital, Jerusalem. But Israel's location made it subject to repeated invasions, and in 586 B.C. the Babylonians destroyed the temple and exiled them. That was the start of the Diaspora, or "dispersing." The formation of a Jewish identity was influenced by the religious beliefs of the Hebrews, and also had a lot to do with the way they were treated after their exile from Jerusalem again in 135 A.D., and the fact that they continued to be exiled throughout their history. Dreams of reclaiming their homeland have also shaped the Jewish identity. Many Jews consider Jerusalem holy because it is the site of the first two Jewish temples and contains the Western Wall. Modern Judaism includes the Orthodox, the Conservative, and the Reform, listed in order of intensity of traditional beliefs. All Jews have the right of Israeli citizenship.

Christianity

Christianity began in the Middle East with the death of Jesus about 2,000 years ago. Christians believe that Jesus was the son of God, that he ascended to heaven after being crucified and coming back to life, and that he was the Messiah, or savior, referred to in the Old Testament. The story of Jesus and his disciples, and the basis of the Christian religion, are in the New Testament. Christians also accept the Old Testament, including the Ten Commandments, especially in terms of ethics, and theoretically stress the Golden Rule: do unto others as you would have them do unto you. The Bible is both the Old and the New Testament put together. The three major branches of Christianity are Catholic, Protestant, and Eastern Orthodox.

Islam

Islam is practiced by over 90 percent of the people in the Middle East. The word Muslim is a religious term, while the word Arab is a cultural term. Islam forms a social foundation; like Hinduism in India, it's a complete way of life. The crescent and the star, symbols of Islam, are found on the flags and currencies of many Islamic nations. There is no central controlling figure for Islam, like the Pope for Catholics.

The word Islam means "submit to God's will." It was founded in Arabia by the prophet Muhammad in 622 B.C. (more about him coming up). Muslims believe that Muhammad was the fourth and most important prophet chosen by God to teach and spread holy ideas and thoughts; Abraham, Moses, and Jesus were just paving the way for Muhammad. All four prophets are believed to have had direct communication with God.

Like Judaism and Christianity, Islam is also a monotheistic religion, and Muslims accept many of the same prophets as Jews and Christians. But Muslims believe that Jesus was a prophet and that Muhammad was the last and greatest prophet of God, or Allah. They accept many of the spiritual beliefs of the Bible, but they follow a holy scripture called the Koran, or Quran. The basic duties of Muslims are outlined in the Five Pillars of Islam, and they are as follows:

1. There is no God but Allah and Muhammad is his prophet.

2. Muslims must bow toward the holy city of Mecca (sometimes spelled Makkah) and pray five times a day: At dawn, noon, mid-afternoon, dusk, and after sunset.

3. Muslims must give alms (charity) to the poor.

4. Muslims must fast during the ninth month of the Muslim calendar, Ramadan, the month when the Koran was revealed to Muhammad (notice that all three of these religions involve some fasting or dietary limitations: Ramadan, Lent, Yom Kippur), from sunrise to sunset each day.

5. Muslims must make a pilgrimage to Mecca, called the haj, once in their lifetime.

The Koran says men are dominant over women. The traditional family is extended and patriarchal; women and children must obey men. Courtship is limited, if not nonexistent, and teenage boys and girls are not allowed to socialize. Marriage is seen as a union between two families, not two people. Parents arrange marriages, and the groom's father gives the bride's family a gift to pay for the loss of her labor. The bride's father gives his daughter a dowry, which the husband cannot claim upon divorce. Islam allows for polygamy, and a Muslim male can have up to four wives if he can afford it. Clearly, women have few rights, and in some nations they still wear veils in public and practice seclusion in the home, which is called *purdah*.

Islam is among the world's youngest religions, but it is also the fastest growing. It is a total way of life; Muslims are not allowed to eat pork, drink alcohol, or gamble. To prevent idol worship, Islamic law forbids its followers from drawing images, and that means no statues or pictures adorn mosques, the Muslim place of worship. Here's something that might account for some of the trouble in the Middle East: Muslims believe that death in a jihad, or holy war fought to defend or spread Islam, guarantees entry into heaven, so fundamentalists are perfectly willing to die for Islam.

LANGUAGES

Muslims believe that the Koran was revealed to Muhammad in Arabic, and for a long time, no translations were allowed. The only way to read it was to know Arabic, so Arabic became a common language for all Muslims, whether Arab (Egypt) or non-Arab (Pakistan, Indonesia). Kemal Atatürk (more about him later) in Turkey broke with tradition in the 1920s with his decision to translate the Koran from Arabic into Turkish; Turkish script being written in Latin letters instead of Arabic was one of his reforms as well. Arabic and Hebrew (which is spoken in Israel) are Semitic languages. Farsi, or Persian, is spoken in Iran. European languages are spoken mostly in areas that were under European influence, so English is spoken in Egypt and French is spoken in Lebanon and Syria (also, two villages in Syria still speak Aramaic, the language of the Bible).

THE ARTS

Islam forbids drawing, so the Muslims developed calligraphy to decorate their holy places with lines from Muslim scripture, and also created stained glass windows, mosaic tiles, and hand-woven carpets. Islamic architecture was expressed in mosques with tall towers, or minarets, which could be square or rounded. The Taj Mahal in India and the Alhambra Palace in Spain are examples of this. The most famous Arab epic poem is the *Rubaiyat* by Omar Khayyam (1048–1122) of Persia, which is now Iran. Other widely read stories include tales of Aladdin and Sinbad from *A Thousand and One Nights*, also known as *Arabian Nights*, a collection of tales drawn from Persia, Egypt and India.

A TIMELINE OF MIDDLE EASTERN HISTORY

10,000–3500 B.C.	Neolithic Revolution
3500–612 B.C.	Early Mesopotamian and Egyptian Civilization
1230–586 B.C.	Hebrew Conquest of Canaan; Kingdom of Israel
334 B.C.–A.D. 395	Greek and Roman Domination
395–1453	Byzantine Empire
750–1058	Golden Age of Islam
1453–1918	Ottoman Empire
1830–present	European Involvement and Arab Nationalism

EARLY HISTORY

The Middle East has the longest recorded history of any region on this planet. The Neolithic Revolution (10,000 B.C.–3500 B.C.), sometimes called the single most important innovation in human history, marked the development of farming and the use of stone implements as tools. The discovery of how to make tools and weapons out of metal radically changed the nature of human society, and led to the building of the first cities and the rise of political systems. Trade in these city-states began in response to the scarcity of resources.

The Egyptian and Mesopotamian civilizations developed in river valleys, just like other "cradles of civilization" did in the river valleys of the Indus River in South Asia and the Yellow River in East Asia. The early empires of Mesopotamia (3500 B.C.–612 B.C., around Iraq) started on the land between the Tigris and the Euphrates Rivers, and included the ancient kingdoms of Sumer, Babylonia, and Assyria. Here, writing was invented, organized religions evolved, and governments were based on kingship. Hammurabi's code of law developed in Babylonia, which is also famous for the hanging gardens of Babylon.

Egypt has been continuously inhabited for over 8,000 years. Ancient Egypt (3500 B.C.–1090 B.C.) developed along the Nile, and cultivated a government and religion centered on a pharaoh, or god-king, who was believed to be immortal and capable of ruling after death. This concept of an afterlife explains the practice of preserving the bodies of pharaohs and building elaborate tombs that resemble pyramids.

Writing

The invention of writing systems made for a more complex civilization and enabled the advancement of technology. Development of writing systems in the Middle East meant that information and ideas pertaining to trade, government and even religion, could be recorded and transferred to other regions, resulting in cultural diffusion. Examples of ancient writing systems include cuneiform from Sumer; hieroglyphics from Egypt; and Phonetics (the alphabet) from Phoenicia (present-day Lebanon).

THE HEBREWS AND ANCIENT ISRAEL

The Hebrews originated in Sumer. Around 2000 B.C. they moved west and settled in Palestine on the Jordan River, the land they called Canaan (again, present-day Israel). Around 1800 B.C., drought forced some of the Hebrews into Egypt. There, the pharaohs enslaved them. Around 1230 B.C., Moses led the Hebrews out of Egypt and back to Canaan. After conquering the Philistines and others, the Hebrew tribes united under a single government, forming the Kingdom of Israel. They achieved great prosperity under King David, and then his son Solomon, who built a temple in the 900s B.C. to glorify God.

Israel's strategic location between Egypt and Mesopotamia made it the target of invasions by the Assyrians, Babylonians, Greeks and Romans. In 586 B.C., the Babylonians conquered Jerusalem and destroyed Solomon's temple. The Jews, as the Hebrews came to be known, were sent into exile, beginning the Diaspora. Though their kingdom was destroyed, they held on tightly to their religion. Eventually they returned to their homeland, but in A.D. 70, the Romans destroyed Jerusalem and a second temple the Jews had built.

INVADERS

Advances in civilization lead to quests for power; the technology of civilization allows one group to control the labor of another. The rise and fall of empires that shaped the area's unique identity and political systems mark the history of the Middle East. In the fourth century B.C., conquests occurred in the Middle East, bringing about great changes. After Alexander the Great united the Greek city-states (see the Western Europe chapter), he swept eastward into Asia Minor, Syria, Palestine, and Egypt, bringing with him Greek culture, thus "Hellenizing" the area. This Hellenistic period lasted from 333 B.C. to 90 B.C.

The word "Palestine" has its origins in the word "Philistine." In 1200 B.C., the Philistines conquered a small strip of land along the eastern Mediterranean coast, which was dubbed "Palestine" by the Romans. Palestine actually describes a geographic region and has never been the name of a nation. Israel is located on most of the land that was called Palestine, and Israelite kingdoms existed there from approximately 1000 B.C. to 70 A.D.

The Romans

By 30 B.C., the Roman Empire controlled most of the Mediterranean region, and all of the Middle East adjacent to the Mediterranean Sea came under Roman control by A.D. 120. Missionaries spread Christianity, which had developed out of Judaism about seventy-five years earlier. It began as a reform movement among Jews and gained converts under the leadership of Paul, a Hellenized Jew. The promise of salvation for all peoples made the Christian concept of one god attractive to non-Jews. At first, Roman emperors persecuted Christians. However, by A.D. 313, Christianity was so widespread that the Emperor Constantine issued the Edict of Milan, which granted freedom of worship. By the end of the fourth century, Christianity was the official religion of the entire Roman Empire.

The Decline and Fall...

In 395 the Roman Empire split into western and eastern halves, with the western part being ruled from Rome, and the eastern part being ruled from the city of Byzantium on the Bosporus. After the fall of the western half in 476, the Eastern Roman Empire, which included those areas of the Middle East from Asia Minor to Egypt, became known as the Byzantine Empire. Emperor Constantine moved to Byzantium, and then built a larger city, Constantinople, which became the capital of the Eastern Roman Empire. The Byzantine Empire inherited the Christian religion, and Christians in this empire called their church Eastern Orthodox to distinguish it from the Catholic Church in Rome. They also inherited Roman law, and the Roman system of government.

THE BYZANTINE EMPIRE

Byzantium was at its height from 527 to 565 under Emperor Justinian and his wife Theodora. It included present-day Greece, Turkey, Israel, Egypt, Jordan, and Syria. The Justinian Code is based on Roman laws, and the justice system of Western Europe and Latin America descended from Justinian's code regarding human rights. The Byzantine Empire dominated the Mediterranean world for eleven centuries, with its unique blend of Hellenistic and Eastern Mediterranean culture, the Orthodox Christian religion, and the Roman political system, all at a time when Europe was fragmented into small feudal units of limited intellectual activity. The political system of Byzantium and the church-state relationships created a model for future power relationships in the Middle East and Russia. Judeo-Christian ethics shaped everything Western. Until Muslim Ottoman Turks captured Constantinople in 1453 and ended Christian dominance in the eastern Mediterranean area, the Byzantines influenced the Middle East, Eastern Europe, and Russia.

MUHAMMAD AND THE RISE OF ISLAM

Muhammad (who lived around 570 to 632) was born in Mecca (present-day Saudi Arabia). Muhammad claimed to have had revelations from God and visions while sleeping in a cave. These revelations, received through the angel Gabriel, were collected and written down in the Koran ("the recitations"), the holy book of Islam. Muhammad began to preach faith in one god, Allah. Facing persecution, he and his followers fled Mecca in 622 to nearby Medina, where the faith grew. The Islamic calendar dates from the year of Muhammad's flight, or haj.

In 630, Muhammad returned to Mecca with an army, captured the city, and proclaimed Allah to be the one God. Mecca was an important city because of its economic activity and because it contained a holy shrine called the Kabbah, a black stone building, standing on the site where Muslims believe God commanded Abraham and his son Ishmael to build a place of worship. Today the Kabbah lies within the Great Mosque at Mecca, so Muslims consider Mecca to be their holiest city, and the Kabbah their holiest site. A haj is a pilgrimage to Mecca, which every Muslim is supposed to undertake at least once in their lifetime. One who makes the haj is called a haji; two million Muslims make the haj each year. Soon after Muhammad's death in Medina (Islam's second holiest city), his teachings were recorded in the Koran. Muslims believe Muhammad rode to Jerusalem on a winged mare and stepped on a rock before going to heaven. He then returned to the rock and rode back to Mecca by dawn; this rock is the one on which Jews believe Abraham was going to sacrifice his son Isaac. In 637, the Muslims conquered Jerusalem and soon after built a mosque over this rock. This building is called the Dome of the Rock, and Jerusalem is Islam's third holiest city.

Islam Spreads

Islam spread successfully because of jihads, skilled warriors, and tolerance of Jews and Christians (as Dhimmis, or "people of the book") because of their similar ways. Muslims also found willing converts. Within a little more than a hundred years, Muslim armies spread Islam west across North Africa and into Spain, east as far as India, and north into Asia Minor.

Despite huge cultural and political changes in the world over the years, Islam has changed very little in terms of religious beliefs, values and ethics. It spread, but it remained strongest in the Middle East, providing cultural unity. It united the whole Islamic world with a common language, Arabic, and a common religion, and helped Arabs conquer diverse peoples and lands. As Arab conquests pushed into non-Arab lands, the Islamic world became a mixture of many cultures. The influence of Islam dominated the religious, cultural, economic and political systems of an interdependent world which stretched from Spain to Sumatra. Now, it's a major religion in many African nations, like Morocco and Nigeria, and Asian nations, like Bangladesh and Indonesia.

Islam Splits

Upon Muhammad's death, Muslims chose a leader called a *caliph*. The first was Abu Bakr, the father of Muhammad's wife, Aisha. After Abu Bakr's death, control of the caliphate was passed eventually to the Umayyad clan. The Umayyad dynasty lasted from 638 to 750, and expanded into North Africa, Western Europe (including Portugal, Spain, and France), and south and southwest Asia. Under the Caliph Muswiyah, they made the capital Damascus in 661, but their leadership was opposed by followers of Ali, Muhammad's son-in-law, who was caliph from 656 until his assassination in 661. Ali's followers eventually formed the Shiite branch (from the Arabic phrase Shi'a Ali, the party of Ali). The other branch is the Sunnis. Shiites believe that Muslims should only be led by a descendant of

Ali, and that true knowledge can only come from an Imam, or religious leader. Shiites are principally found in Iran, where ayatollahs are experts on Islamic law; today Iran is the only Middle Eastern nation in which Shiite Islam is the official state religion (in fact, Iran is the world's largest theocracy). Shiites are also found in Iraq, Lebanon, and Bahrain. They have been called fundamentalists. Today they worry about the growth of materialism, the introduction of Western values, and the changing role of women. But most Muslims are Sunnis, who believe that the first four caliphs were the successors of Muhammad and that there should be no central authority for enforcing Islamic law. They believe that all Muslims are spiritually connected regardless of custom and tradition.

The Golden Age of Islam

The Abbasids defeated the Umayyads and created a dynasty lasting from 750 to 1250, under the Caliph Mansur, with prosperous Baghdad (the capital of present-day Iraq) as the capital. During this Golden Age of Islamic culture, the people preserved the knowledge of Greece and Rome by translating Greek texts into Arabic, and made numerous mathematical and scientific advances. They introduced the concept of zero; devised Arabic numerals, which were based on Indian numerals (and are the ones we use); developed geometry, algebra and trigonometry; increased their astronomical knowledge to calculate the Muslim calendar; invented the astrolabe, which is like a sextant (a navigational instrument) to determine direction at sea; established the earliest hospitals and pharmacies and determined that disease can be contagious; performed surgery; diagnosed diseases like smallpox and measles; manufactured glass; developed chemistry; acknowledged that the earth is a sphere and estimated its circumference; and produced *The Arabian Nights*. Not bad, huh?

At a time when Western Europe didn't like those who didn't adhere to the religious orthodoxy of the Church, the Islamic world was unique with its religious tolerance and acceptance of cultural diversity. The cultural advances of the Golden Age reached Europe by way of Muslim Spain and Sicily, trade, and the Crusades, and influenced modern civilization. European explorers improved the magnetic compass, a Chinese invention that the Arabs had brought to Europe. Arab control of the spice trade caravans in the Middle East motivated Europeans to look for a sea route to the East Indies so they could share in the wealth available from commerce.

INVASIONS

After 1200, the Abbasids declined; it was hard to rule over such a large area, and the different peoples within the empire didn't get along. Also, the Crusades (1095–1291) caused a lot of death and destruction. The Crusades were attempts by Europeans to take Jerusalem and other Christian holy sites from the Muslims. They destroyed many cities and people, and left a legacy of mistrust of Westerners, but also brought about cultural diffusion, both in the Middle East and in Western Europe. In the eleventh century, the Seljuk Turks, converts to Islam, invaded Baghdad and overthrew the Abbasid caliphs. Then they conquered Asia Minor and most of the Byzantine Empire. Christian Crusaders sacked Constantinople and other cities on their way to the Holy Land, which they hoped to seize from the Seljuk Turks. For a time in the 1100s, they controlled Jerusalem and other Mediterranean cities.

THE OTTOMAN EMPIRE (1453–1918)

In the 1300s, Ottoman Turks invaded Asia Minor and were converted to Islam. Constantinople fell to them in 1453, and they changed its name to Istanbul. The name Ottoman comes from "Osman," a Turkish leader in 1300, but the most famous Ottoman ruler, called a sultan, was Suleiman the Magnificent (1521–1566), who was also called the Lawgiver because of his many legal, educational and military changes. The Ottoman Empire was well organized; it was basically a well-functioning army constantly at war. By 1566, Ottoman sultans controlled an empire that included most of the Middle East and part of Europe. The Ottoman Empire attempted to expand farther into Europe and was stopped at the Battle of Vienna in 1683.

The Sick Man of Europe

After the 1600s, Ottoman power dipped and the empire became a pawn in the balance-of-power struggle among European nations. By the 1800s, the Ottomans declined, as ethnic groups within the empire fought for self-rule. One Christian ethnic group, the Armenians, were continually persecuted by the Ottomans, and during World War I, more than a million Armenians were massacred in a genocide attempt.

The Ottomans failed to modernize and keep up with the industrial growth in Western Europe; as a result, the declining empire became known as the "sick man of Europe" (even though only a small part of the empire was actually in Europe; most was in western Asia and North Africa). The industrialized nations of Europe tried to take greater economic control of the Middle East, and the imperialism that resulted formed the basis of much of the anti-Western feelings and resentment in the Arab world today. It increased after France took control of Algeria in 1830. But the European military and technology couldn't really change the Islamic way of life.

Russia was eager to take advantage of the weakening Ottoman Empire on its southwestern border, yearning, as it had for centuries, to take control of the Bosporus and Dardanelles. In 1853, a dispute between Russia and the Ottomans led to the Crimean War (named for the Crimean Peninsula in southern Russia where the major battles took place). Great Britain and France took the Ottomans' side because they were afraid of Russia gaining that much power. As a result, Russia was defeated.

Goodbye, Ottomans

Death came to the Ottoman Empire in 1918 with the end of World War I. Because they were on the losing side of the war, the Turks lost almost everything; all Middle Eastern lands except present-day Turkey were taken away and placed under the control of the newly formed League of Nations. The League created mandates (a mandate is a commission from the League authorizing a member nation to administer a territory) in these lands—Palestine, Iraq, and Syria—placing them under the rule of England and France; they could govern temporarily until the territories were ready for independence. Besides France and Britain and their new mandates, Italy established a presence in the Middle East by taking over Libya in 1912.

In Turkey in 1922, Mustafa Kemal (he was called Ataturk, meaning "father of the Turks") overthrew the sultan and in 1923, he created the Republic of Turkey, of which he was president. He drove all Greeks out of Turkey. He transformed Turkey into a modern, European-style nation. His reforms included abolishing the fez (a headdress), writing Turkish script in Latin letters instead of Arabic, translating the Koran from Arabic into Turkish, ending government support of Islam as the official religion, and replacing Islamic laws with a civil code. These changes led to the rise of Turkish nationalism.

RISE OF NATIONALISM IN THE MIDDLE EAST

Arab nationalism led to the creation of independent Arab states. After World War I, Britain and France divided those former Ottoman territories in the Middle East. Britain took Palestine, Transjordan (now Jordan) and Iraq; France took Syria and Lebanon. The Europeans failed to keep their wartime promises to support Arab nationalist interests and create a Jewish homeland, so resentment grew.

THE SUEZ CANAL

The Suez Canal is a strategic waterway, as well as a "choke-point" to control trade in the area. The canal was completed by the French in 1869. It links the Mediterranean Sea to the Red Sea and the Indian Ocean beyond. Great Britain especially benefited from the canal by giving it access to its crown colony India. To control the canal, Britain sent an army to Egypt in 1882, and made it a protectorate. From the late 1800s until 1922, Egypt remained a British protectorate. In 1922, Egypt became a free constitutional monarchy, though Britain controlled Egypt's foreign affairs until 1936, when Egypt gained more self-government (more on that later). Egypt didn't get the canal back until 1956. Egypt closed the canal to all traffic after the 1967 Arab-Israeli War, and it remained closed until 1975.

MORE MIDDLE EASTERN NATIONS FORM

Saudi Arabia, which was never formally colonized, became a nation in 1927. Its name came from Ibn Saud, the head of a Muslim sect that had established its power in most of the Arabian Peninsula. Algeria came under French control in the nineteenth century, and nationalism grew there in the twentieth century. This posed a problem for the French after the end of World War II. France refused to leave, and a bloody civil war raged from 1954 to 1962. Peace talks in 1962 ended the war, and Algeria became independent, with Ahmed Ben Bella its first leader. After World War I, France held mandates in Lebanon and Syria. After World War II, in 1946, those countries were granted independence. Iraq got its independence from Great Britain in 1923 and Jordan, in 1946.

JEWS AND ARABS

Different Arab dynasties held power in Palestine from the seventh till the fifteenth century; from then until World War I, sovereignty was held by the non-Arab Turks. But Arab habitation in Palestine was continuous during the Ottoman rule. Arabs didn't like the Turks, and sided with the British in World War I. Jews supported Britain in World War I against the Turks.

The Babylonian exile and subsequent exiles scattered the Jews to different parts of the world (the Diaspora, remember?). Many settled in Europe, where they were victims of anti-Semitism and were frequently forced to live in separate areas of cities called ghettoes; here they were the victims of pogroms, which are organized, often officially encouraged massacres or persecution of Jews. There was continuous Jewish habitation in Palestine from the Roman conquest into the nineteenth century.

As a result of the Diaspora, some Jews dreamed of a return to their historic homeland; this desire led to the Zionist movement of the late 1800s, established by Theodore Herzl, an Austrian Jew and journalist who wrote a book called *The Jewish State*. The word Zionist comes from Zion, an area in Jerusalem that was the center of Jewish life in ancient times. The Ottoman Turks refused to grant the Zionists' request for a homeland in Palestine, where Jews were migrating in increasing numbers. Early in the 1900s, Zionist communities were established in Palestine, and the issuance of the 1917 Balfour Declaration by Great Britain supported their cause. In this document the British promised to favor the establishment of a Jewish homeland in Palestine while preserving the rights of the Palestinian Arabs living there. In 1922, acting on their own, the British also carved out over half their mandate area as a separate Arab enclave (called Transjordan, soon to be called Jordan).

Arabs and Jews were in conflict, and Britain couldn't maintain peace there. They were further weakened by World War II, which was also the time of the Holocaust, the attempted genocide of the Jews. The resulting new wave of Jewish immigrants to Palestine was also on everyone's mind; many Jews felt the only place they'd be safe would be their own homeland. By a majority vote in 1947, the UN decided to partition Palestine into two states, one Jewish and one Arab. The city of Jerusalem, holy to both, would be under UN supervision.

ISRAEL

The UN plan for the partition of Palestine was rejected by the Arabs but (reluctantly) accepted by the Jews. When Israel announced its independence in 1948, with David Ben-Gurion as its first Prime

Minister, it was attacked immediately by the neighboring Arab states of Egypt, Iraq, Syria, Transjordan, Lebanon, and Saudi Arabia, who wanted to "drive the Jews into the sea." The UN arranged a truce in 1949, but the Arabs refused to negotiate a peaceful settlement and vowed to drive the Jews out of Israel and restore Palestine as an Arab nation. The Arabs refused to recognize Israel, even though everyone else did.

The 1948 War for Independence had major consequences. Israel defeated the Arabs and took control of half the Arab territory assigned by the UN. Israel got the western half of Jerusalem, and Jordan got East Jerusalem, which contained the city's important holy sites. Jordan promised to permit equal access to these holy Christian, Jewish and Muslim sites for members of the three religions; however, Jordan never permitted Jews to visit their holy sites. Jordan and Egypt divided the rest of Palestine between them; Egypt got the Gaza Strip, and Jordan got the West Bank, which violated the UN Partition Plan, as this area was supposed to become an independent Palestinian Arab state. The Jordanian occupation of the West Bank received international condemnation and was never recognized by any Arab nation; it lasted until 1967. So, there was no Arab homeland, and many Palestinians became refugees.

MORE WAR

The battles were just beginning. In the 1956 War, Egypt's General Gamel Abdel Nasser seized control of the Suez Canal from England and France and sent terrorist raids into Israel. Israeli, French, and English troops responded by attacking Egypt. Israel defeated the Egyptian army in the Sinai Peninsula and occupied that region. The United States and the Soviet Union intervened, bringing about a UN ceasefire. Egypt kept the Suez Canal and demanded that Israel give back the Sinai, and they did, hoping to be recognized as a nation. UN troops were stationed between the borders of Egypt and Israel to keep peace.

The Six-Day War occurred in 1967. Egypt and other Arab nations still refused to recognize Israel, and stepped up terrorist attacks. Nasser demanded the removal of UN troops from the Suez, occupied the Gaza Strip, and closed the Gulf of Aqaba to Israeli ships. Israel attacked Syria, Jordan and Egypt on June 5, and defeated them by June 10. This war enabled Israel to increase its territory. It gained control of the West Bank of the Jordan River, Egypt's Sinai Peninsula and Gaza Strip, and Syria's Golan Heights. It also annexed Jordan's half of Jerusalem, the half with all the holy stuff. Israel held territory occupied by Arabs. The UN passed Resolution 242, calling for all warring nations to recognize one another and make peace, and for Israel to withdraw from occupied lands. The Arabs didn't comply, so neither did Israel.

Then there was the Yom Kippur War in 1973. Egypt and Syria pulled a surprise attack on Israel on Yom Kippur (Judaism's holiest day; Egyptians called it the October War) to regain lost territory. The Soviet Union helped the Arabs, hoping to avoid another Israeli victory, so the United States helped Israel. Oil-rich Arab lands pressured the U.S. not to help, using an oil embargo as their weapon. This was the first example of "oil politics," or the use of oil as a political weapon. A UN ceasefire was declared, and the UN passed Resolution 338, calling for more peace negotiations. Egypt got a little land in the Sinai, and though Israel regained lost territories, the 1973 war is considered one in which Arab pride and nationalism was restored by Anwar Sadat of Egypt.

A LITTLE PEACE

In 1977, Sadat spoke to the Israeli parliament, the Knesset, and after that, Menachem Begin went to Egypt. In 1978, Sadat and Begin got the Nobel Peace Prize. On March 26, 1979, they signed the Camp David Accords, an agreement to end the state of war between Israel and Egypt and return the Sinai Peninsula to Egypt, which also called for negotiations about the status of Palestinian Arabs, and a UN peacekeeping force reestablished on the Egypt-Israel border. President Jimmy Carter negotiated this historic treaty, the first of its kind between Israel and an Arab state. Because of it, Egypt was kicked out of the Arab League, and Sadat was assassinated by Muslim extremists in 1981. Hosni Mubarak became Egypt's new president. In 1982, Israel withdrew completely from the Sinai Peninsula.

THE PLO

Though Egypt signed a peace treaty with Israel in 1979, other Arab nations still oppose the existence of Israel. The Palestine Liberation Organization (PLO) was founded at a 1964 meeting of Arab states to regain Palestine and eliminate Israel. It is led by Yassir Arafat, and it claims to speak on behalf of all Palestinian Arabs. The 1975 civil war in Lebanon between Christians and Muslims (which we'll get to soon) gave the PLO the opportunity to set up bases there, and the Lebanese government wasn't able to control them. Aided by Syrian troops and Soviet ammunition, the PLO launched guerrilla attacks on Israel from southern Lebanon. Israel retaliated in 1982 with a massive assault. An international peacekeeping force negotiated a ceasefire in 1983 (241 U.S. marines and sailors, part of this force, were killed in a terrorist attack on their headquarters in Beirut, Lebanon), and by 1984, the PLO had left Lebanon, but Israeli forces remained in Lebanon till 1985. This attack was controversial among Israelis, and after the 1984 Israeli elections, its army was pulled back from Lebanon except for a small "security zone."

In 1988, in response to the Israeli occupation and control of the West Bank and Gaza Strip, Palestinians in those territories began a revolt called the *intifada*, or uprising. Guerrilla tactics were used, like throwing rocks and handmade bombs at the Israeli military forces, and they were supported by the PLO. The Israeli government responded with force and killed some Palestinians; they refused to negotiate with a terrorist group like the PLO.

An Arab Would Say...

If you asked an Arab about these conflicts, he or she would probably say something like this: The creation of Israel was wrong; it was just another sign of Western imperialism. That land belonged to us, and we never accepted the partition plan of 1947. Palestinians deserve a homeland too; it has been promised. Besides, most Middle Easterners are Arabs and Israel threatens our values. The UN has condemned Israeli actions in occupied territories, and Jerusalem is our third holiest city—it contains the Dome of the Rock, and the El Aksa Mosque. Arab sovereignty in Palestine was more recent than Jewish sovereignty, and Israel seeks to expand beyond its borders. They must give back land gained in wars; the Intifada shows how wrong Israeli occupation is.

An Israeli Would Say...

If you asked an Israeli about these conflicts, he or she would probably say something like this: It is our homeland; it was promised to us in the Bible. The Arabs even sold it to us before 1948, and other Arabs fled from it. The UN Partition Plan was approved by almost everyone. We're too small to threaten all of the Arabs, and those Arabs who reside here are doing quite well, living in the only democracy in the Middle East. A Jewish state is necessary because of all the anti-Semitism in the world. Jordan exists as a state for Palestinians; it was created illegally by the British from 77 percent of the land that Britain got as a mandate from the League of Nations. In fact, most Jordanians today are Palestinians. If the UN does condemn us, it's because of oil politics. Jerusalem was our capital in ancient times, and it's our holy city, containing the Western Wall and the sites of the first two temples, and Jordan restricted us from them when it ruled Jerusalem. Note that today we permit the Muslim holy sites here to be watched over by members of the Israeli Muslim community. Jewish sovereignty in Palestine was earlier in history than that of Arabs, and we wouldn't have all this other land if the Arabs didn't attack us so often. We never intentionally tried to take it away, unlike the Arabs, who have tried to take away and destroy Israeli land. We're willing to negotiate if they would stop warring with us. We're willing to exchange land for peace, like the return of the Sinai to Egypt. The Intifada is just another attempt to destroy us, which would end if they would just recognize our right to exist.

1990S ISSUES

Arabs are worried about the immigration of Russian Jews and the growth of Israeli settlements in occupied territories. They are indirectly boycotting Israel; direct trade is forbidden, so Arabs won't do business with anyone doing business with Israel. Many companies are afraid of losing the Arabs, so they won't touch Israel; Israel has repeatedly asked for an end to the boycott. Iraq's threats of nuclear and gas attacks against Israel cause worry about a possible fifth Arab-Israeli war. Israel was not a participant in the 1991 Persian Gulf War, yet Iraq was responsible for the unprovoked firing of Scud missiles on Israel.

After World War II, the Middle East was an extension of the Cold War between the U.S. and the Soviet Union. The U.S. has been a consistent ally of Israel. The 1990 Iraqi invasion of Kuwait (which we're getting to) is the first major post-World War II struggle in which the U.S. and the Soviets simultaneously supported the same side (which was Kuwait); this was one sign that the Cold War had ended. The Soviet Union, a longtime supplier of weapons to the Arabs, broke up in 1991, so weapons aid for the Arabs was affected, and this also increased U.S. influence as the world's chief superpower. Our prestige increased further with our swift defeat of Iraq's forces in the Persian Gulf War, and President George Bush used the U.S.'s enhanced diplomatic status to organize a historic Middle East Peace Conference. It was held in Madrid, Spain, with representatives from Israel, Egypt, Syria, Lebanon, and a joint Palestinian-Jordanian delegation; it was the first time Israelis and the PLO met formally. Differences were aired, but there were no real solutions.

FINALLY...

In 1993, the PLO and Israel agreed to officially recognize each other. President Bill Clinton, Israeli Prime Minister Yitzhak Rabin, and PLO Chairman Yassir Arafat shook hands and signed a peace agreement that provided the following: Israelis would withdraw from Gaza and the West Bank city of Jericho, there would be a five-year period of Palestinian self-rule with a municipal government in these areas, and talks on a permanent agreement would start later. There were protests in Israel and in the occupied territories by those on both sides who were upset with the pact, some of which protests led to violence. Also in 1993, an agreement was signed in Jerusalem between Israel and the Vatican, whereby diplomatic relations would be established for the first time. The Roman Catholic church would now recognize the state of Israel, reversing its prior policy. In 1994, Rabin and King Hussein of Jordan (the longest-reigning Arab ruler, since 1952) signed a peace treaty that ended forty years of war between them. In 1995, Israel and the PLO signed an accord that transferred much more of the West Bank to the control of its Arab residents. Rabin was assassinated in November 1995 by an Israeli extremist who didn't like these advances toward peace. This endangered the peace process.

OTHER WARS: THE WAR IN AFGHANISTAN (1979–1989)

In 1979, the Soviet Union invaded Afghanistan, claiming it was responding to a request from the Communist Afghan government, which was in danger of being overthrown, but many people believe it was to gain access to oil and gas and possibly to reach through Iran into the Persian Gulf. The Soviets might also have been afraid of the impact that Islamic fundamentalism in Afghanistan and Iran might have on the Muslims in the Soviet Union. The Soviet military action was condemned by lots of nations including members of the Union itself. Afghan fighters, the Mujahadeen, were aided by the United States and thwarted the Soviet victory. In 1989, the Soviets retreated with severe military and political losses. Because of high Soviet casualties and its unpopularity at home in the USSR, Afghanistan is sometimes called "Russia's Vietnam." Afghanistan is still not stable. The civil war there means the country effectively has no government.

LEBANON

When the French mandate in Lebanon (the capital of which, Beirut, used to be known as the "Paris of the Middle East") ended in 1943, a government was created to try to strike a fair balance; Christians were then the majority group, so most of the top positions, like president and armed forces commander, went to them. This was fine until the 1970s, when Muslims became the majority group, and wanted changes to give them more power. Also, Palestinian refugees, including PLO leaders, settled in Lebanon as a result of the Arab-Israeli wars. Palestinians raided Israel from these settlements, remember? Lebanese Christians, represented by the Phalange Party, were against the Palestinian presence in Lebanon. In 1975, Muslims and Christians started to fight each other, and there was also infighting within these groups; each group had militias.

Syria got involved in this civil war at the request of the Arab League (which was formed in 1945 to coordinate the region's political and economic policies), but by 1990 Syria was occupying Lebanon. Iran and Libya also got involved, with some groups carrying out terrorist activities all over the world, like hijacking airplanes and taking hostages. There was no leader in Lebanon to get control of this war, and Lebanon's economy was ruined. It finally ended in 1990 with the National Reconciliation Pact, which provided for a new government in which Muslims and Christians share power equally. The Lebanese army got control of most of the country, with a little help from Syrian forces. Electricity and other basic services were restored, people who had fled came back, and Syria kept its soldiers there and influenced the new government. The Christians want Syria out, but they won't leave. The war between Lebanese Christians and Muslims continues with Syrian forces playing a major role.

THE ISLAMIC REVOLUTION

In 1941, the Shah (the monarch) of Iran, Muhammad Riza Pahlevi, was installed as a figurehead after his father was forced to resign. In a 1953 coup supported by Great Britain and the United States, the Shah assumed control of the government. He spent billions in oil revenues on modernization programs, and ruled as a dictator using his secret police, the Savak, to suppress any opposition. He granted some rights to women that conservative Muslims claimed were forbidden under Islamic law. Ayatollah Khomeini, the Shiite Muslim leader who had organized opposition to the Shah, was exiled. Religious tensions and anti-Western hostilities led to the overthrow of the American-backed Shah in 1979. The Shah left Iran; Khomeini returned and declared Iran an Islamic republic. This was called the Iranian Revolution or the Islamic Revolution. The rise of Islamic fundamentalism, a movement based on the extremely strict following of Muslim religious traditions, swept the nation, and all pro-Western policies were banned. Khomeini supported terrorist activities. Later that year, Iranian militants seized the American embassy in Tehran and took hostages, insisting on the Shah's return from the United States; he never returned, and he died in Egypt in 1980. The 52 hostages were held for 444 days, and were finally released on January 21, 1981 right after Ronald Reagan took power in the United States.

THE IRAN-IRAQ WAR

Shiite Iran, led by Khomeini, and Sunni Iraq, led by Saddam Hussein, went to war in September 1980 over the Shatt-al Arab waterway that divides the two countries, religious reasons, and oil. Although the war had elements of a traditional border dispute, some also think it was an expansion of the fundamentalist revolution of Iran. Each nation wanted to dominate the Persian Gulf area, and Iraq feared the "export" of the Iranian Revolution. They fought eight years of savage war, millions were killed, and oil shipments to and from the Persian Gulf were disrupted. In 1988, the war ended as a stalemate when both sides signed a UN ceasefire agreement. In 1989, the Ayatollah (which means "a reflection of God") died.

THE PERSIAN GULF WAR: OPERATION DESERT STORM

In 1990, Saddam Hussein's Iraq invaded and seized Kuwait and threatened to invade nearby Saudi Arabia, which would have given Iraq control over 40 percent of the world's oil reserves. The UN condemned Iraq and imposed a trade embargo. Hussein refused to leave; Iraqi troops killed, tortured, and raped thousands of Kuwaitis. President Bush and other nations sent troops to Saudi Arabia to protect it from possible invasion, establishing an international peacekeeping force consisting of troops from Egypt, Syria, Morocco, Canada, Great Britain, and France. The UN gave Hussein a January 15, 1991 deadline to withdraw, and he didn't, so on January 16, the United States and its allies began air strikes against Iraq. These lasted until February, when the ground war began, which lasted 100 hours. In February of 1991, Kuwait was liberated from Iraqi control. Eight hundred of Kuwait's 950 oil wells were damaged in the war. Hussein is still in power and still has a large army and weapons; he has failed to cooperate with UN inspection teams. The war upset the ecology of the Persian Gulf, from the burning of oil wells to the release of petroleum into gulf waters. The war caused a split among Arabs: Egypt, Saudi Arabia, Syria and Kuwait sided with the United States; Jordan, Yemen, Tunisia, Algeria, and the PLO sided with Iraq, though they didn't send any fighters.

THE KURDS

The Kurds are a big ethnic group in Iraq who have spread out to parts of Iran, Turkey, and Syria. They want a nation of their own called Kurdistan. But that nation would have to come from land area in these four countries, and that's probably not going to happen. Kurdish people in Iraq have been treated badly by Hussein, and their attempts to break away from Iraqi rule have been suppressed. Many have been killed or forced to become refugees; thousands have been given "safe-haven" areas in northern Iraq under the protection of the United States and the UN. This is an ongoing problem.

LIBYA

Since Colonel Muammar Qaddafi came to power in 1969, Libya has supported terrorist groups. The bombing of Pan Am flight 103 as it flew over Lockerbie, Scotland, killing all 259 passengers and crew members, is the most blatant example. This is state-supported terrorism: A policy that supports, trains, finances, and protects terrorist organizations. Qaddafi nationalized the foreign oil companies and allowed one political party. He also followed Islamic fundamentalism and set up a religious state.

In the 1990s, Libya and Iran have been purchasing intermediate range Silkworm missiles made in China. These are accurate missiles capable of carrying biological, chemical, and nuclear warheads. This puts Western Europe in the range of terrorist states in the Middle East. South Africa is also exporting missile technology to high bidders in the Middle East.

OIL, OIL, OIL

Oil is a non-renewable resource, which makes it all the more precious. The Middle East has oil, but not much else in the way of resources. The expanding population and limited amount of agricultural land has caused the Middle East to import more food than it exports. Leading oil-producing nations include Saudi Arabia, Kuwait, Iraq, Iran, and the Gulf States. From about 1900 to 1970, oil production was largely dominated by the British, French, Dutch, and Americans, because they could supply the factors for production: land, labor, capital (both money and machinery), and management; the things necessary to make a product. The Middle East had the land, but not the rest. These foreigners promised to produce and sell the oil and to give royalties, a percentage of the money earned from selling the oil, to the oil-rich nations. By the 1970s, these Middle Eastern nations wanted higher royalties and more control, which led to the creation of OPEC.

OPEC

The Organization of Petroleum Exporting Countries was formed in 1960, because of the situation described above: industrial nations used their economic power to help Middle Eastern nations develop their oil reserves, and in exchange, Western oil companies controlled the prices and royalties earned from the region's most valuable resource. To break Western influence, thirteen major oil-rich nations in Asia, Africa, and Latin America (dominated by the Arab nations) formed OPEC. Throughout the 1960s, oil companies were able to counter OPEC's power because they owned the technology and the means of producing the oil. Also, back then the production of oil was lower than the demand, and it remained relatively low until the 1970s.

Demand for oil grew in the 1970s, and power shifted from the oil companies to the oil-producing nations. During the 1973 Yom Kippur War with Israel, Arab members of OPEC refused to sell oil to anyone supporting Israel. Included in this embargo was the United States, which in 1973 was getting nearly half its oil from the Middle East. This caused global oil shortages and raised the price of oil on the world market. So the issue was, Who's got the power now? OPEC has the power to affect the whole world with "oil politics." Saudi Arabia's embargo of oil shipments to the United States in 1973 and 1974 was designed to force the United States to behave in a certain way toward Israel. The global recession in the 1980s and increased fuel efficiency in industrial nations helped reduce the power of OPEC. But then the prices dropped, conservation efforts declined, and fuel consumption again rose.

As the 1990s began, the oil-rich nations had achieved complete control over their oil and had become very wealthy in "petro" dollars. Internally, use of this wealth to benefit people has led to a dramatic increase in the standard of living in such nations as Saudi Arabia, where new highways, houses, hospitals, and schools have been built. But this has clashed with some of the traditional beliefs about marriage, child-rearing, and attitudes toward women. In fact, the role of women in Islamic societies is an issue that divides Muslims. Wealth from oil resulted in a secular (emphasis on the worldly, nonspiritual) middle class that is Westernized, and this worries conservative Islamic leaders. Remember, religious tensions and anti-Western hostilities led to the overthrow of the Shah of Iran in 1979.

The wealth from oil has also increased the gap between the "have" and "have not" nations. Not all nations in the Middle East have oil. For example, Egypt and Turkey are the most populous nations in the Middle East, but they produce far less oil than they consume and they lack significant reserves. Therefore, both nations have had to get friendly with the United States, which has led to conflicts with their Arab neighbors. A few nations, such as Libya and Iraq, have bought large inventories of armaments with oil profits. Other governments in the region nationalized foreign oil companies, fortifying the move toward Arab socialism.

ARAB SOCIALISM IN EGYPT

Egypt assumed a leadership role in the Middle East in the post-World War II period because of its more highly developed economy and emphasis on Arab unity; since then, the power has basically shifted to whoever has the oil. Under President Gamel Abdel Nasser, who held power from 1954 to 1970, Egypt broke up its large estates and redistributed the land to Egyptian peasants known as the fellahin. With Soviet aid, Egypt also built the Aswan Dam to control flooding on the Nile and increase its farmland. However, the dam caused unforeseen ecological damage, blocking the accumulation of silt and increasing erosion along the Mediterranean coast. Nasser's dream was to create a unified Arab state; this dream of Pan-Arabism died with him in 1970, and his vice president Anwar Sadat was elected president.

MIXED ECONOMY IN ISRAEL

Israel's economic planners chose diversification and industrialization over agricultural development. It is the most technologically advanced nation in Middle East, but its political isolation has limited its economic interaction with neighboring countries. Israel allows private ownership of some property, but it has also developed the kibbutz, or collectively owned farm, in which people share equally in the work and the profits. Israel has diversified its agricultural production so that it doesn't have to rely on a risky single cash crop. Israel's economy is improving with the growth of high-tech industries, with help from the emigration of Jews from the former Soviet Union, many of whom are engineers and scientists. But one has to house these immigrants, as well as immigrants from Ethiopia, called Falasha Jews. Israel is the only democracy in the Middle East, and although it was established as a Jewish state, it permits religious freedom to all people within its borders. Israel also has a large military budget, and it depends on foreign aid and investment.

Many Middle Eastern nations need foreign aid; Egypt and Israel are among the five largest recipients of U.S. aid. Overpopulation puts a strain on the economy. There is extensive spending on weapons, especially in Libya, Egypt, Syria, Jordan, Iran, Iraq, and Israel, so this money is not as available for social programs. Tourism is a primary source of income, but governments are concerned about terrorist attacks.

MORE PROBLEMS

It's hard to reconcile Arab solidarity with fundamentalism; even Islam itself is divided. Terrorism, like war in past history, is being used to further nationalistic ends and change international relationships. Other problems include the uneven distribution of oil, territorial disputes, and issues of Israeli security and Arab Palestinian nationalism. Water resources continue to be key to settlement locations; strategic geographical aspects like valleys and mountains are also key because both Israel and Arabs want to control these areas.

Western Europe

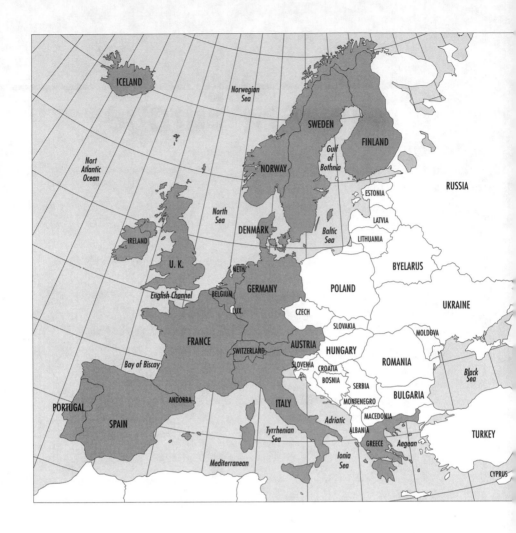

GEOGRAPHY

Western Europe is made up of over twenty nations. Northwestern Europe includes Ireland, the United Kingdom (England, Scotland, Wales, and Northern Ireland), France, and the Benelux countries (Belgium, the Netherlands, and Luxembourg). Southern Europe includes Portugal, Spain, Italy, and Greece. Middle, or Central Europe includes Germany, Switzerland, Austria, and Liechtenstein. Scandinavia includes Iceland, Norway, Sweden, Finland, Denmark, and Greenland. There are also other little countries, like Vatican City, the only state whose official language is Latin.

Europe is the world's second smallest continent; the smallest is Australia. Europe is basically a big peninsula located on a huge land mass called Eurasia; Europe itself has been called the "peninsula of peninsulas" because it has so many peninsulas.

TOPOGRAPHY

Europe is surrounded by the Atlantic Ocean on the west, the Mediterranean Sea on the south, and the Arctic, Baltic, and North Seas on the north. The Caucasus and Ural mountains separate Europe from Asia in the east. The English Channel separates Britain from the European mainland, and has provided protection in the past, but now there's a tunnel called the Chunnel that connects England to France.

Most of Western Europe has easy access to warm water ports and navigable rivers, which always encourage cultural diffusion and economic interdependence. The irregular coastline has tons of excellent harbors; in fact, the coastline is so jagged that Europe has more meters of coastline than any other continent. All parts of Western Europe are pretty close to water, which has influenced its role in world affairs; from the 1600s to the mid-1900s, they set out by sea to build empires. Western European nations have held colonies on every other continent on this planet.

The Alps, the highest mountains in Europe, run through Switzerland and Austria. The Pyrenees run between France and Spain; they have restricted movement between those two countries, separating the Iberian Peninsula (Spain and Portugal) from the rest of the region. The Apennines are in Italy, and the Sierra Nevadas are in Southern Spain. Along the coasts and between the mountain ranges are flat fertile plains. The Northern European Plain reaches from Great Britain in the West to Russia in the east. The greatest population of Europe lives here, and there are no natural barriers to prevent invasion; both Napoleon and Hitler took advantage of that. There are lowlands, especially in the Netherlands, which has built systems of dikes and sea walls to reclaim the land. The Danube River is the longest river in Europe; it starts in Germany and flows to the Black Sea. The Rhine River flows out of the Swiss Alps, across Germany and the Netherlands, and into the North Sea. Other important rivers include the Seine in France and the Thames in England.

CLIMATE

Almost half of Europe is on the same latitude as Canada, but it's warmer and wetter than Canada because it's all so close to the water. Western Europe benefits from the Atlantic Drift: The warm-water Gulf Stream flows out of the Gulf of Mexico and the Caribbean Sea and heads northeast, eventually hitting the shores of Western Europe. This current moderates the climate of Western Europe for most of the year, so its ports are ice-free. Southern Europe has a Mediterranean climate, so in Spain, France, Italy and Greece, the summers are hot and dry, the winters are subtropical most of the time, and there's some rain (kind of like the climates of California and South Africa).

RESOURCES

Western Europe has lots of resources for industry, like coal and iron; in fact, the Industrial Revolution began here. Europeans have used technology to reshape their physical environment. For example, only a small percentage of the land is suitable for farming, but the farms are efficient, using technology and scientific farming methods to produce crops like sugar, beets, and potatoes. Europeans have also exported their technological knowledge and equipment. Europeans have turned to the seas for a living, so fish is big there.

SOCIETY

Western European society is made up of a variety of religious, ethnic, and linguistic groups, from outside Europe as well as inside. Almost all the languages use the Roman alphabet, and share similarities in the way words are put together and spoken, so people in one nation can often understand the language of another, and many Europeans are multilingual because of similarities and proximity of countries; there is frequent travel and economic exchange. French,

Spanish, Portuguese, and Italian are referred to as the Romance languages. English is a Germanic language. German and Dutch have a lot in common, while the Scandinavian languages, except for Finnish, are similar. The Hungarian language is Asian in origin and has qualities not found in any other Western language. Some nations are officially bilingual because of their population, like Switzerland, where both French and German are spoken, and Belgium, where both Flemish and French are spoken.

Before the Industrial Revolution (1750), most Europeans were farmers, and families were extended and patriarchal. The prevailing system of feudalism permitted little social mobility. The Crusades helped revive interest in trade, which led to the emergence of the middle class of merchants, the class that pushed for change because they were wealthy and resented their commoner status. During the Industrial Revolution, the middle class fought for suffrage. Then, with the advent of industrialization, urbanization took place, and the family became nuclear; in the city, you could only support your immediate family. With that, Europe became more egalitarian. Today, the largest nations in Western Europe are Germany, Italy, and France. Overpopulation and overcrowding are not a problem in Western Europe, because it is very industrialized, and there is a high standard of living and modern health care. People live longer, marry later, and have smaller families.

RELIGION

Religion has served both to unify and divide the peoples of Europe. The majority of the people in Western Europe are Catholic, with the largest concentration in the south, in Spain and Italy. Protestants are found mainly in the north, as in England and Sweden. Christianity was founded on the teachings of Jesus, whom Christians believe fulfilled the Old Testament promise of a messiah, or savior, for the Jews. Christianity is rooted in Hebrew religious traditions, like the Ten Commandments, and was based on the idea of love of God and neighbor. Their sacred book is the Bible, which includes the Old Testament and the New Testament. The New Testament tells the story of Jesus and the work of his Apostles, who were his disciples, and the first Christian missionaries (for more details, see the Middle East chapter).

In A.D. 313, the Edict of Milan was issued under Emperor Constantine (more about him later), which permitted religious freedom for Christians; eventually, Emperor Constantine himself converted, and Christianity became the official religion of his empire in A.D. 395. There were different views on religious authority between the church in Rome, led by the Pope, and the church in Constantinople, led by the Patriarch. So the Christian Church split in 1054, with the Eastern Orthodox Church for Byzantine and Russia, and the Roman Catholic Church, the most powerful and influential institution in Europe during the Middle Ages for Western Europe.

Jews have been a minority in Europe for centuries; they share many beliefs with Christians, including the Old Testament. Europe also has Muslims; France's Islamic community come mainly from Morocco and Algeria, former French colonies. Most of the Hindus and Muslims in England come from the Indian subcontinent. The Muslims in Germany are mainly Turks who immigrated for economic reasons.

THE ARTS

Well, we have to start with Ancient Greece and Rome. They stressed secular, or non-religious values. Greek sculptures stressed the love of beauty, perfection, balance, symmetry, and the human body. They often used their gods as subjects; for example, the *Venus de Milo*. The Romans borrowed the style of the Greeks, but made it more realistic, using ordinary people as their subjects. The Greeks created well-proportioned buildings, especially the Parthenon. The Romans were more concerned with the practical, building public buildings and aqueducts. Greek and Roman literature was about history, heroes, and legends; the *Iliad*, the *Odyssey*, and the *Aeneid* are examples.

During the Middle Ages, religion was everywhere. Religious subjects were presented in an unrealistic, two-dimensional style, to show the importance of the soul over the body. The construction of cathedrals was prolific, with the gothic style of vaulted ceilings, stained glass windows, and pointed arches; the style represented worshippers reaching toward heaven. The music was religious, too, but there were also court pieces written for kings and lords. Literature was represented by epic poems like *Beowulf*, which praises the virtues of chivalry.

During the Renaissance, the magic word was humanism, which started as a literary movement, and copied the classical styles of ancient Greece and Rome, in which there was a renewed interest. Literature was secular, and written in the vernacular, the everyday language spoken by people, as distinguished from the literary language. Perhaps the most famous example was William Shakespeare, with his unique understanding of human feelings, problems, and relationships. Some of his works include *Romeo and Juliet*, *Hamlet*, and *Julius Caesar*. Renaissance artists were also inspired by Greece and Rome, but the art was three-dimensional and lifelike, with an attention to detail coming from the fact that people were scientifically studying anatomy. Unlike medieval artists, Renaissance artists painted individual portraits and depicted everyday scenes like landscapes. Man was the center of the universe and earthly life was as important as the afterlife. Da Vinci and Michelangelo were Renaissance artists.

Romanticism reflected the spirit of the French Revolution (1789-1799), which promoted nationalism and individual freedom, and was a reaction to the problems of the Industrial Revolution. Romantics praised beauty, emotion, nature, and past glories. Romantic literature is represented by John Keats, an English poet who wrote numerous odes and sonnets reflecting love of beauty and nature (like *Ode to a Nightingale*, and *To Autumn*). The French painter Eugene Delacroix painted dramatic scenes full of emotion and color (like *Liberty Leading the People*, which was inspired by the Revolution of 1830). German composer Ludwig von Beethoven wrote symphonies, concertos, sonatas, and quartets. The Realism movement confronted the problems of the Industrial Revolution, and was influenced by everyday people and life. Charles Dickens, an English novelist, called attention to industrial-age problems with *Hard Times*, *Oliver Twist*, and *David Copperfield*. Impressionism was a reaction against realism, an attempt to capture feelings or impressions about a particular moment or scene in nature. It was inspired by the Japanese painting style, and Claude Monet is perhaps the best known Impressionist painter.

Europe's contemporary culture is affected by science, technology, and politics. As Western Europe became more industrialized, writers and artists began looking at the human cost. French philosopher Jean-Paul Sartre expressed the idea that life has no meaning. He said that people must create their own standards of what's right and wrong. This is called existentialism, and it has had a lot of influence among mid-twentieth century intellectuals. Another existentialist, Simone de Beauvoir, examined the position of women in society in her book *The Second Sex* (1953). An Irish playwright, Samuel Beckett, portrayed loneliness, alienation, and the futile search for spiritual guidance in modern life in his 1952 play *Waiting for Godot*. Spanish artist Pablo Picasso took impressionism a million steps further by portraying the human body in a cubist and geometric light. Many twentieth century artists were abstractionists, creating paintings, drawings, and sculptures that really had no identifiable subject at all.

A TIMELINE OF WESTERN EUROPEAN HISTORY

Pre-history–3500 B.C.	Emergence of Civilization
2000 B.C.–A.D. 476	Ancient Greece and Rome
500–1500	Middle Ages and Rise of Nations
1350–1650	Renaissance and Reformation
1450–1750	Exploration and Colonization
1500–1789	Establishment of Absolute Monarchies
1500–1800	Scientific Revolution and Enlightenment
1789–1848	Age of Revolutions
1750–1914	Industrial Revolution
1830–1914	Age of New Imperialism
1914–1919	World War I; Treaty of Versailles
1922–1939	Rise of Totalitarianism
1939–1945	World War II
1945–present	Cold War and Recovery

Between 10,000 B.C. and 3500 B.C., the nomadic people of Western Europe developed farming methods that allowed them to settle down and build civilizations with complex governments and religions, social classes, and recordkeeping. The period of classical civilizations is sometimes called the Age of Antiquity.

ANCIENT GREECE (750 B.C.–150 B.C.)

Greece is composed of islands and peninsulas in the Mediterranean. The Greeks were the first people of Western Europe to develop an advanced culture. Unlike other early civilizations, like India and China, ancient Greece did not develop near a river valley.

The mountains in Greece made it hard for the people to unite, so isolated communities developed into independent political units called city-states. One city-state was Sparta, whose society revolved around physical training and the military. Sparta was monolithic, meaning there was only one acceptable way to think or act; it was a totalitarian state, ruled by just a few people, the landowners and nobility. The majority of Spartans, including the slaves, or helots, had no voice; Sparta could be called an aristocracy because it was ruled by a such a small number of people.

Then there was Athens, which, by 450 B.C., had developed the world's first democracy; democracy is a Greek word meaning "rule by the people." It was a direct democracy; all citizens had the right to take part in lawmaking in the Assembly, and citizens voted directly. There were limitations, like the fact that women couldn't vote, and not all men were citizens. But Athens was a pluralistic society, encouraging free expression. A well-rounded education was emphasized, the goal of which was a sound mind and a sound body.

The Golden Age of Greece (461 B.C.–429 B.C.)

The different city-states quarreled among themselves, but they united against the Persians. In the Persian Wars (500 B.C.–479 B.C.), the Greeks stopped the westward expansion of the Persian Empire. Soon after that, the Golden Age of Greece, or the Age of Pericles began. Pericles encouraged the growth of democracy, cultural and scientific achievement, and ordered the building of the Parthenon, a temple to the goddess Athena which was built on a hill called the Acropolis. Greece had an environment conducive to expression and creativity.

Greek Contributions to Civilization

The Greeks invented tragedy and comedy, and two of the big playwrights were Sophocles (*Oedipus Rex*) and Aristophenes (*Lysistrata*). Homer wrote *The Iliad* and *The Odyssey*. In the world of philosophy, there was Socrates, who said "the unexamined life is not worth living" and "know thyself." He believed that truth can be discovered by asking a series of questions and challenging accepted beliefs (this became known as the "Socratic method"). He was accused of corrupting the youth of Athens and was put to death. Socrates' student, Plato, wrote *The Republic*, which attacked democracy and said that philosophers should run the state. Plato's student, Aristotle, wrote his thoughts on reason, logic, science, ethics, and government, which have been influential for almost 2,000 years.

The Greeks crafted well-proportioned marble buildings, and developed three types of columns: Doric, Ionic, and Corinthian. They idealized the human body, and used gods as subjects in their sculpture, where they celebrated beauty and perfection. In mathematics, there were advances in geometry from Pythagoras, regarding right triangles, and Euclid, who gave us geometry based on deductive reasoning. Democritus suggested that matter was composed of atoms. Archimedes was a physicist who discovered the uses of the lever and the pulley, and Hippocrates was the Father of Medicine, whose oath is still used by doctors today. The Olympic Games were held in honor of the god Zeus, and are the basis for today's Olympics. The Greeks set the standard of excellence by which other cultural achievements were measured. They influenced the Middle East, India, China, and Japan.

Meanwhile, city-states like Sparta resented Athens' influence, and this led to conflicts which have been referred to as the Peloponnesian Wars (431 B.C.–404 B.C.). In the conflict between Athens and Sparta, Sparta won, and brought Athens under its control, but it couldn't unite all the city-states. Most of the city-states were united by the conquests of King Philip II of Macedonia, the region to the north of Greece, in 338 B.C. He was able to step right in and conquer Greece because it had been weakened by the Peloponnesian Wars. When Philip died, he passed everything on to his son Alexander.

ALEXANDER THE GREAT (356 B.C.–323 B.C.)

Alexander extended his territory from Greece, forming an empire that stretched all the way to India in the east and Egypt in the south; this was the largest world empire up to that time. Alexander, an admirer of Greek culture, was taught by Aristotle, and he helped spread Greek culture throughout this whole area. The resulting unique blend of Greek, Asian, and Middle Eastern cultures was known as the Hellenistic Period (336 B.C.–150 B.C.).

Hellenistic Advances

In philosophy, Diogenes founded the school of Cynics. Cynicism included criticism of materialism and social conventions and a distrust of human virtue. Zeno founded Stoicism, which advocated freedom from passion and desires, and detachment from the outside world. Epicurus founded Epicureanism, which advocated the search for pleasure and happiness while maintaining a sense of moderation. Big names in math and science at the time include Aristarchus (in astronomy), Euclid (in geometry), Archimedes (in physics), and Eratosthenes (in geography).

When Alexander died, his empire was divided into three parts, each ruled by one of his generals. In less than 200 years, these parts reunited under the Roman Empire.

ROME (500 B.C.–A.D. 200)

While the geography of Greece divided the people, the Italian peninsula's geography allowed people to unite, so there was a monarchy in Rome from 753 B.C. to 509 B.C., when the kings were overthrown. By 500 B.C. the Latin peoples of central Italy, also known as Romans, had created a republic.

Over a 200-year period, democracy expanded as the plebeians, or lower class, attained more power. Important political gains were made by the plebeians, the farmers and workers, who won the right to become members of the assembly and to vote for tribunes, who could take action against the Senate. Plebeian gains also included the codification, or writing down, of laws into the Twelve Tables of Law, which protected the rights of citizens. The Roman Republic's population was much larger than that of Greece, and the citizens couldn't directly take part in government, so there was an indirect democracy with representatives. The real power was held by the Senate, which represented the patricians, or upper class, and two consuls, who served as the heads of state.

Becoming an Empire (340 B.C.–27 B.C.)

After conquering the Italian Peninsula, Rome took control of lands bordering the western Mediterranean; it had success in the Punic Wars (264 B.C.–146 B.C.) against Carthage, a rival city in North Africa. Next they conquered the eastern Mediterranean and acquired the Greek lands that were once Alexander's: Greece, Egypt, and the Middle East. So, through a series of wars, Rome expanded and dominated the Mediterranean area, selectively borrowing from those they conquered, and improving their society. The Mediterranean Sea had pretty much become a Roman lake ("Mare Nostrum" for you Latin-speakers).

Julius Caesar

As Rome grew, so did the gap between rich and poor. People tend to support strong leaders during times of crisis, and conflicts within Roman society set the stage for Julius Caesar, a dictator, and then Augustus, an emperor. Under Julius Caesar, Rome held land on three continents, and by 50 B.C. was the largest empire known to the world. The Roman army changed from a civilian force to a selectively trained group of professional soldiers, so they were more loyal to their generals than to the republican government. Military commanders got more power and fought in civil wars for control of Rome. The republic changed into a dictatorship, and in 46 B.C., Julius Caesar became the dictator. He was succeeded by three generals, one of whom was Octavian, who became the first emperor of Rome when he took the title Caesar Augustus and established the Roman Empire.

The Roman Empire (27 B.C.–A.D. 476)

The Roman Empire was an autocracy in which power was held by one man—the emperor. Augustus ruled from 27 B.C. to 14 A.D. as an absolute ruler who believed in governing for the good of the people; he brought about fairer taxation and a civil service. The so-called Augustan Age was the start of 200 years of stability, peace, and progress called the Pax Romana (27 B.C.–180 A.D.).

Rome flourished during the Pax Romana ("Roman Peace" in Latin), which led to a Golden Age, the peak of the civilization. In architecture, Romans perfected the arch and the dome, and were the first to use concrete. Massive concrete structures like the Colosseum were built, symbolizing the strength and power of the Empire. Roads and bridges were built, promoting unity and interdependence, as well as aqueducts to carry water from countrysides to cities. The Latin language was the basis for the Romance languages, which include Spanish, Italian, French, Portuguese, Romanian, and half of all English words. In law and justice, the code of law centered on those Twelve Tables, which were carved onto stone and displayed in the Forum, or public square. This ensured public knowledge of the law and fair treatment in the courts; the Romans came up with the concept of innocent until proven guilty. This is the time when Cicero wrote speeches and Virgil wrote *The Aeneid*.

Unlike the Greeks, the Romans were able to govern a large Mediterranean empire, which strongly influenced the development of European political systems; but in terms of arts, literature and drama, they relied on the cultural patterns of the Greeks. The Roman concepts of justice, natural law and human equality played a major role in shaping thought during the Middle Ages and the Enlightenment.

The Growth of Christianity

Initially, Roman law offered limited human rights to citizens, including the Christians, who were perceived as a subversive, dissident group, but whose ideas of brotherhood and equality sounded good to slaves and the poor. Roman authorities were mad because people weren't worshipping the emperor, and although Christians faced persecution, or perhaps because of it, the religion grew, spread by St. Paul and other followers of Jesus.

The Decline of the Western Roman Empire (180–476)

In 395, the Roman Empire split into East and West. The Eastern Roman Empire, or the Byzantine Empire centered around Constantinople and regained strength (see the Middle East chapter). This was not so in the Western Roman Empire, which was centered around Rome. At its height, Rome had actively participated in a globally interdependent economic system, which ultimately led to its downfall as unfavorable balances of trade increased, which lowered the value of Rome's money. The rulers wasted money, the government was weak and corrupt, and because there was no orderly way to choose the next emperor, the role often fell to the strongest general. Assassinations were commonplace. There were heavy taxes, high unemployment, and a decline in trade. The people had developed a selfish attitude, and the resulting lack of patriotism forced the government to rely on a mercenary army of non-Romans who were only interested in the spoils of war. Slaves were badly treated, the class system was rigid, and the teachings of Christianity conflicted with the dictatorial policies of Roman emperors. All of this made Rome vulnerable to invasion. Meanwhile, Germanic peoples were gaining power which they used to create new economic and political arrangements based on the Roman system. These Germanic tribes invaded and took Roman territory in the third century. Rome itself fell to the Ostrogoths in A.D. 476.

THE MIDDLE AGES (500–1500)

The Middle Ages is the period between the end of the Roman Empire and the start of modern European history. "Medieval" describes this period of transition when the people of Western Europe tried to rebuild what had been lost with the fall of Rome. The first 500 years (500-1000) are called the Dark Ages, because there were lots of invasions that shaped the character and direction of the culture. The Vikings, or Norse, came from the north, the Magyars from the east, and the Muslims from the south, leaving lots of fear in their wake.

The Vikings were especially feared. They were a Germanic farming people who lived in Scandinavia. Viking sailors gained a reputation as fierce raiders. The first Vikings who came south were mainly interested in plunder, but later, some settled in the conquered areas to live and rule. For example, Danish Vikings conquered and ruled England several times. Norwegian Vikings sailed west and established colonies in Iceland, Greenland, and yes, North America. Swedish Vikings set up trade routes through lands that later became Russia; they were called the Rus (more in the Russia chapter). Most Vikings remained in Scandinavia as farmers, becoming more a part of the mainstream of Western European society after Christian missionaries converted them. Eventually, they set up the independent kingdoms of Norway, Sweden, and Denmark. Denmark is actually Europe's oldest kingdom; the monarchy dates back to the tenth century.

When the invasions ended in about the year 1000, political power was decentralized, or held by several small weak groups throughout Europe: the Franks in Gaul, or France, the Visigoths in Spain, the Ostrogoths in Italy, and the Angles and Saxons in England. People felt more loyal to their local ruler than to some larger political system. There was no strong central government, so there was lots of warfare. Roads deteriorated, and merchants were afraid to travel, so trade declined; the use of money nearly ceased, and people resorted to bartering. There was a decline in learning because the constant warfare destroyed libraries, schools, and museums. People concentrated only on survival, neglecting culture and education. The Christian Church, which maintained a centralized organization based in Rome, moved right in and became the center of literacy and a link with the past culture of Rome. It helped to preserve Western civilization and kept learning alive. Meanwhile, the Eastern Roman

Empire, now the Byzantine Empire, maintained schools, etc., and Constantinople became the center of trade (more about that in the Middle East chapter).

Charlemagne (771–814)

Charlemagne was the king of the Germanic tribe known as the Franks, and he was able to create a strong kingdom by the fifth century. He established a great empire in Europe, conquering and uniting lands in parts of present-day Italy, Spain, France, Germany, Czechoslovakia, Austria, Belgium, and Holland. He converted to Christianity and spread it. In 800, the Pope at the time, Leo III, crowned him "Emperor of the Romans" and his empire became known as the Holy Roman Empire (or, as the Germans would call it, the First Reich). Charlemagne ruled effectively and built schools. After Charlemagne's death in 814, his empire fell apart, and Western Europe was again vulnerable to attack. The feudal system developed as a way of restoring order and protection.

Feudalism

Feudalism grew out of Germanic customs, the breakdown in central authority after Charlemagne's death, and the chaos of the invasions in the ninth and tenth centuries (especially those dreaded Vikings). It was a political system of local government based on control of land. Kings granted land, a fief, to nobles, called lords or vassals, in return for their pledge of military support and loyalty. Lords became more powerful than kings as they got more land. The system lacked a strong central authority; the lords made their own laws and had their own armies of knights. Feudalism was also an economic system of manorialism where land, rather than trade or commerce, was the major source of wealth. The manor was the basic economic unit of society, replacing cities; peasants couldn't own land, so they lived under the protection of the lord of the manor, worked the land, and provided food for the upper classes. The manor was self-sufficient, so there was really no need for trade. There were also many agricultural advances, such as the three-field system (crops were planted on two of the fields while the third field was left fallow; then, by rotating the crops, nutrients in the soil would be replenished), the iron-tipped plow (an iron-tip on the end of a wooden plow made it easier to turn over the soil), and the horse collar (oxen had been used to plow the fields, but this collar enabled the faster-moving horse to take over).

Feudalism was also a social system of classes: there were greater lords, lesser lords, knights, peasants or serfs, and townspeople. One's class was determined at birth, and there was little social mobility; kings, lords and knights were the noble elite and were bound by oaths of loyalty and chivalry (a code of behavior). The Christian promise of heaven as a reward for a good life was the only hope of any relief from poverty for the serfs. Feudalism provided cohesion in a chaotic Western Europe; there were sharp class distinctions that everyone understood.

The Medieval Church

Feudalism was not the only thing providing stability in the Middle Ages. Most people of Western Europe belonged to the Catholic faith, which unified the people and provided order in this highly fragmented world. The Church was a place of refuge and hope, but if you violated its laws, you could be excommunicated, or barred from services and the rites believed to help insure salvation from punishment after death for past sins. Excommunication was a huge threat. In the thirteenth century, the Church created a special court, called the Holy Inquisition, to investigate anyone who disobeyed, and tortured and killed people. The Church had a political function, including the power to crown Charlemagne as the Holy Roman Emperor. It also educated Church leaders, kept records of births, marriages, and deaths, and made religious laws. Schools were set up in churches and monasteries, and the Church supported universities, and influenced music, art, and architecture, like those Gothic cathedrals whose statues and stained glass tell the stories of the Bible. The Church preserved classical learning, and ministered to the sick and poor. Bishops and priests were looked to for guidance, especially because they could explain the Bible and were usually the only people around who could read or write. The Church had an economic function, too; it was an important landowner, having acquired wealth through the collection of the tithe, a 10 percent tax on a person's income.

Anti-Semitism

Christians were not permitted to become bankers; the Church forbid usury, or the charging of interest on loans, because its role in the economy was so great that it was able to forbid it. This prohibition on interest only applied to Christians; Jews were permitted to become moneylenders and to charge interest and, because they were prohibited from engaging in most other trades, many Jews created banking houses, and some became wealthy, but they suffered prejudice because of their financial activities. The Roman Catholic Church taught that only those who believe in the teachings of the Church will be saved, and because Jews didn't follow those teachings, they were the targets of prejudice and expulsion; some were forced to live in ghettoes, and sometimes were even forced to convert. These were gross violations of human rights for Jews in Medieval Europe. By losing citizenship rights, Jews lost the political power to protect their choice of livelihood and their right to remain in their own countries. Because of superstition, religious zeal, negative stereotyping and popular distaste for different cultures, Christians made Jews scapegoats for natural disasters. The Jews were even blamed for Bubonic Plague, or the Black Death, which devastated much of Europe during the Middle Ages. This tradition of anti-Semitism in Europe would reach its peak during World War II.

The Crusades

Muslims were also considered enemies of the Church. In the late Middle Ages, 1095 to be exact, Pope Urban II called for a Crusade, or holy war, against the Seljuk Turks, the Muslims who had captured Palestine, the birthplace of Jesus, and were threatening the Christians of the Byzantine Empire. The Crusades were mostly about increasing Church power and wealth and uniting the Western and Eastern branches of Christianity, but these goals were not achieved. Over a period of 200 years, there were eight Crusades, ending in 1291 with the Muslims winning and keeping control of the Holy Land until World War I.

The Revival of Trade Ends Feudalism

The Crusades failed to "liberate" the Holy Land completely, but they resulted in cultural diffusion and the revival of trade. Those centuries of no trade brought about by the self-sufficiency of feudalism were ending. The Crusades created a demand for goods previously unavailable to Europeans, and thus stimulated trade. The Europeans wanted more of the stuff from the East, like silks, spices, and perfumes, which they had gotten a taste of from the Crusades. The stimulation of trade also stimulated the growth of cities, which replaced manors as centers of society; Italian cities became especially wealthy due to their Mediterranean location.

Coined money came back, and a new middle class of merchants and craftsmen grew. They formed organizations called guilds, which regulated trade or crafts in a town. Members of guilds became wealthy, and serfs ran away to towns or bought their freedom and became tenant farmers. The shift from land to money led to the decline of lords and increased the power of kings; also, some feudal lords were either killed in the Crusades or sold their land to go on them. As a result, kings were able to create nation-states, which they then ruled. It didn't hurt that the new middle class needed the protection of a strong ruler, and supported the king. The wealth of the middle class also allowed the king to hire an army so he wouldn't have to rely on the loyalty of lords. Strong kings led to nationalism. By the year 1500, nation-states had been formed in England, France, Spain, Portugal, Denmark, and Sweden (but not in Italy or Germany; keep that in mind).

The scarcity of Asian goods in Europe, particularly after Constantinople fell to the Turks, led Europeans to expand outward in search of new trade routes. The travels of such European traders and missionaries as Marco Polo and John de Plano Carpini within the Mongol Empire increased the Europeans' knowledge of China, India, and the East Indies, and prepared Europeans for overseas expansion. Developments from the more advanced Muslim culture and the Golden Age of Islam also made their way into Europe, including developments in math, science, art, and literature. Europeans also found many Greek and Roman writings that had been lost to them but had been preserved by Muslim scholars, and the combination of the renewed interest in classical civilization and the new ideas from abroad helped bring an end to the Middle Ages and led to the period we call modern history, starting with the Renaissance.

THE RENAISSANCE (1350–1650)

The Renaissance was the "rebirth" of culture and learning in Western Europe. It began in Italy in the fourteenth century. Italy had a rich heritage in the traditions of Greece and Rome, and Italian city-states such as Florence and Milan had grown rich from trade between Europe and the Middle East, again with the help of its swanky Mediterranean location. Members of the middle class and nobility, like Lorenzo de' Medici and his family of Florence, used their wealth to become patrons of the arts. This is how increased trade, greater affluence and the rising power of the middle class created the preconditions for the Renaissance.

Officials of the Church employed artists to decorate cathedrals and monasteries. But the major influence of Renaissance art and literature, secular humanism, had a questioning attitude that was often in conflict with the Church. Humanism focused on man and his world, and on everyday relationships and problems, not on religion and the afterlife, like medieval arts. The emphasis was on the uniqueness and worth of the individual. So the Renaissance marked the move away from the influence of the Church.

Accomplishments

Writers started using the vernacular, the language of the people (like Italian instead of Latin). The invention of the printing press in the 1400s in Germany by Johannes Gutenberg helped spread humanistic books, and also spread traditional religious works; Gutenberg's first printed book was the Bible, which remains the most widely published book in the world. In Renaissance Italy, Niccolo Machiavelli (1469–1527) of Florence wrote a handbook for rulers called *The Prince*, promoting the idea of "power politics;" he said that the "end justifies the means" in gaining and keeping power. This sometimes ruthless approach has been the model for future leaders. Francesco Petrarch (1304–1374) created the sonnet, a fourteen-line poem. Renaissance England produced William Shakespeare (1564–1616), the playwright and poet who explored the depths of human emotions and relationships, and could very well be the greatest writer of all time. Renaissance Spain produced Miguel de Cervantes (1564–1616), who wrote *Don Quixote*. And let's not forget Dante (Italian; wrote the *Divine Comedy*) and Chaucer (English; wrote the *Canterbury Tales*).

Renaissance art used Greco-Roman styles and humanist themes, and took a realistic approach to religious subjects, rather than the two-dimensional Middle Ages style. Leonardo Da Vinci (1452–1519) is recognized as a genius today; he was an inventor, a scientist, a sculptor, an architect, and a painter (he painted the *Last Supper* and the *Mona Lisa*). Michelangelo (1475–1564) did the sculptures of David and the Pieta. He also designed the dome of St. Peter's Basilica in Rome, and painted Biblical scenes on the ceiling of the Sistine Chapel. Other Renaissance painters include El Greco (Spanish; painted *Views of Toledo*) and Rembrandt (Dutch; painted *The Night Watch*).

Renaissance science changed the way people looked at the world, and is sometimes considered the start of a Scientific Revolution. In the thirteenth century, a monk named Roger Bacon encouraged the use of reason to solve problems, and developed the scientific method. Scientists made discoveries that challenged existing theories. Nicolaus Copernicus (1473–1543) was a Polish scientist who developed the heliocentric theory; using math formulas, he figured out that the earth was not the center of the universe. Galileo Galilei (1564–1642) was the Italian scientist who improved the telescope and proved Copernicus right. Church leaders, who taught that the sun revolved around the earth, didn't like this challenge to their authority, and tried Galileo as a heretic and forced him to admit his "error," or face death. Other prominent Renaissance scientists include Harvey (English; discovered circulation of blood in the body), Leeuwenhoek (Dutch; invented the microscope), and Newton (English; discovered the laws of motion and gravity).

THE PROTESTANT REFORMATION (1517–1650)

The Renaissance led people to question the authority of the Church and place greater faith in human reason. The rise of nation-states led some monarchs to resent the power the Pope wielded in their countries; they felt that the Pope had too much power over political and other secular matters. The growing sense of nationalism made people feel more loyal to their king than to the Pope. The ban on usury created opposition among the new middle class, and people, not to mention rulers, also resented the tithe. The corruption of the Church caused a crisis of faith.

The Protestant Reformation was the challenge to the Roman Catholic Church that ended Western Europe's religious unity. In 1517, a German monk named Martin Luther posted on a church door in Wittenburg, Germany, a list of complaints against the Church, called the Ninety-Five Theses. He condemned the Church's practice of selling indulgences (paying money for church pardons), simony (selling of church offices), and nepotism (giving church positions to relatives). He believed that the Bible was the supreme religious authority, not the Pope; he protested against the materialistic life led by some Church officials, and the Pope's power. He wanted the Bible translated into German so that people could read and interpret it for themselves. He believed that salvation was achieved through faith alone, not both faith and good works. Faith was a free gift given to humans through God's grace, and only God's mercy permitted humans to be saved. Rejecting the power of the Pope and priests, he made a break with the Church, and the pope excommunicated him, declaring him a heretic.

The printing press had been invented in 1450 in Germany, which helped Luther's ideas spread, and he gained followers. Gradually, a new worship service and a religion developed that followed Luther's ideas. Lutheranism spread from the German states to Scandinavia and some parts of central Europe. The Reformation increased literacy and education, and also increased the persecution of non-Christians in Western Europe, particularly Jews.

All Christian religions that deny the universal authority of the Pope, and rest on the Bible as the source of truth are called Protestant, and Lutheranism was the first. Lutheranism replaced Catholicism as the established religion throughout Germany, Sweden, Denmark, and Norway. Some German rulers became Lutherans in order to seize properties of the Roman Catholic Church. They also saw it as a way to weaken Charles V, the Holy Roman Emperor.

In Geneva, Switzerland, French religious thinker John Calvin (1509–1564), who agreed with Luther's ideas, established a religion based on the idea of predestination and the theory of the elect. Predestination means that whatever happens to you after death was determined by God beforehand, and you couldn't do anything about it. The elect, or those who would be saved from punishment for sins, would be known by their moral lives and by the success they achieved through hard work; God chose certain people, called the elect, to be saved, and not others, and it didn't matter what you did on earth. According to Calvin, a moral life did not include dancing, music, or even playing cards! These ideas won acceptance in Switzerland, Scotland (the Presbyterians), Holland, England (the Puritans), and parts of France (the Huguenots).

Protestantism was popular with the middle class, who liked the idea of business and hard work as a sign of salvation. Henry VIII of England was excommunicated from the Catholic Church after he defied the authority of the Pope by divorcing his wife, Catherine of Aragon, to marry a woman he hoped would give him a male heir. Supported by his people, Henry convinced Parliament to pass the Act of Supremacy (1534), which created a national religion independent of the Pope, the Anglican Church of England, with the English monarch as its head.

THE COUNTER-REFORMATION

The Counter-Reformation was an attempt by the Catholic Church to retain its authority. In 1545, the Pope convened the Council of Trent (1545–1563) to uphold the Church's traditional beliefs and practices, and to end the sale of indulgences and simony. The Index, a list of books Catholics were forbidden to read, was created by the council to prevent the spread of heresy. The Inquisition, the Church courts established during the Middle Ages, took measures against heretics which were very effective in southern Europe, especially Spain and Italy. The Jesuit order, known officially as the Society of Jesus, was founded in 1534 by Ignatius Loyola; they helped defend and preserve Catholic teachings. But the Counter-Reformation was unable to restore the Church's former power.

The Protestant Reformation enabled monarchs and civil government to increase their power at the expense of the Catholic Church, which would never again have the power it had during the Middle Ages. But the resulting religious differences led to a century of warfare. In 1588, Protestant England was at war with Catholic Spain—as usual, competing for trade was also a factor; this time, it was about colonial territory. An attempted invasion of England resulted in the defeat and near destruction of the Spanish Armada. Through this victory over Spain, Queen Elizabeth I preserved Protestantism and helped her country become a huge power.

By 1600, almost all of Western Europe was divided into Catholics and Protestants, with each group hostile to each other. The Thirty Years' War (1618–1648) involved most major European nations, and was essentially Catholic versus Protestant, except for Catholic France, which joined with the Protestants in order to get land from Austria. There was also a civil war in France. Finally, Catholic France issued the Edict of Nantes (1598), which permitted Protestants to practice, and in England, the Toleration Act of 1689 granted some freedom to various Protestant groups.

THE AGE OF EXPLORATION AND COLONIZATION (1450–1750)

The Age of Exploration truly ended Western European isolation. The Crusades had brought on an explosion in trade and the desire to find a new route to the riches of Asia; Byzantium had fallen by now, which had an effect on access to Eastern goods. The Renaissance awakened the spirit of curiosity, and Marco Polo's tales made Europeans itchy to travel. Technological advances like the astrolabe and compass for navigation, not to mention gunpowder, enabled them to get where they wanted to go, and conquer almost anyone they found. Many adventurers were stirred by the desire for gold, God, and glory.

The big idea was to find an all-water route to Asia; other routes were dangerous, especially after the fall of Constantinople to the Muslims in 1453. An all-water route would be safer and less expensive. Italy wasn't too interested in finding it, because they had the monopoly on the existing Mediterranean trade. So the new nation-states of Spain and Portugal led the way. In Portugal, Prince Henry the Navigator set up a school for sailors, got money, and sent explorers down the coast of Africa. In 1488, Bartholomeu Dias reached Africa's southern tip, later called the Cape of Good Hope. In 1498, Vasco da Gama rounded the cape and got to India. This route was longer, but it was safer and more profitable. In Spain, Queen Isabella wanted wealth, power, and the spread of Christianity, so she sponsored the voyage of Christopher Columbus. Columbus sailed west trying to get to the East. In 1492, thinking he had gotten to the "Indies," he "discovered the New World" and mistakenly called the inhabitants "Indians." In 1519, Ferdinand Magellan completed the first circumnavigation of the world (other explorers are named in other chapters).

This was the beginning of European global domination in much of Latin America, Africa, Southeast Asia, and China; the raw materials obtained from the colonies spurred the economic development of Western Europe for centuries to come. Spain, Portugal, England, France, and Holland were the leading colonial powers in the seventeenth and eighteenth centuries. Overseas expansion led to increased power and wealth for European nations, but the resulting competition led to war, such as the French and Indian War, from 1754 to 1763, in which France lost most of its North American possessions to England. European rivalries grew out of expansion and trading practices. Conflicts like the Thirty Years War began as religious conflicts but had political overtones; rulers wanted to increase and consolidate their power bases, and they were in competition over the colonies abroad.

European expansion had a huge effect on the indigenous peoples of Africa, North and South America, and Asia. The Atlantic Ocean replaced the Mediterranean Sea as the center of economic activity, and there was a shift in European economic power from the Mediterranean area to Northern Europe. The Europeans, thinking that they had "discovered America," were extremely Eurocentric, mistreating native people as they spread Christianity. The expansion gave Europeans access to raw materials, making possible the start of a commercial revolution.

THE COMMERCIAL REVOLUTION

"Commercial Revolution" refers to the changes made in trade and business practices beginning in the 1400s and continuing throughout the Age of Exploration. The raw materials from the colonies brought about the growth of trade within Western Europe and worldwide, which brought about mercantilism. Mercantilism is an economic system in which the nation-state carefully controls most economic activities, especially the development of colonies, in order to strengthen the nation's economic wealth and power, which was measured by gold and silver. Strict government control was established in order to create a favorable balance of trade, which is when a country exports more than it imports. The government would promote domestic industry, place tariffs on imports, and obtain colonies to be used as sources of raw materials and markets. Mercantilist policies strengthened the power of Europe's absolute monarchies.

Increased trade and the greater supply of gold and silver taken from the New World led to the expansion of industries like banking and investment, part of the economic system called capitalism, which was based on the idea of private ownership of property. The result was the emergence of a middle class of merchants, businessmen and bankers who became a powerful force. Capitalism grew with joint stock companies like the Dutch East India company, which were privately owned and which sold stock to investors who were willing to risk their money hoping to make a profit.

Western Europe, unlike the cultures of the East, had all the preconditions necessary to achieve the transition from an agrarian, or farming economy to a capitalistic one, including the existence of a class of merchants and bankers powerful enough to initiate change. Mercantilism spurred the Industrial Revolution by providing increased resources and by encouraging consumer demand for finished products. Mercantilism also fostered resentment in colonies, and was a big cause of the American Revolution in 1775. Back in the mother countries, the European middle class became dissatisfied with mercantilist policies; in France, the bourgeoisie, or middle class, thought they could make more money with fewer restrictions, but they didn't have the power, so they grew discontented. Keep that in mind when we get to the French Revolution.

Other effects of this commercial revolution included huge world population shifts. African slaves were brought over to work in the colonies, devastating Africa's population, and Europeans left their homelands to settle in the colonies, and their culture spread. Also, a new production system, the domestic system, developed in Europe, in which goods (well, basically cloth) were produced in the home rather than in a shop. This enabled merchants to increase production, but was replaced by the factory system during the Industrial Revolution. Finally, the power of several European nation-states and their absolute monarchs increased, changing the international order.

THE RISE OF NATION-STATES

Besides the cultural (Renaissance), religious (Reformation), and economic (Commercial revolution and exploration) changes taking place, there were also political changes. In the sixteenth and seventeenth centuries, the monarchies of Western Europe sought to centralize the political power of their respective political systems. The term "nation-state" refers to a specific area of land with fixed boundaries, united under the rule of a central government. During this Age of Absolutism (1500–1789), almost all nations were ruled by monarchs who had total power, called autocracies.

THE STORY OF SPAIN

After the Moors invaded the Iberian Peninsula in the eighth century, it was ruled by various Christian kingdoms and Muslim states. Gradually, Christian kingdoms like Aragon and Castile defeated the Moors and expanded the area. In 1469, the royal heir of Castile, Isabella, married the royal heir of Aragon, Ferdinand, and with that union, united most of Spain. Their armies conquered Granada, the last Muslim state in Spain.

THE STORY OF ENGLAND

While most of Europe was experiencing absolutism, England was undergoing a big lurch toward democracy. Rule by the people came gradually, in a series of steps, until a limited constitutional monarchy was established. Here's how it happened.

William the Conqueror, the Duke of Normandy in France, crossed the English Channel with his Norman Army and invaded England. After his victory at the Battle of Hastings in 1066, he was crowned king of England. He introduced feudalism to England, but made the lords and knights swear loyalty to him. His successors became even more powerful.

Democracy Forms

The jury system began under William's grandson, King Henry II (1154–1189), who ruled over England, Scotland, Wales, and a large chunk of France. In 1215, the basis of English democracy, the Magna Carta (Great Charter) was signed by Henry's son King John (he was forced to sign). It limited the power of the king by law, forcing him to consult the Great Council, the legislature full of nobles and bishops, in order to raise taxes. The document made sure that the king was not above the law, that he had to obey like everyone else. The Great Council got more powerful under King Edward I; in 1295, he added the middle class to it, and it was known as the Model Parliament; afterwards, all Parliamentary meetings included representatives from nobles and "commons." Eventually, the Parliament was divided into two parts, the House of Commons and the House of Lords. During the later Middle Ages (1000–1500), court verdicts were written down and collected, becoming the basis for future legal decisions, and forming a body of law called the English common law.

The Tudors

The Hundred Years' War (1337–1453) was fought between England and France, and the British lost some territories in France. During the period of Tudor Rule (1485–1603) there were two big monarchs, both of whom have been mentioned: Henry VIII (1509–1547, established the Anglican Church) and his daughter, Queen Elizabeth I (1558–1603, beat the Armada, encouraged the growth of the navy). These two rulers weren't absolute; they followed the limits that had been set by the Magna Carta.

The Stuarts

Then, in the seventeenth century, the Stuarts, who succeeded the Tudors, became absolute rulers of England. James I (1603–1625) said "the king is from God and the law is from the king." This might remind you of the Chinese Mandate of Heaven, except in this case, the people didn't have the right to overthrow the king, because he was above the law. Obviously, this idea brought about conflicts with Parliament, which can be summed up in the age-old question, Who's got the power? In 1628, Charles I was forced by Parliament to agree to the Petition of Right, which limited the power of the monarch, in exchange for granting more revenues, but as soon as he got the money, he dissolved Parliament and ruled for eleven years (1629–1640), ignoring all previous democratic advances.

In 1640, when Scotland invaded England, Charles was forced to call Parliament into session. Led by Puritans, a group of English Protestants who advocated strict religious discipline along with simplification of the ceremonies and creeds of the Church of England, this Parliament was known as the Long Parliament, and it sat from 1640–1660. This Parliament changed English history by limiting the absolute powers of the monarchy. In 1641, the Parliament denied Charles' request for money to fight the Irish rebellion, and in response he led troops into the House of Commons to arrest some of the members. This sparked a civil war, as the Parliament raised an army, called the Roundheads, to fight the king. The Roundheads, under the leadership of Oliver Cromwell, defeated the armies of Charles I, who were called the Cavaliers; the king was tried and executed.

This civil war was part of the Puritan Revolution (1642–1660). Between 1649 and 1660, there was a republican form of government in England led by Oliver Cromwell, but then in 1653, supported by his army, Cromwell took the title of Lord Protector and ruled as a military dictator with religious intolerance and violence against the Irish (more about that later). All of this caused much resentment, and after Cromwell died, Parliament invited Charles II, the exiled son of the now-beheaded Charles I, to take the throne and restore a limited monarchy. This is called the Stuart Restoration (1660–1688). Charles II was careful, and he acknowledged the rights of his people. In 1679, he agreed to the Habeas Corpus Act, which provided everyone with a fair trial and the right to know the charges of one's arrest. On Charles II's death, his brother James II took over.

The Glorious Revolution (1688–1689)

James II was Catholic, and he was unpopular; he believed in the divine right of kings. In a bloodless revolution which was referred to as Glorious, he was driven from power by Parliament, who feared he'd make England a Catholic country, and fled to France. He was replaced by his son-in-law and daughter, William and Mary, the Protestant rulers of the Netherlands (William was William of Orange, a Dutch Prince). They shared power with the people, and the Glorious Revolution ensured that England's future monarchs would be Anglican, and their powers would be limited. The English Bill of Rights (1689) placed further limits on the power of the king to tax and make laws, and listed the civil liberties of the people, including trial by jury; it became the basis for its American counterpart. Also issued in 1689 was the Toleration Act, which provided all Protestants with freedom of religion. All major decisions were made by Parliament. In the centuries that followed, England became more democratic and the monarch became more of a figurehead.

John Locke, a seventeenth-century English philosopher, was a font of democratic ideals that influenced the Declaration of Independence and the French Revolution, including the social contract between a government and its citizens, in his book *Two Treatises on Civil Government* (1690). He wrote in defense of the Glorious Revolution, saying that all people have natural rights to life, liberty, and property, and that the king gets his power from the people, who were entitled to rebel. The American and French Revolutions used this concept of "government by the consent of the governed" to justify their rebellions. Thomas Paine, the American who wrote *Common Sense*, also claimed it was right and natural for Americans to revolt.

THE STORY OF FRANCE

In 987, King Hugh Capet ruled only a small area around Paris. Later French kings expanded the territory, but beginning in the twelfth century, the English gained large parts of what now belongs to France. It wasn't until the end of the Hundred Year's War in 1453 that the English were driven out of all but a small part of France. After the Hundred Years' War, royal power in France became more centralized. Louis XI (1461–1483) increased his power, and so did his successors. Henry IV (1589–1610), the first Bourbon ruler, ended the religious wars in France; he was a Protestant but he adopted Catholicism to avoid bloodshed, and issued the Edict of Nantes in 1598, which granted some religious freedom to the French Protestants, called the Huguenots. The Bourbons ruled France until the French Revolution in 1789. Louis XIII, Henry's son, made Cardinal Richelieu his advisor and chief minister; this monarchy was absolute, and Richelieu's foreign policy made France the strongest power in Europe.

Louis XIV (1643–1715)

Louis XIV is said to have claimed "L 'etat, c'est moi," or "I am the state." He believed that his power and right to rule came from God, and used the wealth of his kingdom for his own benefit. At a time when many French people didn't have food or shelter, he built the lavish Palace of Versailles and hosted huge banquets. He got the name "Sun King" because of the luxury and brilliance of his court, and his symbol, the sun; like the earth revolves around sun, the destiny of France revolved around him. Louis never summoned the Estates-General, his lawmaking body, to meet. He increased French nationalism and revoked the Edict of Nantes, forcing many Huguenots to leave France. France became the center of culture and an important trading power, but Louis waged costly wars. When he died in 1715, he left bitterness, debt, a bankrupt treasury, and unrest, which are some powerful ingredients for revolution.

Let's Get Ready to Revolt

In 1789, France was bankrupt; the Sun King's debt grew larger under his successors. Louis XVI couldn't deal with this economic crisis, and he was very unpopular; he imprisoned anyone who spoke out against him, and he and his wife Marie Antoinette provided the spark that ignited the French Revolution.

There were all kinds of reasons for revolution. People were fed up with absolutism; enemies of the king were jailed without trial. Under Louis XVI there were rigid social classes, or estates, creating inequality and limited social mobility. The First and Second Estates, made up, respectively, of the Roman Catholic clergy and the French nobility, accounted for 2 percent of the population, but they received rights and privileges denied to the majority in the Third Estate, who were middle class (bourgeoisie), peasants, and city workers. The Third Estate was always outvoted; it represented the biggest part of the population, but the First and Second Estates always voted together, and each estate only got one vote. There was unfair taxation, which fell heaviest on the Third Estate, causing discontent. There were also restrictive mercantilist laws, causing the bourgeoisie to lose profits; they also had to pay the tithe and feudal dues to certain lords. The bourgeoisie, that wealthy and educated middle class, resented their lack of status, and they knew about the growth of democracy in England and the successful revolution in America. Inspired by the Enlightenment, they led the revolution.

THE ENLIGHTENMENT OF REASON (1500–1800)

The Enlightenment was a movement among writers and intellectuals that was inspired by the Scientific Revolution of the previous age, which represented a new approach to solving stuff that set the West apart from other regions. This approach changed the way Europeans viewed themselves. It represented a "secularization" of scientific inquiry—theological explanations were rejected—and a revolt against traditional authorities. With its emphasis on observation, experimentation, investigation, and speculation, it became synonymous with modern thought throughout the world. The writers of the Enlightenment applied this scientific method of observation and investigation to social problems and challenged traditional authority, saying that everything should be open to criticism. They encouraged the improvement of society through the use of reason. Because they urged change, they were supported by the bourgeoisie and opposed by the nobility and the clergy. The writers pointed out the abuses of the Old Regime, the system that supported absolutism, and called for democracy, inspired by the successful Glorious and American Revolutions. Europe's middle class rejected the medieval class structure that denied them political power; they insisted on their right to participate in a government controlled by an elected representative legislature.

Laissez-faire Capitalism

Besides democracy, another big Enlightenment idea was "laissez-faire" (French for "let people do as they choose") capitalism, an economic system in which the government has little control, which clearly opposed mercantilism. A Scottish philosopher and economist named Adam Smith proposed this system and challenged mercantilism in his book, *The Wealth of Nations*, written in 1776. He rejected the idea of government regulation of the economy because it stifled economic growth, and promoted the "hands off" economic policy, arguing that the "invisible hand" of the market would spur individuals to seek profit for their own good. He argued that consumer demand would guide producers to supply only the best and cheapest goods, which in turn would benefit the welfare of the nation. This became the prevailing economic system, with governments allowing the business cycle—prosperity followed by recession followed by depression followed by recovery followed by prosperity—to operate with pretty much no interference.

Other Enlightenment Ideas

The Philosophes, a mostly French group of thinkers, put forth some of the Enlightenment's most thought-provoking ideas. Voltaire, who wrote *Letters on the English*, liked the idea of a limited monarchy, and said, "I may disapprove of what you say, but I will defend to the death your right to say it." Jean Jacques Rousseau wrote the *Social*

Contract, calling for the equality of all people. He supported government based on the "general will" or what the majority wants, and he wrote, "Man is born free, and everywhere is in chains." Baron de Montesquieu wrote *The Spirit of Laws*, and he called for the separation of government into three branches, judicial, legislative, and executive, to prevent dictatorship (sound familiar? It should—it became part of the U.S. Constitution). The Enlightenment resulted in greater religious tolerance, and inspired revolutions all over the world.

STAGES OF THE FRENCH REVOLUTION

Let's digest the French Revolution in stages. In Stage One (1789), Louis XVI called a meeting of the Estates General, the French Parliament that hadn't met in 175 years, to solve France's economic problems. The representatives of the always-outvoted Third Estate took this opportunity to demand the creation of a more democratic National Assembly. The king rejected this and ordered them to disband. Locked out of their meeting hall, the new National Assembly met on a tennis court, and in what became known as the Tennis Court Oath, they vowed to stay together until they had a new constitution. Hearing rumors that the king was going to send troops to break up the assembly, mobs stormed and captured the Bastille, a former jail for political prisoners, symbolizing the end of the Old Regime and the start of the revolution.

In Stage Two (1789–1791), the provisional National Assembly adopted the Declaration of the Rights of Man, which was based on the English Bill of Rights and the Declaration of Independence, which said that "men are born free and remain free and equal in rights." "Liberty, Equality and Fraternity" was the word on the street. The class structure ended, and with it, what remained of feudalism. This also ended the special privileges of the clergy and the nobility. The National Assembly wrote the Constitution of 1791, establishing a limited monarchy and three branches of government.

In Stage Three (1791–1792), that limited monarchy was a government in which the king shared his power with a Legislative Assembly dominated by the bourgeoisie. This was an unstable period. Radicals called Jacobins, led by Georges Danton, Jean Marat, and Maximilien Robespierre, favored extreme change, wanting to abolish absolute monarchy and establish a republic dominated by the working classes. Neighboring countries invaded France in 1792 to stop the spread of revolution, which only intensified French nationalism. The limited monarchy came to an end when Louis XVI, accused of treason, was arrested and executed, and the birth of the Republic was announced.

In Stage Four (1792–1795), the Jacobins seized power and established the Committee of Public Safety. Using all means possible to safeguard the Revolution, they instituted the first draft in European history. See, the execution of the king had brought on more invasions, so they needed an army, and nationalism ensured its success. The Committee of Public Safety, including Danton and Robespierre, began a Reign of Terror in which those suspected of opposing the revolution were executed (sound familiar?). Marie Antoinette, Louis XVI's wife, was among the thousands who died on the guillotine in 1793. Though it was supposed to protect the revolution, it led to the downfall of the radical leadership as people turned on the Jacobins.

Finally, in Stage Five (1795–1799), the moderates regained power as Danton and Robespierre died on the guillotine in 1795. They wrote a new constitution that made France a republic, and set up the five-member Directory government. It was inefficient and weak; it couldn't defeat Russia and Austria in war, and the economic problems were worsening. So it was overthrown in a coup d'état by ambitious revolutionary general Napoleon Bonaparte. Though Napoleon claimed to be a "true son of the Revolution," he established a military dictatorship which ended the revolution.

NAPOLEON'S REIGN (1799–1815)

France was chaotic from the Revolution, so they were pretty much ready for the absolute rule of Napoleon. He came to power in a new, efficient, centralized government called the Consulate, restricting personal freedoms, but promoting equality. He established the Napoleonic Code, a code of law that preserved some of the revolutionary changes in the legal system; it guaranteed equal treatment before the law, trial by jury, and religious freedom (for example, the Concordat of 1801 provided a peaceful relationship between the French government and the Catholic Church). He also abolished discrimination against Jews, which had been going on for centuries. He strengthened the French economy through new tax laws and the creation of the Bank of France; his system of public schools encouraged nationalism. Napoleon took the title Emperor Napoleon I in 1804.

Napoleon also dominated most of the European continent by 1808. France had taken lots of land, and its military potency upset the balance of power in Europe. Other countries tried unsuccessfully to stop Napoleon. In 1812, his disastrous invasion of Russia weakened him to the point where a strong alliance, led by England's Duke of Wellington, defeated him at the Battle of Waterloo near Brussels in Belgium in 1815. Napoleon was exiled to St. Helena where he died in 1821.

Effects of the French Revolution and Napoleon's Rule

Absolutism was over in France; after the downfall of Napoleon, a limited monarchy was installed. His social equality reforms stuck around, and those revolutionary ideas of "liberty, equality, and fraternity" spread. The American and French Revolutions, models for political action, represented a basic change in the Western relationship between government and the governed; with these two revolutions, the West moved toward a more democratic system in which equality and human rights of citizens were recognized and the power of government was based not upon divine right but on the consent of the governed. This had a huge impact on Europe and Latin America.

THE GROWTH OF NATIONALISM (1815–1871)

After Napoleon's defeat, England, Russia, Prussia, France, and Austria got together at the Congress of Vienna (1814–1815), a meeting held by the leaders of Europe to draw up peace plans and pretty much redraw the map of Europe. Led by Prince Klemens von Metternich of Austria, this crowd was reactionary; they wanted Europe to return to pre-revolutionary conditions, and stuff like absolutism and special privilege. Their goal was for no nation to be powerful enough to threaten the security of another's. To reach this goal, shifts of territory were necessary, not to mention compensation, or providing one state with territory to pay for territory taken away.

All of this reactionary thinking clashed with Napoleon's ideas and the ideals of the French Revolution, and the people of Europe wanted to move forward, not backward. This conflict brought about nationalistic revolutions among the Germans, Italians, Poles and Greeks from 1815 to 1848, with autonomy as the goal. Most of them failed, except for Greece and Belgium in 1830. An international government called the Concert of Europe was formed, suppressing nationalism by trying to maintain the balance of power established by the Congress of Vienna. But nationalistic ideas stuck around, and the spirit of nationalism influenced the political history of Europe from 1815 to 1914, when World War I started.

THE UNIFICATION OF ITALY

In the nineteenth century, Italy was divided, with much of it being dominated by Austria, which controlled the states in the northern part, and was against any kind of unity. In fact, in 1815, there was no actual nation called Italy; Italy was a geographic expression. The Italian Peninsula was divided into large and small states, such as the Lombardy province and the kingdom of Sardinia-Piedmont. Nationalism ("risorgimento") was reawakened by the armies of Napoleon.

Giuseppe Mazzini, the "soul" of Italian unification, inspired people through his writings and speeches, and formed "Young Italy" in 1831, an organization dedicated to the removal of Austrian control and the establishment of an Italian republic. Count Camillo Cavour, the "brains" of unification, orchestrated the plan. In 1852, he became the prime minister of Sardinia-Piedmont, a limited monarchy under King Victor Emmanuel II. Sardinia-Piedmont represented democracy and became the center of the reunification movement. Cavour formed an alliance with France in 1859 and Prussia in 1866, and this allowed him to drive the Austrians out of northern Italy. This inspired other Italians to rebel, and eventually to vote by plebiscite to join Sardinia-Piedmont. Giuseppe Garibaldi, the "sword" of unification, organized an army called the "red shirts," which carried out a successful rebellion in the Kingdom of the Two Sicilies in Southern Italy in 1860. He encouraged Sicilians to unite with Cavour's Sardinia-Piedmont, and later joined with Cavour to take control of most of the Papal States, the Church-owned land in central Italy. The formation of the Kingdom of Italy was announced in 1861, and King Victor Emmanuel II became its limited monarch. In 1870, French troops that had been guarding the Pope in Rome were withdrawn to serve in the Franco-Prussian War, and Italian troops took over the city and claimed it their capital. Italian nationalism kept growing beyond unification, which led to future problems.

THE UNIFICATION OF GERMANY

The same feelings were swimming around in Germany as in Italy, and again, in 1815 there was no nation called Germany. There were more than thirty independent German states that had their own traditions and laws. The largest and strongest German state was Prussia, in the north, and it led the unification movement. The chief obstacle was Austria. In 1848, the liberals attempted to achieve unity and democracy and failed. The conservatives took control, and Germany was united under a strong, autocratic ruler, Otto von Bismarck, the Prime Minister of Prussia. Bismarck's policy of "blood and iron" was the foundation for the totalitarian Nazi regime. After the Seven Weeks War (1866), Austrian domination of the German states ended, and the northern states combined into a confederation. To give the southern states a reason to join in, Bismarck provoked France into declaring war on Prussia. During this Franco-Prussian War (1870–1871), the four southern German states, getting that nationalistic feeling, came to Prussia's aid and eventually agreed to permanent unification. As a result of these wars, Prussia gained Schleswig-Holstein from Denmark and Alsace-Lorraine from France. This was a humiliating defeat for France, and the French vowed revenge; keep this in mind.

In 1871, the second German Empire, or Reich, was formed; remember, the first had been the Holy Roman Empire. The government was authoritarian, with the power resting with Kaiser Wilhelm I and Bismarck, his chief minister. Under Bismarck, the "Iron Chancellor," there was nationalism, militarism, industrialization, and social reform. Bismarck was able to prevent France from forming alliances, but France was isolated and unable to threaten Germany, which continued to grow in power, and was allied with Austria and Italy. In 1888, the new Kaiser, Wilhelm II, young and unwilling to share his power, forced Bismarck to resign, but the Kaiser wasn't as skillful and his policies gave France the opportunity to form alliances with Russia (in 1894) and England (in 1904). These two opposing alliances, France-Russia-England and Germany-Austria-Italy, set the stage for World War I. But meanwhile...

INDUSTRIAL REVOLUTION (1750–1914)

Like the Neolithic Revolution, the Industrial Revolution brought a radical change to the nature of human society. It began in England, a country that had the natural resources needed for industrialization—coal and iron ore. An island with an irregular coastline, England had many natural harbors, and navigable rivers that were good not only for transportation but as sources of power for factories. England's many colonies provided raw materials, like cotton, and markets for finished products, like clothing; wealthy English merchants had the money to invest in business and industry, money made from the triangular trade system discussed in the Africa chapter. In the late seventeenth century, Parliament passed the Enclosure Acts, which fenced off the "common lands" and deprived small farmers of land; these unemployed farmers went to cities to work in factories. There you have it, all the preconditions: natural resources, increased demand, labor supply, investment capital, and transportation.

KEY INVENTIONS

England's James Watt invented the steam engine in 1775, which meant that factories no longer had to be built along rivers. Robert Fulton, an American, built the first steamboat in 1807, and soon steam-powered boats and ships carried stuff on rivers and oceans. George Stephenson of England invented the steam locomotive in 1814, a faster and easier means of transporting goods. In 1831, England's Michael Faraday gave us the Dynamo, the electrical generator that provided a new source of power. In 1856, England's Henry Bessemer perfected the process of making steel, which became the most important metal in industrialization.

THE FACTORY SYSTEM

A major effect of all this industrialization was the rise of the factory system. The method of manufacturing went from domestic to factory, handmade to machine-made. In the factory system, all means of production are in one place. Parts of machines or tools are made alike or are interchangeable. Workers specialize in one task to speed up the completion of a job; this is called the division of labor. Mass production, or production of large quantities of identical goods became possible, especially with the assembly line, a conveyor belt with each worker adding a part.

The result was a higher standard of living; prices came down and there was more variety available. At first, there were also changes in the working environment, like long hours, low pay, and poor conditions. The response was the rise of labor unions and collective bargaining, in which union representatives negotiated with factory owners on behalf of workers, and organized strikes. Governments, pressured by the public, passed regulations curbing the power of big business. The Factory Act (1833) and the Mines Act (1842) were passed to improve working conditions; people felt empathy for those suffering injustices, and humanitarianism grew; concern for the welfare of all people led to the abolition of slavery, more public education, and the improved treatment of the mentally ill.

There was a population explosion due to the rising birth rate and declining death rate caused by the increase in food supply and the advances in medicine. There was also rapid urbanization, and with it, more pollution and crime, and housing problems from all the families moving to the cities. The concentration of the middle and working classes in cities furthered the development of democracy. Changes in the European power structure brought about by the Industrial Revolution were reflected in the expansion of suffrage in Europe throughout the late nineteenth and early twentieth centuries. In England, the Reform Bill of 1832 extended suffrage, and by 1918, the right to vote was extended to all adult males, and then to women in 1928.

CAPITALISM

The capitalist system became fully formed. Its tenets are private ownership of all property, including the means of production; free enterprise with no central control; supply and demand, where a price is determined by the scarcity of a product (a large supply and a reduced demand brings the price down; a small supply and an increased demand raises prices); competition, which ensures high-quality goods at low prices; and the profit motive, which dictates that businesses operate to earn money, so they'll always look for ways to lower costs and increase production to compete more effectively.

CHALLENGES TO CAPITALISM

The free enterprise, or market economy, where decisions are made by wealthy private individuals, was king due to the Industrial Revolution, but there were challenges to the king. One major challenge was socialism, the idea that the major industries should be owned and operated by and for the people rather than for the profit of individuals; this is also called a planned or command economy. Utopian socialists like British manufacturer Robert Owen and French philosopher Charles Fourier believed that a socialist society would emerge peacefully and that even capitalists would be willing to help create it. It would be an evolutionary change rather than a revolutionary one.

MARXISM

Karl Marx, a German writer and economist, and Friedrich Engels, a German socialist, responding to the evils of the Industrial Revolution and the factory system, predicted that Europe's industrial economy would be plagued by increasingly more frequent periods of unemployment and depression and that the conditions of labor would worsen until the proletariat (the workers) were driven to revolution. Marx and Engels proposed that the competitive capitalist economic system based on the private ownership of the means of production would be replaced by an economic system in which the means of production are publicly owned. Marx predicted that a revolution by the workers would bring down capitalism, and his ideas became the basis of communism. He believed that socialism was inevitable.

Marxism, or scientific socialism, embraced an economic interpretation of history, saying that the history of the world is a series of class struggles between the haves and the have-nots, or rich and poor, like master versus slave, capitalist versus proletariat. Those with economic power are generally those with political power and military power. The surplus value theory stated that surplus value was the difference between the price of a good and the wage paid to a worker. Marx said the difference was the profit, kept by the capitalist, and was unfair exploitation. This continued exploitation of workers would lead to more frequent depressions and eventually the overthrow of capitalism by workers seizing the means of production. Each person would contribute to a communist society "according to his ability and receive according to his needs." Workers would then assume political power as well as economic, and based on public ownership and true democracy, a classless society would emerge. There would be no need for government, so the state would just "wither away."

Marx predicted the revolution would happen in Western Europe, but instead it happened in Russia. It never won control in industrialized nations in Western Europe and North America.

IMPERIALISM (1830–1914)

Imperialism is the domination by one country of the political, economic, or cultural life of another country to increase its own power. The old imperialism in fifteenth and sixteenth centuries took place mainly in the Western Hemisphere; in the nineteenth century, it was mostly in the Eastern Hemisphere, and it was spurred by the Industrial Revolution. Industrializing countries wanted to gain more colonies to provide raw materials for factories, markets for finished products, places to invest surplus capital, and places to send the surplus population to relieve overpopulation.

But that wasn't the whole story. Many agreed with British poet Rudyard Kipling, who said it was the "white man's burden" to educate the underdeveloped, spread their "superior" Western culture, and convert everyone to Christianity; otherwise, the souls of non-believers wouldn't be "saved." Also, nationalism sometimes promotes feelings of superiority, and countries wanted power and respect from other nations, so they tried to obtain strategic military bases. They also wanted tons of wealth.

Great Britain liked to boast, "The sun never sets on the British Empire," and they were right; they controlled the South Asian subcontinent, the Malay Peninsula, Burma, Singapore, Hong Kong, New Zealand, Australia, and many African colonies. The scramble for African colonies had begun with King Leopold II of Belgium (see the Africa chapter).

Nineteenth century imperialism took different forms. With a sphere of influence, a nation gained sole economic power in a region, like in China. With a concession, a country got special privileges, like the Arabs letting the British drill for oil in the Middle East. With a protectorate, a country allowed the native ruler to stay in office as a figurehead, like France in Tunisia. With a colony, there was total control, like the British in India. (See other chapters for more details.)

The effects of imperialism were a double-edged sword. Imperialists provided stability and unification, and improved transportation, communication, education, and medical care. But they also undermined native cultures, drew boundaries randomly, destroyed traditional industries and patterns of trade, introduced Western vices and diseases, and exploited people and resources. Colonial nationalist movements developed, like the Boxer Rebellion in China. Some ex-colonies still retain ties to their foreign ex-rulers.

WORLD WAR I (1914–1918)

The Congress of Vienna had brought about peace in Europe for years, but the Industrial Revolution triggered competition for new sources of raw materials, and markets for finished goods fueled nationalism and economic rivalries. This competition led to the outbreak of World War I, which began the decline of European world dominance.

The buildup of strong armies caused fear and suspicion in Europe, especially since there was nothing like the United Nations around to resolve disputes. England's number one naval status was challenged by Germany, and these two countries also had an economic rivalry in the competition for trade. France, hurt in the Franco-Prussian War, wanted revenge against Germany (remember?). Ethnic minorities, such as Slavic people of Eastern Europe, wanted independence, and Austria-Hungary attempted to stop the spread of these ideas. Bosnia-Hercegovina wanted to be free from Austria-Hungary so they could unite with Serbia. And again, let's not forget the imperialistic competition for trade and colonies: Britain and Germany rivaled for Africa, France and Germany clashed over Morocco, Russia and Austria-Hungary were competing for the Balkans, otherwise known as the "powderkeg of Europe" because of all the foreign interest and the Slavs seeking independence there.

The Powderkeg Explodes

In 1907, Europe was divided into the Triple Entente—Great Britain, France, and Russia—and the Triple Alliance—Germany, Austria-Hungary, and Italy. The spark that set off the "powderkeg" was the assassination of Austrian Archduke Ferdinand in June of 1914 in Sarajevo (a city in Bosnia-Hercegovina). The assassin was a member of the Black Hand, a Serbian nationalist group. Germany gave Austria-Hungary a "blank check" in whatever action it wanted to take in revenge, so they threatened Serbia, which angered Russia, the "big brother of the Slavs" who supported Serbia. Sure enough, the system of alliances went into effect like dominoes. The Triple Entente turned into the Allies, growing to over twenty nations. Germany and Austria-Hungary became part of the Central Powers. Italy didn't get involved until 1915, when it joined with the Allies with the hope of gaining Austrian land.

So, the attempt to maintain a balance of power by means of opposing alliance systems actually ended up escalating limited regional crises into major international war. The stirring up of nationalism among the diverse ethnic groups of Eastern Europe weakened the political system of Austria-Hungary and became a major factor leading to war.

The Great War

First called the Great War, World War I was the most violent European conflict since the Napoleonic Wars almost 100 years before. It was also the first modern war, incorporating machine guns, grenades, poison gas, and flame throwers. The military technology introduced in World War I dramatically changed the nature and character of modern warfare and killed millions of Europeans. The main theaters of combat were in Eastern Europe and along a western front in France and Belgium. The method of fighting was known as trench warfare since opposing armies dug in, in trenches dug into the ground, on either side of a "no man's land" over which they fought.

Germany's failure to win a total victory produced a stalemate in the West. On the eastern front, Russia suffered heavy losses, and by 1917 its soldiers were deserting. This led to the Russian Revolution and the rise of Communism, which pulled Russia out of the war. This allowed Germany to fully concentrate on the Western front, but U.S. participation on the side of the Allies was a new problem for them. The United States declared war on Germany in April 1917; it tried to remain neutral, but the Germans' policy of using submarines to sink the ships of neutral nations suspected of carrying supplies for the Allies pushed the United States to get involved. President Woodrow Wilson thought that freedom of the seas and the rights of neutral countries were good reasons to fight; he also thought that if autocratic Germany won, it would be a threat to democracy around the world. The entry of the United States into the war had a big effect on its isolationist tradition, and set the stage for more intervention in European affairs. It also strengthened the Allies until Germany agreed to an armistice, with the fighting ending on November 11, 1918.

THE TREATY OF VERSAILLES (1919)

In 1919, the "Big Four" got together. They were Great Britain's David Lloyd George, France's Georges Clemenceau, Italy's Vittorio Orlando, and the U.S.'s President Wilson. Of the four, President Wilson was the only one who didn't want to punish Germany or gain territory. The Fourteen Points was Wilson's idealistic plan for arms reduction, freedom of the seas, the right of self-determination for all nationalities, and the formation of the League of Nations to help settle disputes and prevent future wars. Many of his ideas were ignored; the other three thought he was a dreamer.

The Treaty of Versailles applied to Germany alone. It called for loss of territory, some of which was used to recreate the country of Poland, and loss of colonies, taken by the League of Nations and becoming "mandates" of the Allies, to be prepared for independence. Also, Germany's army and navy were drastically reduced, there were no troops allowed in the Rhineland, an industrial area along the French border, and all war industries were shut down. Finally, there was the War Guilt Clause, in which Germany was forced to accept all responsibility for the war and pay for damages; this hurt Germany's national pride and caused some major bitterness. Keep this in mind.

The United States never became a member of the League of Nations; the Senate thought that participation in the League would involve the United States in future European conflicts, so it signed a separate treaty with Germany. This lack of support from the United States contributed to the League's weakness in enforcing the Versailles treaty. From other treaties with other members of the Central Powers, Austria-Hungary was divided, and both resulting countries had to limit arms and pay reparations. Any future union between Austria and Germany was forbidden, and new nations were created from land taken from the Central Powers and Russia.

World War I was a turning point in world history. European global domination began to weaken in the face of an increasingly hostile and nationalistic climate in its colonized nations. By 1918, democracy had become the dominant form of government in Western Europe. In Great Britain in 1911, the House of Lords, the symbol of the privileged position of the nobility, was stripped of almost all its power, and the House of Commons, which represented the majority, became the dominant branch of Parliament, signifying the democratic transfer of power to the people. In France, many revolutions had led to the permanent adoption of a republican form of government. Italy had become a constitutional monarchy in 1861, but in the 1920s and 1930s came the rise of totalitarianism, emphasizing the glorification of the state, authoritarian rule by a dictator or party, and control of the individual citizen's life, a system where the individual exists to serve the state's interests.

GERMANY

Germany's defeat in World War I led to the collapse of the Kaiser's government, and in 1918 the democratic Weimar Republic was established, even though Germany had little experience with democracy (it was really an experiment). The government appeared weak for having accepted the Versailles treaty and there were big economic problems like severe inflation, unemployment, and street violence. Germany received loans from the United States, and by the mid-1920s had made a slow recovery.

The Industrial Revolution led to greater global interdependence, so the 1929 stock market crash in the United States had global repercussions, causing widespread economic despair. The German government was unstable and its leaders seemed helpless. This made the people think that democracy was just not going to work for them. The end of the Weimar Republic paved the way for Adolf Hitler and the Nazi Party.

Hitler

Adolf Hitler was born in Austria, and he served in the German army during World War I. He joined the National Socialist German Workers (Nazi) party, speaking out against the Weimar government. He was arrested at the Munich Putsch of 1923, an unsuccessful attempt to overthrow the government. While in jail, Hitler wrote *Mein Kampf* (My Struggle), in which he encouraged the unity of all Germans in Europe, and outlined his theory of the "master race." He believed that Germans were a pure Aryan race, therefore superior to everyone. This is an example of the "big lie technique": The idea that a lie repeated often enough is eventually believed. Hitler advocated German expansion because they needed "lebensraum," or living space, which was there for the taking in Eastern Europe. The people they conquered would become German slaves. This racist policy justified all kinds of aggression.

The Nazis Rise

Nazism, with its simple solutions to complex problems, was accepted by people who felt great despair and anger concerning their economic and political systems. The Nazis had answers for everything, and they promised to restore law and order. They said the Versailles Treaty was unfair and promised to improve the economy by breaking it. Unemployment would be alleviated by reopening war materials factories and increasing the size of the army, in order to expand to places where people of German descent lived, like Austria, Poland, and Czechoslovakia. They refused to accept the War Guilt Clause, and they wanted to regain land that Germany had had before the war, justifying violence to achieve their goals. They controlled education and culture in order to teach Nazi principles, and stressed the importance of looking back and glorifying the mythical German race (the so-called Volk) as the source of all strength and power. They claimed that Nordic Germans were destined to rule the world, and that undesirables must be eliminated.

The Nazis claimed that the Weimar Republic was forced to accept the Versailles Treaty by Jews, Communists, and others, and that the Germans hadn't really lost World War I, but instead were stabbed in the back. Anti-Semitism had a long tradition in Germany; it had been around for hundreds of years, but Hitler's was fanatical—he blamed them for his own personal failures. He believed that Aryans were the master race naturally entitled to control people of less "pure" blood, like Slavs and Jews.

Hitler also cashed in on the fear of Communism and Soviet Russia, which is how he got the bankers and industrialists to follow him: His pro-capitalist philosophy appealed to the middle class businessmen who were afraid they'd lose their property in a communist revolution. Hitler's followers organized into private armies called the Brown Shirts, who used scare tactics and violence to terrorize Jews and "enemies" of the Party. Citizenship was measured by service to the state, and the expression of human rights was suppressed. The Nazis had no real opposition. Hitler was a stirring and charismatic speaker when addressing large crowds, and no one spoke out against him; some were afraid, some were apathetic, and internationally, no one really knew what the deal was.

The Third Reich (1933–1945)

The formal takeover occurred in 1933 when the president of the Weimar Republic, Paul von Hindenburg, appointed Hitler as chancellor. The Nazis never won the majority in any election, but they were the largest party and formed the single largest bloc in the Reichstag, or parliament. Hitler promised to preserve the Weimar constitution, but he destroyed the democracy. He became the Fuhrer, creating a totalitarian state where only the Nazi Party was allowed to exist, and the Gestapo, or secret police, crushed any opposition. His ideas spread through indoctrination; most German children were taught Nazi ideas in school and were encouraged to join the "Hitler Youth." He won support through a huge propaganda campaign of speeches, rallies, and military parades; newspapers, radio, and movies promoted Nazism.

The Holocaust

The Nuremberg Laws of 1935 deprived Jews of their German citizenship and made discrimination against them legal. All Jews were required to wear a yellow Star of David to identify them. They were sent to slave labor camps and then to death camps as Hitler implemented his "final solution" of genocide. The Holocaust was the intentional persecution and systematic murder of European Jews by the Germans from 1933 to 1945. Jews from Germany and German-held lands were taken from their homes, and taken to concentration camps; they were then led to gas chambers disguised as shower rooms and murdered with poison gas. Other groups that Hitler considered inferior, such as Communists, Gypsies, Poles and other Slavic peoples, and homosexuals, were also killed in concentration camps.

To say the least, the Holocaust drastically changed the population makeup of Europe, especially Central Europe. By the end of the war, the Jewish population of Europe had been almost wiped out (for example, Poland's Jewish population of 3 million in 1939 was reduced to about 120,000 by 1945). Concentration camps claimed 12 million lives: Six million Jews, as well as homosexuals, gypsies, the mentally ill, Jehovah's Witnesses, and Slavs. The discovery of the Nazi death camps such as Auschwitz, Dachau, and Treblinka, equipped with gas chambers and crematoria, revealed how brutal Hitler was, and makes one wonder how people stood by and allowed this to happen.

MEANWHILE, IN ITALY...

Hitler's fascist ideology was created by Benito Mussolini, who came to power in Italy in 1922. Mussolini was Hitler's model and Nazism was the German form of fascism. The word *fascist* comes from the word *fasces*, an axe-like weapon that was a symbol of the ancient Roman Empire. Mussolini wanted nationalism, and he and his Black Shirt followers came to power for many reasons. Post-World War I Italy suffered from high unemployment, inflation, strikes, low morale, and the mourning of many war deaths. The weak and divided government of King Emmanuel III was unable to provide leadership. There was no strong democratic tradition in Italy, and they feared communism. As a result of his famous March on Rome in 1922, supposedly to save Italy from a communist revolution, Mussolini came to power with no opposition and established a police state. He destroyed civil liberties, demanded that people recognize him as Il Duce (the Leader). There was a command economy but Mussolini allowed some private ownership, so the middle class was happy. He encouraged people to make sacrifices, especially of their freedom, for the good of the state. Mussolini also annexed Ethiopia in 1935. He was executed in 1945, at the end of World War II.

WAR BREWS

The aggressive nationalism of these fascist dictators led to World War II, which nearly destroyed Europe. Military strength was seen as a source of national pride, and the leaders of the Axis nations were always seen in military dress. The Axis Powers also thought they were superior, what with the German "master race" theory, Italy reveling in Ancient Rome, and Japanese pride based on Shinto teachings. Let's not forget imperialism: the Axis wanted land, so Japan moved into China, Italy conquered Ethiopia, and Germany annexed Austria (the *anschluss*, or union) and Czechoslovakia. Collective security failed; the League of Nations didn't take any action to curb the Axis Powers, and neither did the U.S. or the rest of Europe. Americans, disillusioned from World War I, were also preoccupied with the Great Depression, and following public opinion, they passed a series of Neutrality Acts, which forbade the shipment of arms to nations involved in war. Russia's Joseph Stalin didn't believe that his country's military forces could successfully fight Germany without the support of the Allies.

THE WAR BEGINS

In 1938, as promised, Hitler took control of Austria, violating the Versailles Treaty, but the former Allies did nothing. Later that year, Hitler threatened war if he was not given the Sudetenland region of Czechoslovakia. The Munich Pact, signed by Great Britain, France, Italy, and Germany in 1938, authorized the annexation of the Sudetenland in return for Hitler's promise to leave the rest of Czechoslovakia alone. This policy of giving in was called appeasement, and it was promoted by British Prime Minister Neville Chamberlain. Unfortunately, it only encouraged more aggression. In 1939, Hitler violated the pact and took all of Czechoslovakia, and, anticipating a conflict with Great Britain and France, he secured the eastern border. The Nazi-Soviet Nonaggression Pact signed that year, which said that Russia would take over eastern Poland and the

Baltic states, and not fight with Germany, eliminated the possibility of a two-front war, and allowed Hitler to invade Poland on September 1, 1939, signaling the start of World War II.

The Allies finally took a stand against Germany when it invaded Poland. The United States declared neutrality, but it helped the Allies in non-fighting ways until the Japanese surprise attack on the Pearl Harbor naval base in Hawaii on December 7, 1941. That's when the United States entered the war. Hitler's "blitzkrieg" or lightning war tactics made victory easy against Poland and France. He had overrun most of Europe, except England (which was saved by the Royal Air Force shooting down enough German planes to cause Hitler to call off the invasion), by 1941. Then he made a fatal mistake by violating the Nazi-Soviet Nonaggression Pact and invading the Soviet Union. The Soviet Union joined the Allies.

This war between the Allies (Great Britain, France, the United States, the Soviet Union, and China) and the Axis (Germany, Italy, and Japan) dwarfed all previous wars in geographical extent, and human and material losses. There was fighting on three continents with over fifty nations involved. This was a "total war." Civilian areas were targets for bombings. There were tanks, planes, aircraft carriers, battleships, sonar, radar, and offensive weapons capable of mass destruction.

With the invasion of Normandy in western France (June 6, 1944, D-Day), the Allied forces began to retake German-held land and pushed them eastward. Russia entered the German-held Eastern European nations and pushed westward. On May 8, 1945 (V-E Day), Germany surrendered, but the war in the Pacific went on. Meanwhile, in 1945, the United States had secretly tested the first atomic bomb, and President Harry Truman ordered the dropping of atomic bombs on the civilian cities of Hiroshima and Nagasaki, resulting in enormous destruction and hundreds of thousands of casualties. Japan surrendered on September 2, 1945 (V-J Day), 1945, ending the war.

At the Nuremberg War Crimes Trials, Nazi war criminals were brought to justice. Hitler had committed suicide, but other Nazi leaders were tried for "crimes against humanity" like torture, the execution of prisoners, and the attempted genocide of the Jews. Similar and more extensive trials were also held in Tokyo regarding Japanese war crimes.

THE AFTERMATH OF THE WAR

This was the most costly war ever fought; more people were killed than ever before, not to mention all of the refugees. Poland's boundaries with the Soviet Union changed, giving it more land. Italy returned to democracy with the overthrow of Mussolini, and became a republic in 1946. Communism spread in Eastern Europe, and the Atomic Age had begun. In 1949, four years after the U.S. dropped the first bombs, the Soviet Union tested one, and soon Great Britain, France, and the People's Republic of China joined the "atomic club." Nuclear proliferation raised all kinds of fears all over the world.

The war marked a major shift in global power. Even though Great Britain and France were on the winning side, they lost their status as great powers because they had to recover from all the destruction, and their empires were beginning to disintegrate. Colonial nationalism and independence movements abroad started or intensified because the war had weakened the imperial powers. There was no more SuperEurope, but instead two Superpowers emerged—the United States and the Soviet Union. This is often referred to as a "bipolar world."

THE UNITED NATIONS

The Allies helped to create the United Nations in 1945 to promote peace. Led by the "Big Five"—the United States, the Soviet Union, Great Britain, France, and China—its purpose was to provide a forum for discussion and a means of settling disputes, and, well, so far, there's been no World War III. The UN can take action against those who threaten world peace. There are six bodies in the UN. The General Assembly, which now has representatives from 184 nations, is a forum for discussion; each nation has one vote, and a two-thirds majority is needed for a vote to be passed. The Security Council has fifteen members, of which five are permanent—Great Britain, France, the United States, Russia, and China. It deals with threats to peace and functions as the UN's executive body. To pass something you need nine votes, including all five permanent members, so each permanent member has veto power. The head of the Security Council is the most important UN official, the Secretary General.

The General Assembly and the Security Council are the two most important bodies in the UN; there is also the Secretariat, headed by the Secretary General, which handles administrative work; the International Court of Justice, which sets the rules on international legal disputes; the Trusteeship Council administers territories that were not self-governing when the UN was established; and the Economic and Social Council promotes human rights. There are also specialized agencies: UNESCO (United Nations Educational, Scientific, and Cultural Organization), WHO (World Health Organization), and FAO (Food and Agriculture Organization). Geneva, Switzerland is the home of many UN agencies, although Switzerland itself is not a member of the UN.

The UN has been more successful dealing with economic and social issues than with political issues. It helped eliminate smallpox, it fights famine, and it champions women's rights. It sometimes seems weak because of member countries pursuing national interests instead of cooperation, and blocs of countries voting the same way can be an obstacle to progress.

CONTAINMENT

After the war, the United States and the Soviet Union emerged as superpowers, and there were vast differences in their political and economic philosophies; basically, it was capitalism versus communism. The West feared that Communism would spread, and the United States led the "free world" in adopting the policy of containment, or "let's make sure Communism stays where it is." With the Truman Doctrine in 1947, President Truman instituted a successful economic and military aid program designed to help people resist Communist aggression, which was aimed chiefly at Greece and Turkey.

In 1948, the Marshall Plan offered economic aid to all European countries as a means of lessening the appeal of Communism; Europe was a vulnerable economic mess after the war. The United States believed economic recovery was essential to the future of Western Europe, so it approved this massive package of aid aimed at containment, and thus Europe was caught up in the Cold War. The Marshall Plan was named after George C. Marshall, the U.S. Secretary of State, and was officially known as the European Recovery Act. Aid was offered to all, but it was refused by Communist nations, who instead accepted aid from the Council of Mutual Economic Assistance, a Soviet version of the Marshall Plan.

POST-WAR GERMANY

After World War II, Germany and its capital, Berlin, were temporarily divided into four zones of occupation—American, British, French, and Soviet. The Allies couldn't agree on a plan for German reunification. In 1948, the Soviet Union wanted to drive the Allies out of Berlin, so they cut off all land access routes to the city. The Allies didn't want to lose control of the city to the USSR, so they conducted a successful airlift (the Berlin Airlift), flying in tons of food and supplies for almost a year. Eventually the Soviet Union lifted the blockade, but Berlin remained divided and occupied by foreign powers.

The Western nations permitted their zones to come together in 1949 as the Federal Republic of Germany, or West Germany, with the capital at Bonn. The Soviet zone became the German Democratic Republic, with the capital at East Berlin. West Berlin, though surrounded by East Germany, became part of West Germany. The Soviet Union's leader at the time, Joseph Stalin, never allowed free elections to take place in Eastern Europe, so Eastern European countries, including East Germany, became Communist "satellites." So, West Germany became a democracy, and East Germany a Communist satellite, causing a division of Europe described by British Prime Minister Winston Churchill as an "iron curtain" descending across Europe. This set the stage for the Cold War. West Berlin became a showplace for democracy and prosperity, and thousands of East Germans wanted in. Embarrassed by this, the East German government built the Berlin Wall to prevent more loss of people in 1961.

NATO

The Berlin Blockade made the Western Allies form a collective security agreement called the North Atlantic Treaty Organization, or NATO. Today it has sixteen nations, including the United States, Canada, and most of Western Europe. NATO's policy was containment, and it was answered by the Warsaw Pact in 1955, made up of the Soviet Union and the Eastern Bloc (or satellites). In the 1990s, the Communists fell, and the Warsaw Pact was dissolved in 1991. The question now is: What's the purpose of NATO now that there's no Soviet Union? Since the Cold War ended, some Eastern European countries are being granted membership in NATO. In 1994, some of the nations of Eastern Europe and Russia established a friendly relationship with NATO called the "partnership for peace." NATO carried out its first bombing raid, bombing Serbian positions in Bosnia-Hercegovina to protect the UN officials under fire and protect the people in the town of Gorazde.

EUROPE LOSES ITS COLONIES

In 1947, Great Britain lost India, the "jewel in the crown." In the French-Indochina War (1945–1954), France tried to hold onto its empire in Southeast Asia, but was defeated, and the 1954 Geneva Agreement gave Indochina its independence, dividing it into Laos, Cambodia, and North and South Vietnam. In 1956, Great Britain and France, along with Israel, invaded Egypt to block the nationalization of the Suez Canal. The UN stepped in and ordered the invaders out, which was a big humiliation for these former global giants. The independence movement in Algeria was another bloody conflict for France, resulting in domestic turmoil and the creation of a new French government headed by World War II hero Charles de Gaulle, who ended the war by granting Algeria its independence in 1962. Great Britain withdrew from its African colonies in the late 50s and 60s.

MODERN RELATIONSHIPS

Charles de Gaulle, president of France from 1959–1969, tried to reassert French power by following nationalist policies. France developed its own atomic weapons instead of relying on the United States for protection, and it stayed a member of NATO but withdrew French troops from NATO forces in 1966. de Gaulle consistently vetoed Great Britain's entry into the Common Market, in order to preserve France's dominant role in the affairs of the continent. de Gaulle set the tone for the future leaders of France.

Many European nations set up mixed economies, which means capitalism with a little socialism to correct economic inequalities among citizens. An example is Great Britain's social welfare state. In 1945, the British Labor Party won control of Parliament and instituted socialist policies. They nationalized key industries and increased the taxation of the wealthy. The government also increased the amount of tax money used for social programs. The British National Health provides free dental and medical benefits, paid for with taxes on employers and workers. Denmark and Sweden also have extensive social welfare programs.

"Iron Lady" Margaret Thatcher, British Prime Minister from 1979 to 1990, was a conservative who lessened the role of government in Great Britain's economy. Greater prosperity resulted, but social programs were cut back quite a bit. She promoted Great Britain as a world power. As an ally of the United States, Britain supplied the second largest number of troops to UN forces in support of Kuwait in the 1990 Persian Gulf War.

IRELAND

During Oliver Cromwell's reign, many Irish were killed by the British. Protestants from Scotland and England took over land in Northern Ireland, and until 1829, when the Catholic Emancipation Act was passed, Irish Catholics could not hold public office and were taxed to support the Anglican Church. In 1905, the Sinn Fein Party was formed as a nationalist group to press Britain for Irish independence. In 1922, the southern four-fifths of the island became a free nation known as the Republic of Ireland, and the remaining one-fifth, known as Ulster, stayed part of the United Kingdom. Catholics in Northern Ireland and the Republic of Ireland wanted unification, but Britain turned them down, mostly because the majority of Ulster citizens were Protestants and wanted to stay under the British Crown. In 1985, the Hillsborough Agreement tried to end the "Troubles," stopping discrimination toward the Catholic minority in the North, and giving the Republic of Ireland some involvement in the governing of Northern Ireland. This had mixed results. Today the Catholic minority in Northern Ireland is still the target of economic and political discrimination. Many want to reunite with the Republic of Ireland, and some support the outlawed Irish Republican Army (IRA), which uses terrorist tactics. In 1993, Prime Ministers John Major of Britain and Albert Reynolds of Ireland signed a declaration of principles, saying that all groups that promise to renounce violence, like the IRA and Protestant guerrilla organizations, would be invited to join negotiations on the future of Northern Ireland. Northern Ireland remains a province of Britain for as long as the majority of the people want it to; the Irish government agreed to amend its constitutional claim to the northern territory. Since the beginning of the "Troubles" in 1969, there has been no real solution.

SPAIN

In 1936, civil war broke out in Spain between the Left Wing, which included the socialists, Communists, and anarchists, and the fascists. The fascists, supported by Italy and Germany, toppled the Spanish Republic and established a dictatorship under General Francisco Franco. Spain was the only fascist country to survive World War II due to its position of neutrality. Franco served till his death in 1975, when Spain was restored to a constitutional monarchy.

GERMAN REUNIFICATION

In 1989, the Berlin Wall came down. Poland wanted to be in on all reunification talks because it had suffered more from the German occupation in World War II than any other European nation. Poland wanted assurance that Germany would respect Polish sovereignty, not retake land, and respect the Oder-Neisse boundary line between East Germany and Poland. Chancellor Helmut Kohl, head of West Germany, made that promise, and Germany was reunited in October 1990. The first all-German elections since 1932 took place in December of that year, and the winner was the Christian Democratic Union (CDU) coalition party and its leader, Kohl, who became the first leader of a united Germany since Hitler. An economic merger occurred when the West German mark became the unit of currency in East Germany, and people were allowed to move. (See chapters on Russia and Eastern Europe for more on this.)

THE POST-INDUSTRIAL WORLD

The term *post-industrial society* refers to a society in which more people work in service industries, like accounting and health, than in production industries, like steel and textiles. Technology and service industries are highly developed in Europe, despite its relatively narrow resource base. Western Europe depends on outside areas for raw materials; its dependence on the Middle East's oil is a major consideration. Modern technology has made Western European agriculture among the most productive in the world, but Southern Europe remains less economically developed than the North. Increased developments in other parts of the world have meant more competition for European economies and a slower growth rate for the more mature economies.

The end of imperialism greatly reduced Europe's power and market base. To compete with the superpowers, in 1957, led by France, six Western European nations—Belgium, France, Italy, Luxembourg, the Netherlands, and West Germany (the Inner Six) formed the European Economic Community (EEC), also known as the Common Market. It encouraged free trade and uniform economic policies, the sharing of industrial technology, and greatly reduced the threat of Communism. It originated in 1951 as the European Coal and Steel Community (ECSC). Today it includes almost all Western European nations.

The EEC came to be known as the European Community (EC), and by 1985, Denmark, Ireland, England, Greece, Portugal, and Spain were accepted for membership. In 1987, a plan was discussed for one large common market in which nations could sell their goods more easily to each other, subject goods coming into the EC from outside to tariffs, and create a frontier-free Europe. Twelve nations would make up a single economic unit, which could compete with the United States and Japan, and might even join together politically, creating the United States of Europe. Since 1994, the EC has been known as the European Union. In 1994, it voted to admit four more nations, Austria, Finland, Norway, and Sweden (which has been neutral since 1815).

UNITY

Europe is a bunch of sovereign states that make their own choices on issues of national concern but are moving toward greater interdependence. As single sovereign nations, the countries of Western Europe cannot compete, but united, they're a major economic power. Today, Western Europe is trying to bring about more unity, with a plan that builds upon the structure of the EEC, which includes almost all the countries of Western Europe and has become a powerful economic force in the world. Not everyone in Europe wants unity; the major opposition wants to keep its national sovereignty.

The European Parliament deals with issues of concern to the whole region. Other plans include the adoption of a common passport and a uniform currency for members of the European community. Nationalism stands in the way of unity, with Britain's Margaret Thatcher having been the most vocal in expressing concerns. She was seen as an obstacle to the creation of such a united Europe. In December 1990, she was forced to give up the leadership of the Conservative Party and resign as Prime Minister. Her Chancellor of the Exchequer, John Major, became Prime Minister in 1990, followed by Tony Blair, the leader of the Labour Party, in 1997.

In 1991, the Maastricht Treaty, agreed to at the Maastricht Summit, committed members of the EC to a closer union. Its goals include the development of common foreign and defense policies and the creation of a single European currency by 1999. The European Parliament, a 518-member assembly, primarily a consultative body, would get some legislative say in internal trade, the environment, education, health, and consumer protection. There would be common rules on immigration, and the "Citizenship of the Union" would be introduced, guaranteeing free movement within the Community. As of 1993, virtually all restrictions on the movement of people, capital and products were eliminated within the EC. Maybe someday there will be a United States of Europe, since there is already a European Parliament, a European Court of Justice, and a European Commission.

Increasingly, the peoples of Eastern and Western Europe have rejected war as a means of resolving international conflict. Western Europe has achieved a high degree of security and prosperity based on voluntary cooperation. But not everyone in Western Europe respects the rights of others. There are Neo-Nazis in Germany, and Turks, Arabs, Africans, Gypsies, and refugees from Eastern European countries have been subjected to firebombings, beatings, and other attacks. Similar attacks have taken place in France, Spain, Italy, and Greece.

CHAPTER 7

Russia and Eastern Europe

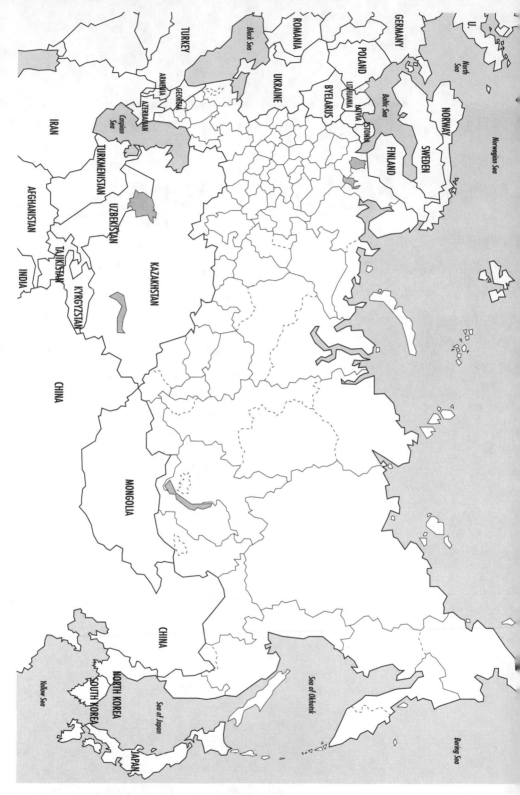

GEOGRAPHY

We're talking here about the nation of Russia, the nations of Eastern Europe, and the nations of Asia that were once part of the Russian and Soviet Empires. The area is made up of the Commonwealth of Independent States (C.I.S.), which includes Russia, Ukraine, Moldova, Uzbekistan, Turkmenistan, Armenia, Azerbaijan, Kazakhstan, Georgia, Tajikistan, Kyrgyzstan and Belarus. Latvia, Estonia, and Lithuania are independent nations that are not part of the C.I.S. and are sometimes called the Baltic countries because of their proximity to the Baltic Sea. Armenia, Azerbaijan and Georgia form a distinct subregion in the area. Azerbaijan is predominantly Muslim and has a lot of oil, while the other two are predominantly Christian and don't have oil. Another distinct subregion is made up of the five countries south of Russia with Muslim majorities whose names end in "stan:" Uzbekistan, Turkmenistan, Kazakhstan (where Russia's space program is based, in the city of Baykonur), Tajikistan, and Kyrgyzstan.

Russia is the largest nation in the world and takes up more than a quarter of the globe. It is more than twice the size of the United States and spans two continents; 25 percent of it lies in Eastern Europe and 75 percent is in Asia. Since the population of Russia is a little more than that of the United States, two and one-half times the size, it's relatively underpopulated.

Eastern Europe is between Western Europe and Northern Eurasia; for many years the countries here were Soviet satellites. Eastern Europe has served as an invasion route throughout history. European Russia, where most Russians live, is included in what is known as Eastern Europe. Eastern Europe includes Albania, Poland, Romania, Hungary, Bulgaria, the Czech Republic, Slovakia and the parts of the former Yugoslavia: Serbia, Montenegro, Bosnia-Hercegovina, Croatia, and Slovenia and Yugoslavian Macedonia. Another former Eastern European nation, East Germany, reunited with West Germany in 1990. (You can refer to the map in the Western Europe chapter to see Eastern Europe.)

TOPOGRAPHY

Although Russia is large, much of it is landlocked because its ports to the north are frozen much of the year. Consequently, Russia has always wanted to conquer and control warm-water ports. This desire to gain access to the sea for trading purposes led many Russian rulers to adopt a policy of expansionism.

About 10 percent of Russia is along the Arctic Circle; this tundra is frozen all year (permanently frozen land is called permafrost), and there's little vegetation. The taiga is south of the tundra; it extends in a band of pine forests from Russia across Asia, and is also not suitable for agriculture. The tundra and the taiga make up Siberia. The steppes, vast plains of grasslands, are south of the taiga; the southwestern region of the steppes, now the nation of Ukraine, was known as the "breadbasket of Russia." Fifty percent of the land in Russia is steppe, and the Russian and West Siberian steppes are an extension of the North European Plain. The North European Plain stretches from the Atlantic Ocean, across Western Europe and Eastern Europe until it reaches Russia, where it becomes the Siberian plain, and runs from the Ukraine in the west to China in the east. Plains are easy to cross; the lack of natural barriers provides easy passage across Russia. In the 1200s, invading Mongols crossed the steppes from the east; later, both Napoleon's and Hitler's armies used them to invade from the west. Russia's vast size hurt travel and communication and trade, but helped save Russians from invaders: both Napoleon and Hitler's armies were defeated by Russia's size and harsh climate.

The desert stretches from south of the steppes from the Caspian Sea—the largest inland body of water in the world—to the border of China. The Volga River in European Russia is important for internal transportation, but it empties into the landlocked Caspian Sea. The longest river in Russia is the Ob-Irtysh. Other rivers include the Yenisey, Amur, and Lena. These rivers are of limited use because they mostly flow north to the Arctic Ocean and are frozen most of the year. Mountains separate Northern Eurasia from other nations. The Pamir Mountains separate Tajikistan from Iran and Afghanistan, the Caucasus Mountains help isolate Armenia and Azerbaijan from Turkey and northwestern Iran, and the Urals divide the European and Asian portions of Russia.

In Eastern Europe, the Danube River, the "Mississippi of Europe," connects Hungary, Slovenia, Croatia, Serbia, Bulgaria, and Romania. It runs through the center of Eastern Europe into the Black Sea, and is a major commercial route. The Balkan Peninsula is surrounded by the Black Sea, the Adriatic Sea (a rich source for fishing and tourism), the Mediterranean Sea, and the Aegean Sea. As in Russia, mountain ranges divide and encourage cultural and language differences in Eastern Europe: the Carpathian Mountains stretch through Romania, Hungary, the Czech Republic, Slovakia, and Poland; the Balkans run from northern Bulgaria to eastern Serbia; the Sudeten Mountains are in the Czech Republic; and the Julian and Dinaric Alps run through Slovenia, Croatia, and Bosnia.

CLIMATE

Russia has a varied climate, ranging from frigid subzero temperatures (its winters are the coldest in the populated world) to warm weather around the Black Sea. Much of Russia has the same latitude as Canada, but it doesn't benefit from the Atlantic Drift that warms Western Europe; its summers are short and its winters are long and cold. Eastern Europe is cooler than Western Europe.

RESOURCES

Northern Eurasia has coal, iron, oil, and gold. Siberia supplies the area with 90 percent of its coal and half its natural gas; it also has oil, iron and other minerals, but the climate makes them hard to get. The abundance of natural resources helped Russia industrialize. Up until the twentieth century, Ukraine was able to grow enough grain to supply the entire Russian Empire with enough surplus to make it a food-exporting nation. The C.I.S. is the world's largest producer of coal, iron and manganese. The steppes make good farmland, but harsh climates elsewhere make land uncultivable. Wheat, rye, corn, potatoes, oats, and sugar beets are grown in Russia, but Russia still needs to import a lot of grain to meet its needs.

Eastern Europe has coal, iron, lead, and bauxite, and it grows potatoes, grains, sugar beets, tobacco, and corn. The Czech Republic is Eastern Europe's most industrialized nation; rich in coal and ores used in the production of atomic energy, it also produces beer, glass, china, machinery and light aircraft.

SOCIETY

Russia is made up of more ethnic groups than any other place. Northern Eurasia is made up of fifteen countries and over 100 ethnic groups. The largest groups, the Great Russians, Ukrainians, and Belarussians ("White Russians") share a common culture and religious heritage, and common linguistic roots in Slavonic, the ancient language of the Slavic Eastern Orthodox churches. The Georgians, also Orthodox Christian, and the Armenians share a cultural heritage, but the Armenians have their own Eastern Orthodox Church that's a little different (in the fourth century, it was the first country to adopt Christianity as the state religion). The Tartars are descendants of the Mongols, and the Azerbaijanis, Turkmen, Uzbeks and Kazahks are descended from Turkish invaders. The Latvians and Lithuanians share a common cultural, linguistic and religious heritage, while the Estonians speak a language closely related to Finnish and Hungarian.

In Eastern Europe, the largest and most dominant ethnic group is the Slavs, which includes Great Russians, Belarussians, Ukrainians, Poles, Serbians, Croatians, Bulgarians, Slovenes, Slovaks, and Czechs. Non-Slavic peoples include Magyars (the proper name for Hungarians), Romanians, Albanians, Greeks, Germans, Turks, and Gypsies.

The traditional Russian family was extended and patriarchal; several generations lived together and worked the land, the eldest male dominated the family, and fathers arranged children's marriages. After the Russian Revolution of 1917, the focus was more on urbanization; collectivization broke up extended families, and the nuclear family became more prevalent. The communist doctrine of equality extended to women, who took on a greater role in the family. Following World War II, Eastern European nations became satellites and adopted similar changes, though not as dramatic as those in the Soviet Union, because Eastern Europe didn't reach the same level of industrialization.

RELIGION

In the tenth century, the Russian czar, Prince Vladimir of Kiev converted to the Eastern Orthodox religion of the Byzantine Empire. He made it the official religion of Russia, and had the people of Ukraine, Russia and Byelarussia (now Belarus) baptized along with himself. The Russian language is written in Cyrillic letters and was influenced greatly by the Slavonic language used by the Church. Russian folk music and polyphony (using four-part harmony) were incorporated into church hymns. Building churches and painting icons were the main obsessions, and monasticism became popular. The church was placed under the control of the czar's government during the reign of Peter the Great, and church officials became part of the elite class, providing a source of comfort and guidance.

Marx called religion the "opiate of the people;" that is, religion makes people unjustifiably satisfied with their lives and unwilling to bring about social change. After the Communist Revolution, the Church lost its land and power, and worship was discouraged.

Gorbachev's Glasnost relaxed this policy, resulting in a resurgence of religious activity in Northern Eurasia. In fact, in 1995, Russian leader Boris Yeltsin returned to the Russian Orthodox Church himself.

The Eastern Orthodox Church is headed by a bishop known as the Patriarch of Moscow. He is not like the Pope; he is one of many bishops who consult with each other. Ukraine and Georgia have their own patriarchs too. There are Roman Catholics, called Uniates, or Eastern Rite Catholics, who are Orthodox in ritual but officially under the authority of the Pope, in Ukraine. Lithuania has a large Roman Catholic population. Those descended from the conquering Mongols are Muslims; also, as Russia expanded, some Muslim territories became part of the empire. Glasnost allowed its spread, and today, countries with large Muslim populations want independence.

Jews are a sizable minority in Russia. They were used as scapegoats in both czarist and Communist Russia, despite the fact that Leon Trotsky, one of Russia's revolutionary leaders, was a Jew.

EASTERN EUROPE

Roman Catholicism is practiced in Poland, Hungary, and Czechoslovakia. The majority of Czechs became Roman Catholic while under Austrian rule. The majority of Albanians became Muslim under Turkish domination. Parts of Yugoslavia (Croatia, Slovakia, and Slovenia) as well as Hungary and Poland, were converted to Christianity by Roman Catholic missionaries. Roman Catholic officials spoke out against Communism, and supported Solidarity in Poland. But the majority of Eastern Europeans are Eastern Orthodox Christians because they were once part of the Byzantine Empire. In the former Yugoslavia, most Serbs are Eastern Orthodox, and Islam has a following in Bosnia-Hercegovina and Albania. There are also some Protestants and Uniates. Before World War II, Jews were a large minority, but the Holocaust nearly destroyed Eastern European's Jewish population.

THE ARTS

Kievan Russia felt the strong influence of the Byzantine Empire; the Eastern Orthodox religion was a major influence that can be seen in the icons, or small religions paintings, and domes. In czarist Russia, the spirit of nationalism pervaded. The literature was written in Slavonic, the language of the Church, and was mostly chronicles and hagiography (the lives of the saints). The music and literature at that time were mostly written by monks.

The Russian authors of 1800s used their creativity to point out social injustices. Alexander Pushkin's work was based on folklore; his famous poem was *Boris Gudonov*. Count Leo Tolstoy was a member of the nobility, and despite his criticism of Russian society, there is a deep sense of nationalism in his work. *War and Peace* recounts Napoleon's invasion of Russia in 1812. Theodor Dostoyevsky wrote psychological novels like *Crime and Punishment* and *The Brothers Karamazov*. Anton Chekov wrote plays, such as *The Cherry Orchard* and *The Seagull*. The music of this time was nationalistic, and included romantic themes of beauty, love and nature; Peter Tchaikovsky wrote *Swan Lake*, *The Sleeping Beauty*, and *The Nutcracker*. Nikolai Rimsky-Korsakov was another famous Russian composer. These musical giants composed all kinds of works with traditional melodies. In Eastern Europe, Frederic Chopin, a Polish composer famous for his piano concertos, expressed nationalist sentiments in his polonaises and mazurkas.

Soviet arts were an expression of Communist ideology and Soviet nationalism, or "socialist realism." When Soviet totalitarianism took over, musicians, including Sergei Rachmaninov and Igor Stravinsky were exiled by the Revolution. Writers criticizing the system faced exile or death; some escaped to the West. Boris Pasternak won the Nobel Prize in literature in 1958 for his book *Dr. Zhivago*, but Soviet authorities opposed his interpretation of the Revolution of 1917 and banned him from accepting the prize. The novel was not released in the Soviet Union until recently. Alexander Solzhenitsyn wrote works criticizing Stalin and the Soviet system. *One Day in the Life of Ivan Denisovich* describes life in a Soviet concentration camp; Solzhenitsyn was himself sent to one for being critical of Stalin. In 1973, he wrote *The Gulag Archipelago*, which exposed the Soviet police state. It was published in the West, and Solzhenitsyn was deported from the Soviet Union; he took up residence in the United States, but returned to Russia in 1994.

A TIMELINE OF RUSSIAN HISTORY

800s–1240	First Russian State at Kiev
1240–1480	Mongol Control of Russia
1480–1598	Muscovite Rule
1613–1917	Romanov Dynasty
1917–1991	Communist Rule
1991–present	Democratic Rule

EARLY SETTLERS

Before the ninth century A.D., tribes of Slavic people from Eastern Europe moved to what is now Ukraine, Belarus, and Russia. They couldn't really farm there, so they became traders. The cities they established depended on the Vikings, whom the Slavs called Varangians, to protect the trade routes. The Varangians soon became a ruling class, intermarrying with the Slavs, and founding both a royal dynasty called the House of Rurik and a new state called Rus (hence the name Russia).

Eastern Europe's settlers were ancestors of Romanians and Albanians, who were first brought under the influence of the Romans (Romania is the only nation with a Romance language without a Roman Catholic background). Then waves of Slavic tribes arrived, and nomadic tribes from central Asia followed the Slavs, most notably the Magyars in Hungary and the Bulgars in Bulgaria (where, incidentally, shaking your head means "yes" and nodding means "no"). They mixed with and were absorbed by the Slavs living there.

KIEV

The site of the first Russian State was Kiev, and by 879, it was the center of trade. Kiev is in the Ukraine, the most fertile part of Rus. Kievan princes led a loose federation of Russian cities for mutual protection and the expansion of trade, bringing it into a close relationship with the Byzantine Empire. From the ninth to the thirteenth centuries, Kiev traded with the Byzantine Empire, causing cultural diffusion in both directions.

CHRISTIANITY

In 988, Vladimir of Kiev converted to Orthodox Christianity. Two Byzantine missionaries, Cyril (826–869) and Methodius (815–885) were instrumental in converting the Slavs in Eastern Europe; they preached and conducted worship in the vernacular, or common spoken language. These brothers were quite successful in converting tribes of Slavs in Moravia (the present-day Czech Republic). Cyril created the Cyrillic alphabet, based on Greek and Coptic letters; it was the language of Christian Egypt letters and grammar for the spoken Slavic language. This evolved into Church Slavonic, the liturgical language that unified early Slavic literature and culture. (Today, Croatia uses the Roman alphabet, while Serbia uses the Cyrillic). The brothers' followers converted both Slavic and non-Slavic nations throughout Eastern Europe—Bulgaria, Serbia, Romania, and Rus/Ukraine. Poland and Hungary were converted by German missionaries and came under the influence of the Roman Catholic Church.

THE BYZANTINE COMMONWEALTH

By the year 1000, the Byzantine Empire and its Orthodox satellites, including Hungary, formed the Byzantine Commonwealth. This was an alliance to promote trade and economic expansion in Eastern Europe, and to provide a common defense against Arabs, Turks, and Germans. It was also a political triumph for the Greek East over the Latin West in the development of Eastern Europe as a sphere of influence. Poland joined with the Baltics, particularly Lithuanians, and became a Roman Catholic rival to the Byzantine Commonwealth nations. The Byzantine belief in autocracy, or absolute rule, set an example for future Russian and Soviet leaders.

THE MONGOLS (1240–1480)

In 1240, the Mongols, nomadic warriors on horseback from Central Asia, invaded under the leadership of Batu Khan, Genghis Khan's ("Great Ruler") grandson, and took control of Russia. They were called Tatars by the Russians, and established a harsh, autocratic rule by the Khanate of the Golden Horde (that's what the Mongol princes who ruled Russia were called) from the capital city of Sarai, located in the steppes. They collected tribute from local inhabitants. Only Novgorod, a city of the legendary Rurik, was able to repulse the Mongols and remained free of their rule; it did the same with the

Swedes and the Teutonic knights (German crusaders) who attacked from 1240–1242.

The harshness of the Mongol political system nurtured a fear of foreign exploitation and domination among the Russians which has survived to the present day. Mongol rule had lasting implications: land became the most valued possession, a noble class emerged, and peasants gradually lost their freedom and became legally bound to land as serfs (sounds like feudalism, huh?). The Mongols isolated Russia from Western Europe, so the Russians were not exposed to the Renaissance or the Commercial Revolution, and the fall of the Byzantine capital of Constantinople to the Muslim Turks in 1453 isolated them even more. Absolutism and feudalism, two major themes in subsequent Russian history, developed in response to the needs of the times as they developed in other areas (like Western Europe, China, and Japan) in response to similar needs.

MUSCOVITE RULE

In the fourteenth century, the Mongols began their decline as the Russian princes of Muscovy grew in power. Muscovy was centered around the city of Moscow, the headquarters of the Russian Orthodox Church after the fall of Kiev. Moscow was an important commercial and religious center. Local princes copied the autocratic and efficient methods of the Mongols, and by the end of the fifteenth century, the Mongols had been forced out of power and Moscow had become the heart of a new Russian feudal state. The policy of Russification, a means of forcing the national identity and unity on an ethnically diverse (non-Russian) population, began.

A UNIFIED RUSSIAN NATION

Ivan III (or Ivan the Great, 1462–1505) extended Muscovy territory, united lands, and declared himself czar, the Russian word for emperor or Caesar, in imitation of Byzantine Emperors. He declared Moscow to be the "Third Rome," or the center of the Eastern Orthodox Church—czars considered themselves the defenders of the Orthodox Church—and Constantinople took the title of "Second Rome." Ivan IV (Ivan the Terrible, 1533–1584) continued to expand the empire, and strengthened his own power at the expense of his nobles. His nickname came from his use of a secret police and his harsh methods in dealing with people he felt were disloyal. He made the aristocracy subservient to an autocratic central monarchy, and created a new "service nobility" that was loyal only to the czar. He was succeeded by several weak czars; Theodor died without an heir, thus ending the House of Rurik and beginning a thirty-year period of upheaval called the "Time of Troubles" (1584–1613).

THE ROMANOV DYNASTY

The Time of Troubles ended with the election of Czar Michael Romanov in 1613, who established a dynasty that would rule for 300 years. Peter I (Peter the Great, 1682–1725) was a true absolute monarch. He controlled the nobility and the Russian Orthodox clergy and created an extremely loyal army. He expanded his empire westward to the Baltic Sea, and for the first time in its history, Russia was no longer landlocked.

Following a year's tour of major Western European countries, Peter, the first czar to leave Russia, liked what he saw, and began a policy of Westernization. He modernized the army and established a large and impressive navy with which he expanded to the north and south. He established a new capital, St. Petersburg, on newly acquired land, a seaport he called his "Window to the West." St. Petersburg is located on the Baltic Sea, and was the Russian capital until 1918. Peter helped transform Russia into a commercial power by escalating manufacture and trade; he created a Western-style bourgeoisie, or middle class. He even forced Western customs like smoking and beard shaving on Russian nobles. Peter made Russia a major power, but at a considerable cost. The people had no rights, and all opposition was put down. Peter used forced labor, and he raised taxes. The economy improved, but a Russian serf's life was worse than before. Because of Peter, Russia would always be involved in European affairs.

The German-born wife of Peter III (she converted to Eastern Orthodox when she married), Catherine II (Catherine the Great, 1762–1796) became czarina and continued to expand the empire; in a series of "partitions," Russia, Austria, and Prussia divided Polish territory among them, pretty much erasing it from the map. Poland couldn't do anything to stop this because it had been weakened by internal problems and lacked geographic barriers. Catherine also expanded to the south and by 1796, Russia was huge; it included Lithuania, the entire Crimea, much of the northern coast of the Black Sea, and parts of Ukraine and Belarussia. She also continued to raise taxes. She tried to rule as an "enlightened despot," claiming to base her policies on the liberal ideas of the European Enlightenment, and encouraging art, literature, and science. In spite of her interest in reform, respect for justice and human rights, particularly for serfs and peasants, declined during her reign, and all of their protests were crushed.

Alexander I (1801–1825) was the monarch who defeated Napoleon, due to the "scorched earth policy" the Russians adopted in response to Napoleon's invasion; the policy consisted of retreating and burning anything that could not be taken rather than leaving it for the enemy. France's lack of supplies and Russia's extremely cold winter also helped. At the Congress of Vienna, Russia got most of Poland. Alexander also got Finland from Sweden in 1809. After his death in December 1825, a group of Russian army officers with liberal ideas attempted to take over (they were called the "Decembrists"). The new czar was supposed to be Nicholas I, but the Decembrists wanted his brother Constantine, who had already denounced his claim to the throne. The revolt failed. Nicholas I (1825–1855), was an autocrat who fought change because he was afraid that reform would undermine his authority; this is how he earned the title "policeman of Europe."

ALEXANDER II'S ATTEMPTS AT REFORM

Following Russia's defeat in the Crimean War (1854–1856), the people were discouraged by their country's failure as a world power. The plight of the serfs got the attention of middle-class intellectuals, and an uprising was feared. Czar Alexander II (1855–1881), the son of Nicholas I, was known as the "czar liberator," and tried to calm everyone down by agreeing to the emancipation of the serfs. In 1861, he issued a decree freeing millions of serfs and granting the opportunity to buy and work their own land. But in reality, the nobles kept more than half of their former estates, releasing only the wasteland to the peasants. Alexander also instituted reforms in government, education, and the military that ended many abuses.

The liberation of the serfs created a lot of small farmers who couldn't pay off their debts, leading to mass foreclosures and migrations. The abundance of unskilled labor allowed factory owners to exploit the proletariat (workers), and that exploitation resulted in poverty, slums, and unsafe working conditions. These exploited workers became strong supporters of revolutionary ideas and parties, like Communism, socialism, and anarchism. The assassination of Alexander II in 1881 resulted in the end of reform and the return of repression. Alexander III (1881–1894) reacted to his father's murder by enforcing strict control. He reestablished Russification and created resentment and those revolutionary feelings.

Alexander III's son, Nicholas II (1894–1917), tried to change things. From 1904 to 1905, Russia was at war with Japan (the Russo-Japanese War), and expected to win, but lost. This humiliating defeat served to point out the problems of czarist rule. Peaceful demonstrations turned bloody when soldiers fired on a group of workers marching in protest to the palace. This massacre, known as "Bloody Sunday," touched off the Revolution of 1905. To calm everyone down, Czar Nicholas II agreed to establish a Duma, or legislature. However, he disregarded his promises of basic civil rights and lawmaking powers to the Duma once the revolution was put down, which pretty much ensured the inevitability of more revolution. Revolutions are more likely to happen when many different groups in a country become dissatisfied at the same time.

THE ROAD TO REVOLUTION

The French Revolution and the Industrial Revolution changed Western Europe in the eighteenth century, and Russian czars wanted that wealth, but didn't want the ideals of liberty, equality, and fraternity to reach the people. Russia's lack of progress laid the groundwork for a huge revolution in 1917. So did the rigid class structure limiting social mobility (even the middle class couldn't move), the poverty, and the fact that the upper classes, composed of the Russian Orthodox clergy and nobility, controlled the wealth and got special privileges.

The guiding principles of the Romanov dynasty were nationality, orthodoxy, and autocracy. Regarding nationality, by the end of the nineteenth century, Russia contained lots of ethnic minorities, and the "Russification" that was going on was an attempt to destroy native cultures in the name of nationalism. The only acceptable belief was orthodoxy, or the teachings of the Russian Orthodox Church, and hatred of other religious groups was common at this time. Anti-Semitism was prevalent throughout Russia and Eastern Europe. Jews were an ethnic and religious minority, so they were an easy target, and were used as scapegoats for all the problems of the nations whenever an uprising was feared. The government played on the fears and the anger of the people, channeling them into attacks on Jews, called pogroms, which helped the people forget about their own problems and allowed the government to avoid confrontation. Millions of Jews were forced to flee Russia during the nineteenth century to escape the pogroms. While other countries were incorporating democracy, autocracy in Russia was the rule, and this also bred discontent. The majority of people, especially the educated middle class, began to feel that an end to absolutism was the answer. The czar repressed as much as he could with his secret police.

MEANWHILE, IN EASTERN EUROPE...

Despite the establishment of the Byzantine Commonwealth, by 1450 Ottoman Turks had captured much of the Byzantine Empire and Eastern Europe. Eastern Europe was under Turkish domination from 1453 to 1821. During the nineteenth century, a rivalry developed between Russian czars, the Romanovs, and the Austrian emperors, the Hapsburgs, to lead the Slavs out of Turkish rule. Each claimed to be the rightful heir to the Byzantine Empire. Both rulers used the double-headed eagle in their coat of arms. The Orthodox nations favored Russia, and the Catholic ones favored Austria.

In 1821, the Greek struggle for independence sparked a movement throughout Eastern Europe to end Turkish domination. Revolutions broke out in every country, and the rivalry between Russia and Austria intensified (remember, in 1815, Russia and Austria divided Poland at the Congress of Vienna after the Napoleonic Wars). By 1900, Austria also gained Bohemia (the modern-day Czech Republic) and Croatia. Austria-Hungary was formed after Hungarians revolted against the Austrian empire in 1848 (the revolution was crushed) and again in 1866, after Austria lost a war against Prussia. The Hungarians settled for a compromise, a dual-monarchy, where the Austrian emperor also served as the Hungarian king, and the Hungarians could have their own capital city and parliament (though Austria dominated the union).

Russia, "big brother of the Slavs," financed wars for independence in Greece, Serbia, Bulgaria and Romania. As a result of the Russo-Turkish War of 1877–1878 and the Conference of Berlin that followed, three nations in the Balkans—Serbia, Montenegro, and Romania—gained their independence from the weakening Ottoman Turks (Bulgaria broke away in 1908). The concept of Pan-Slavism, the political, religious, and cultural unity of all Slavs and/or Orthodox Christians, was developing, and the czars were in conflict with the British, the Germans and the French, as well as the Austrians and the Turks.

WORLD WAR I

By 1914, tensions had grown so much in Eastern Europe, especially in the Balkans, that it was called the "powderkeg of Europe." People throughout Eastern Europe wanted their own independent nations, while Russia and Austria-Hungary wanted to keep control over minorities and keep expanding their empires. World War I broke out following the assassination of Austrian Archduke Ferdinand by a Serbian nationalist, and Russia joined Great Britain and France against Germany and Austria-Hungary. Russia was not militarily or economically ready to fight; the German forces were technologically superior.

PROBLEMS IN RUSSIA

Another problem Russia had was a scandal within the royal family. Czarina Aleksandra had fallen under the influence of a fraudulent "holy man," Grigory Efimovich Rasputin, who was able to control Czarevitch (Prince) Alexis, possibly through hypnosis. While the czar was away at the front, Rasputin was a bad influence over the German-born czarina, who was already suspected of being a spy. His interference produced corruption and inefficiency.

The Russian troops met many defeats; the soldiers lacked supplies, and those serving behind the lines began to desert. The czar himself was on the battlefront neglecting civilian problems, which resulted in low morale and the collapse of his authority in St. Petersburg (then called Petrograd) and other cities. In March 1917, the czar's troops refused to fire on a group of protesters, and instead joined them in sympathy, resulting in widespread rioting, and bringing the country near anarchy. Realizing he couldn't control his troops without the support of the people, Czar Nicholas II abdicated. In this way, World War I provided the spark for the Russian Revolution.

THE MARCH REVOLUTION

The March Revolution was a spontaneous uprising which brought about the downfall of the czar, but it lacked strong leaders and a plan. A Provisional Government was set up, led by Aleksandr Kerensky and dominated by the middle class. They intended to write a constitution and establish a democracy, but they only brought about moderate change. They were cautious about examining the peasants' problems. This caution angered the people whose representatives, the soviets (or councils of workers and soldiers, and later intellectuals and peasants), demanded action and results. Remember, Russia did not have a democratic tradition, so no one really understood the goals of the Provisional Government, and it couldn't provide what the monarchy had provided, that is, unity of the empire. Plus, the Provisional Government's leaders decided to honor Russia's commitment and continue participation in World War I, which was a very unpopular decision. The war wasted their best troops, and those who remained to protect the Provisional Government were inferior. All of this contributed to the Bolshevik Revolution of November 1917.

THE NOVEMBER REVOLUTION

The new, more open atmosphere in Russia following the March Revolution allowed the exiled to come home, and among them were Nikolai Lenin (born Vladimir Ilyich Ulyanov) and Leon Trotsky, leaders of the Bolshevik Party (*bolshevik* means *majority*, though the Bolsheviks were never really a majority). They were "professional revolutionaries," radical socialists who followed Karl Marx' ideas and who struggled for a dictatorship of the workers (the majority) in place of the owners (a minority), that is, for Communism.

Marxist-Leninist Philosophy

Karl Marx had predicted that a communist revolution would first occur in an industrial society like Great Britain, that exploited factory workers would be driven to overthrow the capitalist owners and take control of the country. In 1917, Russia was still industrializing, and Lenin didn't think it was possible to wait until it was completely industrialized before establishing a Marxist state. The revolution was to bring about a "dictatorship of the proletariat," which would rule temporarily during the transition from capitalism to Communism. Once that was accomplished (they thought it would take around 100 years), the state would "wither away." In a society where everyone was equal and contribute according to their ability, there would be no need for government.

The Bolsheviks immediately tried to gain support by capitalizing on the unpopularity of the war. They offered the people a program of peace (an end to Russia's role in World War I), land (the peasants could seize the land of the nobles) and bread (an end to shortages; better conditions for workers; and city workers would get a greater share of the wealth they worked to produce). All of this was exactly what the people wanted, and it was better understood than the goals of the Provisional Government, so Bolshevik support grew. In November 1917, the Bolsheviks led a second revolution: the Provisional Government was overthrown, and a new government was installed with Lenin as Premier and Trotsky as Minister of War.

THE RISE OF THE MODERN TOTALITARIAN SOVIET STATE

Lenin was in charge from 1917 to 1924, when he died. The Bolsheviks became known as Communists, and they immediately took steps to establish peace with Germany and take Russia out of the war. They were counting on the German workers to revolt, following Russia's lead. The Treaty of Brest-Litovsk (1918) was harsh; Russia was forced to give up a lot of territory. Despite the objection of others, Lenin accepted the treaty, since he thought that peace at any price was necessary for the survival of the revolution and the state. Industries and land were nationalized (or put under government ownership). Opposition grew because the people weren't familiar with communist philosophy and didn't understand Lenin's actions. He found it hard to get their cooperation, and they thought the promises of land and bread weren't being fulfilled.

THE CIVIL WAR (1918–1921)

Civil war raged in Russia between the "Reds," or Bolsheviks, who supported the revolutionary government, and the "Whites," who represented many different groups who shared the same goal, to overthrow the Bolsheviks and regain power. The White Army was helped by Great Britain, France, Japan, and the United States, who wanted Russia to rejoin allies and who feared the spread of Communism. The Bolsheviks used a secret police to uncover opposition, and thousands of people suspected of being anti-Bolshevik were executed. They also executed Czar Nicholas II and his entire family. The Whites, who were also suffering from disunity among the leadership, were no match for the Reds, and after years of fighting, the Reds won.

Lenin eased up on his economic programs to help the economy damaged by the civil war. His New Economic Policy (NEP) allowed for some private control of land and business. In 1922, the Communists organized the government into the Union of Soviet Socialist

Republics (USSR), or the Soviet Union, which became the new name of the country.

MEANWHILE, IN EASTERN EUROPE

With the exception of the Bulgarians, who fought against the Greeks, Serbians and Romanians over territory in the Second Balkan War (1912–1913), the Slavic/Orthodox nations joined Russia against Austria in World War I. When it was over, Ukraine and Poland were independent, as were the Baltic states of Finland, Lithuania, Latvia, and Estonia. Three new nations were created by the Treaty of Versailles: The independent states of Hungary and Czechoslovakia (Bohemia, Moravia, Slovakia, and the Sudetenland) from the Hapsburg empire, and Yugoslavia (now Serbia, Croatia, Slovenia, Yugoslavian Macedonia, Montenegro, and Bosnia-Hercegovina).

BACK IN THE USSR

Lenin died in 1924, and you can still see him on display, as a symbol of the state, in Red Square. Once a month, special undertakers inject his body with stuff that keeps it from rotting. His death led to a struggle for power between Trotsky and Joseph Stalin (born Dzhugashvili, and called Stalin, "man of steel"), the ruthless and ambitious Communist Party secretary. By 1925, Stalin forced Trotsky out of office and the country; Trotsky was assassinated in Mexico by Stalin's agents in 1937 after publishing numerous criticisms of the Stalinist regime.

THE MAN OF STEEL

Stalin had unlimited power, and created a totalitarian police state that was more efficient and brutal than even czarist Russia had been. He increased the size and the power of the secret police and ruled through terror, trusting no one. Stalin's paranoia was brutal: from 1935 to 1936, he conducted a series of show trials, hearings where the verdicts were decided in advance, known as the purges. Purges were his moves to clean out the Communist Party of "disloyal" members; even those closest to Stalin were not safe. People were arrested, forced to confess to crimes they didn't commit, and executed; even close friends and relatives of Stalin's were killed. Only recently has Soviet leadership fully acknowledged Stalin's atrocities.

The Soviet Constitution

Theoretically, the Soviet Union had a constitutional government, but in practice its government was a dictatorship of the Communist Party; just because you have a constitution, doesn't mean you have a democracy. The Constitution of the USSR placed greater emphasis on social cohesion and law and order than on individual rights; it guaranteed human rights, but, for example, Communist ideology opposed the free practice of religion in the USSR, especially proselytization. Religion competed with Communist efforts to obtain allegiance. The constitution did guarantee equal rights for men and women. In the 1980s, about 70 percent of Soviet doctors were women. In fact, the percentage of women employed as doctors, lawyers and engineers was higher in the USSR than in the United States.

The Communist Party was the only political party allowed to exist, and only a small percentage of the entire population could belong to the Party. The Politburo, or inner circle, was the fifteen men responsible for making policy. The leader of the Communist party, the general secretary, was the most powerful man in the Soviet Union. Voting was a responsibility required by law, and you had to vote for a Communist candidate. The legislature, called the Supreme Soviet, was merely a rubber stamp for policies made by the Communist Party.

Five-Year Plans

Stalin transformed Russia into a modern, industrial nation by putting the needs of the state first. Under Stalin, the government had complete control over production and distribution, and put the emphasis on heavy industry, especially war materials, not on light industry goods and food and consumer goods. He exhibited little empathy for human costs. The economy was severely strained during the years of Stalinist rule; a lot was spent on national defense, and the standard of living for citizens was lowered.

The Reign of Terror

The 1917 revolution promised land, but Stalin viewed individual farms as inefficient. In 1928, he abandoned Lenin's NEP and went for centralized planning. He forced peasants to give up small farms and join collective farms controlled by the government. Many peasants, especially the more affluent ones known as kulaks, resisted. Some killed their livestock and destroyed machinery rather than turn it over to the government. Stalin hit back by sending millions of people to prison labor camps in Siberia or Soviet Central Asia, and by conducting executions. In Ukraine, where farmlands were rich, opposition was strong, and food was seized by the government; thus, if you stood in Stalin's way, you starved to death. During this forced famine in the Ukraine, between 4.5 and 9 million Ukrainians died of starvation. Stalin claimed he was eliminating the kulaks, those wealthy peasants who were exploiting their neighbors, but, in fact, few of those who were killed were kulaks (besides, that's not an excuse for murder).

The failure of collectivization, which reduced agricultural output, was demonstrated by the success of the small garden plots that Stalin allowed farmers to work for themselves. These small parcels consistently out-produced the collectives and state farms. World War II interrupted Stalin's Third Five-Year Plan in 1941, during which only heavy industry made any progress, at the cost of huge human suffering and death.

WORLD WAR II

The USSR was not the only totalitarian state in Europe in the 1930s. On September 1, 1939, Hitler invaded Poland, and the war began. This gave Stalin the opportunity to expand. In the Nazi-Soviet Non-aggression Pact (1939), the USSR and Germany promised not to attack each other; there was also a secret provision for the division of Poland between them. In 1940, through military pressure, not democratic choice, the Baltic nations of Estonia, Latvia, and Lithuania were annexed to the Soviet Union as separate Republics. In 1941, Hitler violated the Nonaggression Pact with a surprise attack on the Soviet Union, forcing Stalin to join the Allies against Germany. Following the Battle of Stalingrad (1942–1943), the Soviet army went on the offensive, freeing Czechoslovakia, Poland, Hungary, and Romania from the Nazis. The Russians used the scorched earth policy again, and that combined with the harsh climate wore down the German forces. By 1945, the Soviet army had pushed the Nazis out of Russia and Eastern Europe and into Germany, and occupied the eastern part of Germany. Germany surrendered in 1945 with the fall of Berlin.

MEANWHILE, IN EASTERN EUROPE...

The history of Eastern Europe is marked by the domination of foreign powers; remember, most of Eastern Europe is made up of flat plains, which are easy to invade. Poland was formed in 1918 with land taken from Russia, Germany, and Austria-Hungary. In the years between World War I and World War II, Eastern Europe developed constitutional monarchies and democratic governments, but only Czechoslovakia was able to maintain a democracy. During World War II, Eastern Europe fell under Nazi control, and fascist governments were set up. Then, as the Germans retreated, the Soviets took over. At the Yalta Conference (1945), the Allies agreed that the Soviets would occupy Eastern Europe until free elections could take place.

Satellites

At the end of the war, guided by nationalism, Stalin made sure he'd never be vulnerable to invasion again. He took control of the countries that had been liberated from the Nazis, even though he promised the Western Allies that those countries would have free elections. These became known as satellites; they were not truly independent, and they revolved around the Soviet Union. They provided a buffer zone against future Western European attacks; remember, the Soviet Union lacked geographic barriers in the west; these satellites served that purpose. This action also violated the Yalta Conference, because there were no free elections, just the installation of Communist regimes.

The Iron Curtain

Stalin isolated his satellites from the free Western countries. The Soviets blocked Western efforts to reunite Germany, and East Germany became a satellite. Winston Churchill, the Prime Minister of England during World War II, likened this to an "iron curtain" descending across Europe, and it was the basis for the Cold War. Eastern Europe was cut off and was totally dependent on the Soviet Union. Poland and East Germany tried to break away, but were stopped.

THE COLD WAR (1948–1990)

Following World War II, the Soviet Union emerged as a superpower, and helped to create the United Nations. The Soviet bloc included Hungary, Czechoslovakia, Bulgaria, Albania, Poland, Romania, and East Germany. When the Soviets tried to force the Allies out of Berlin by blocking access routes, the Allies responded with a massive air lift. This was the first incident of the Cold War, the political, economic and diplomatic struggle between the Communists and the West without open military conflict. The Cold War was more than a military rivalry, it was a struggle for survival and supremacy by two basically different ideological and economic systems. No one could really isolate themselves from this confrontation.

In 1949, Western Europe and the United States formed the North Atlantic Treaty Organization (NATO) in response to Stalin's take-over of Eastern Europe and his unsuccessful attempts to install Communist governments in Greece, Turkey and Iran. NATO's policy was "containment," or "let's make sure Communism stays where it is." This was answered by the Warsaw Pact (1955), made up of the Soviet Union and the Eastern Bloc (or satellites). Europe was split into two camps, East and West.

In 1949, the Soviet Union organized the governments of Eastern Europe into COMECOM (Council for Mutual Economic Assistance), which was later joined by Cuba and Vietnam. The Soviet Union used COMECOM to promote regional independence, but it didn't quite work because the combination of food shortages and the desire for Western technology led them to seek trading relations with capitalist nations like the United States. The Soviet Union turned to the Middle East for oil, sometimes trading weapons for oil, and escalating tensions in the Middle East.

The Final Frontier

There was a lot of government support for technological progress in the USSR, including agricultural research, military research, space stations and telecommunications, and education, which was a Soviet priority. Industrial and technological progress was made, often at the expense of social progress; there was great diversity in living standards within the Soviet society. In 1949, Soviet scientists exploded the nation's first atomic bomb, triggering the nuclear arms race with the United States. In 1957, the Soviets launched the first space satellite, Sputnik I, setting off the space race. The launching of Sputnik was a great blow to American morale and represented the tremendous leaps the Soviets had made in military and space technologies. Since the 1960s, the Soviet Union made progress in lunar exploration, telecommunications, and established the Salyut space stations.

Cold War Mentality

The United States and the Soviet Union distrusted each other for many reasons. Both superpowers had huge spy networks (the CIA and the KGB) and were conducting propaganda campaigns (such as the United States' Radio Free Europe, which broadcast information unavailable to the people of Eastern Europe). Of course, there was the arms race, where, year after year, the superpowers spent huge amounts of money building up their nuclear arsenals and inventing new weapons systems. And the Cold War rivals influenced the politics of third world nations in Latin America, Africa, Asia, and the Middle East. Although the United States and the USSR never fought each other, they did engage in "proxy wars," or giving military support to opposing sides in wars going on elsewhere, like the Korean War and the Vietnam War.

A Loyal Soviet Citizen Would Say...

If you asked a loyal Soviet citizen during the Cold War about his or her distrust of the United States, he or she probably would have said something like: I regard the anti-Communist policies of the United States, like the Truman Doctrine, the Marshall Plan, and NATO, as hostile. The ideology of Soviet Communism taught me that there were bound to be violent conflicts between a capitalist nation, like the United States, and a Communist one. From 1945 to 1949, you guys were the only nation in the world who had nuclear weapons, which was scary. I oppose the unification of the three western zones in Germany; we've already suffered immeasurably from German invasions during the two world wars, so I'm afraid.

A Loyal U.S. Citizen Would Say...

If you asked a loyal American citizen during the Cold War about his or her distrust of the Soviet Union, he or she probably would have said something like: I believe in democracy; I don't trust your totalitarian system. Soviet troops hung around in Eastern Europe even after the war, which violated wartime agreements and spread Soviet power over a large area. I don't like how Communist parties are gaining strength in Greece, Italy, and France. I don't like your aiding revolutions and nationalist uprisings; after all, by 1949, Communists had taken over China and North Korea, and were threatening to take over French Indochina. And Soviet troops in Eastern Europe threatened the security of Western European nations.

KHRUSHCHEV

After Stalin died in 1953, the Great Thaw from Stalinism (1953–1958) allowed some freedom, but this was short-lived. There was also a power struggle, and Nikita Khrushchev (1953–1964) emerged as the undisputed leader. He stunned people by denouncing Stalin's excesses, but he was still a dictator. He tried to increase industrial and agricultural production, but his plans didn't work because of the inefficiency of the bureaucratic system, the lack of incentives, and those severe forces of nature in Russia. He encouraged a policy of "peaceful coexistence" with the West.

TROUBLE IN PARADISE

Starting with riots after Stalin's death in 1953, the Eastern bloc began to oppose USSR control. In 1956, the Hungarian Revolt was Hungary's attempt to rise against the Communist puppet government; it was crushed. Then there was the U-2 Incident in 1960: A U.S. spy plane was shot down over the Soviet Union. The United States said it was a weather plane, but the Soviets produced a pilot and proof that the United States was lying. As a result, a summit between Khrushchev and President Dwight Eisenhower was canceled. In 1961, Albania's extremist Communist government left the Soviet world and joined forces with Communist China; Albania was once the world's only official atheist state. Also in 1961, a wall was built in the middle of Berlin to stop the flow of East Germans and Eastern Europeans trying to move West. And in 1962, there was the Cuban Missile Crisis: the United States learned that the Soviet Union had installed missile bases in Cuba from which it was possible to launch an attack. President John Kennedy ordered a naval blockade of Cuba, and Khrushchev removed the sites.

BREZHNEV (1964–1982)

Khrushchev's failure in the Cuban Missile Crisis, plus the poor Soviet economy and the split between the Soviet Union and Communist China, led to his removal from office in 1964. He was replaced by Leonid Brezhnev, a hardline Communist who took a Stalinist approach, but unlike Stalin or Khrushchev, he didn't have complete power and had to answer to top Communist Party officials. The Brezhnev Doctrine had the goal of suppressing popular, democratic movements in the satellites.

PRAGUE SPRING

In 1968, the Czechoslovakian government attempted to improve conditions, calling these reforms "socialism with a human face."

They allowed people greater rights and freedom, and greater contact with the West. Brezhnev sent in troops and stopped it. After the Soviet invasion ended the Prague Spring, they installed a more obedient government in Czechoslovakia.

DÉTENTE

The massive nuclear arsenals controlled by the Soviet Union and the United States made everyone nervous. By 1972, the antagonism between the Soviet Union and Communist China and the fear brought about from China's improved relations with the United States forced Brezhnev to adopt détente (which means "understanding"). Détente was an easing of Cold War tensions that involved arms control talks and cultural exchanges. There were Strategic Arms Limitations Talks, arms treaties known as SALT I and SALT II, limiting production of nuclear weapons. In the Helsinki Accords of 1975, the United States and its NATO allies agreed to respect the Soviet sphere of influence in Eastern Europe, and the USSR and its Eastern European allies agreed to respect the human rights of their citizens, such as freedom of travel (though they were accused of violating the accords by preventing thousands of Soviet Jews from leaving the country).

Improved United States-Soviet relations were hurt in 1979 with the Soviet Union invasion of Afghanistan. Soviet troops invaded Afghanistan in an attempt to prevent the fall of a friendly Communist government. In response, the United States refused to approve the SALT II arms reduction treaty (though it adhered in principle), saying the Soviets could not be trusted. The United States also placed a grain embargo on the Soviet Union and boycotted the Summer Olympic Games in Moscow. After Ronald Reagan became president in 1980, he built up the military, which came as a direct challenge to the USSR. He even referred to the Soviet Union as the "evil empire."

SOLIDARITY

Poland was the first satellite to break away from Communism and Moscow. It had economic problems in the 70s, and in 1980, a 10-million-member labor union called Solidarity was formed, led by Lech Walesa. Walesa demanded an end to the Communist monopoly of power, and pushed for economic reforms. Pressured by the USSR, the Polish government imposed martial law; as a result, Solidarity was outlawed, and Walesa was jailed. These actions were condemned by the Catholic Church in Poland, a long-time opponent of Communism, and by the Pope and Western leaders.

Walesa was freed in 1983, and leading a fight for freedom by peaceful means, he got the Nobel Peace Prize. Suppressions of protests in Poland continued until 1988. Walesa was elected the leader of Poland in 1990, the first non-Communist to have that role in forty years. The Solidarity-led coalition government embarked on a radical course to change Poland to a market economy by ending price-fixing and canceling subsidies to industries. In the short term, this caused inflation and high unemployment, and people weren't willing to wait for the long-term changes. Former Communist Aleksander Kwasniewski defeated Walesa in 1995.

GORBACHEV (1985–1991)

After brief periods of rule by Yuri Andropov (1982–1984) and Konstantin Chernenko (1984–1985), Mikhail Gorbachev assumed the role of leader of the Soviet Union as general secretary in 1985. He was young and energetic, and he wanted change because he knew the economy was weak. He didn't, however, plan on the collapse of the whole system. That collapse happened despite his reforms, not because of them.

Glasnost

Glasnost means *openness*. The policy of glasnost allowed more contact with other countries, and more freedom to criticize. Dissidents were treated better, there were meetings with Western leaders, and previously banned items like literature were now allowed back in the country. Gorbachev lifted many restrictions on religion just as Russian Orthodoxy celebrated its 1,000-year anniversary.

The entire Soviet political system was reorganized, including the addition of some democratization. People got a more meaningful voice in government, a freely-elected government body was created, and parties other than the Communist Party were allowed to exist. The Congress of People's Deputies, for which anyone could run, met to discuss issues. There was an end to the Communists' monopoly of power; and new executive powers were established for the president, who would replace the general secretary as the most powerful person in the USSR. Gorbachev was elected as the first and only president of the Soviet Union. In 1987, Gorbachev and President

Ronald Reagan had summits resulting in the Intermediate-Range Nuclear Forces (INF) Treaty, the first agreement to eliminate some types of existing nuclear weapons. In 1988, Gorbachev began to reduce the number of troops in the satellite countries, which helped to bring about the collapse of Communist regimes there a year later.

Perestroika

When Gorbachev came to power in 1985, he inherited an economy on the verge of collapse. Soviet citizens waited in long lines for almost everything, even bread and milk. Food shortages and the failure to meet industrial objectives led to *perestroika*, the restructuring of the economy that helped accelerate changes leading to the dissolution of the Soviet Union. Gorbachev sought to expand trade. There was less central planning in industry; the Enterprise Law of 1987 decentralized industrial and agricultural management and allowed citizens to set up private businesses free of state control and keep the profits. The Agricultural Reform Law of 1988 broke up collective farms, and replaced the collective system with the private leasing system. Gorbachev won the Nobel Peace Prize in 1990 for his part in bringing about the end of the Cold War, but he still had the mindset of a socialist, and he wrapped the economy and his reforms with a thin coating of democracy. His reforms helped hasten the end of the Cold War, the collapse of Communism in Eastern Europe, and the breakup of the Soviet Union in 1991.

THE WALL COMES TUMBLING DOWN

In the fall of 1989, Hungary allowed thousands of East Germans to escape to their country, and the East German government, faced with enormous pressure, allowed free travel. Citizens began to dismantle the Berlin Wall in November of that year. Gorbachev wouldn't support the East German Communists, so they resigned their monopoly of power. The reunification of Germany became official in 1990. East German currency was exchanged for West German currency, there were joint ventures with West German firms, entrepreneurship with economic help from West Germany, and social and political problems from the merger. Germany's liberal immigration policies were criticized as instances of violence against foreigners increased; some Germans viewed immigrants as threats in the job market. After Germany eschewed Communism, other satellites followed like dominoes. Hungary, followed by Czechoslovakia, began free elections and reforms and by 1990, they were Communist-free.

BACK IN THE USSR

Russian Republican president Boris Yeltsin was among a group of radicals who pointed out the slow pace of Gorbachev's reforms and wanted even bolder action—there was bureaucratic caution because government planners and military leaders resisted giving up their former privileges. There was fear among workers of no job security, as well as consumer frustration. They expected to see an increase in goods and services, but instead saw homelessness and continually empty shelves.

THE AUGUST COUP

By the middle of 1990, the large and powerful republics of Russia, Ukraine, and Belarus joined the Baltic republics and several smaller republics, and declared independence from Soviet central control. An overwhelmed Gorbachev gave them more autonomy, which frightened the Soviet conservatives into attempting a military coup d'état in 1991. Gorbachev was put under house arrest, but the coup lacked public or military support, and it collapsed after three days. Yeltsin, who had denounced the takeover, became a national hero. Gorbachev returned to power, and the coup leaders were either arrested or committed suicide.

The coup made Gorbachev look incompetent, and the Communist party and the KGB (the secret police) were discredited. By the end of August 1991, all activities of the Communist Party had been suspended and the Soviet Union had ceased to be a Communist state. Yeltsin declared Russia an independent state, and one by one others claimed independence. Gorbachev couldn't stop it, and resigned from the presidency of an empire that no longer existed on December 25, 1991. The Soviet Union disbanded, and Yeltsin emerged as the leader of a new Russia.

THE ARTIST FORMERLY KNOWN AS THE SOVIET UNION

When the USSR disbanded, each republic held its own election and established its own government. Russia, as the largest, took the lead in creating the Commonwealth of Independent States. The United Nations recognized each new government, allowing each one representatives. The twelve republics of Russia, Ukraine, Moldova, Uzbekistan, Turkmenistan, Armenia, Azerbaijan, Kazakhstan, Georgia, Tajikistan, Kyrgyzstan, and Belarus are independent countries that are members of the Commonwealth of Independent States.

Three other republics—Latvia (the most urbanized Baltic state), Estonia (which has the highest standard of living of any former Soviet republic), and Lithuania (the first Soviet republic to declare its independence, in 1991) are not part of the commonwealth, but they are independent. They've officially declared their sovereignty and have been accepted as members of the UN as well. Of course, this transition was not all smooth; there was civil war in Georgia, and the fighting continued between the Christians of Armenia and the Muslims of Azerbaijan that had started in the last years of the Soviet Union.

At first, it was unclear what role the C.I.S. would play. Originally, it was supposed to help member nations coordinate their military defense systems and economies. So far, the C.I.S. (an organization more in name than in fact) has been weak; there's no common currency (not everyone uses the ruble), there's no single military policy (Ukraine and Russia have disputes concerning the control of the nuclear weapons in the Ukraine), and there's debate about the role of Russian troops in other Commonwealth nations. As the dominant member of the C.I.S., Russia has taken over the seat once held by the USSR in the UN Security Council. The C.I.S. continues to weaken due to economic problems, nationalism, the promise of NATO and European Union membership, and the influence of Islam.

YELTSIN

Yeltsin made the transition to a free-market economy and a democratic government, but he also sent Russian troops into the independence-seeking province of Chechnya. This war cost a lot of lives and damaged Yeltsin's support; crime and corruption rose.

In 1993, Yeltsin dismissed the Congress of People's Deputies, which was leftover from the Communists, but it refused to stop meeting and barricaded itself in the parliament building. Yeltsin brought in troops to storm it, and this increased his popularity. He took steps toward creating a new constitution and giving greater powers to the presidency. Some people were afraid he was creating a dictatorship, but most people still liked him. He has looked to the West for both cooperation and aid in finishing the transition to a free market economy. All of the countries are still struggling to solve all the economic problems and make a smooth transition to capitalism and a free market, which seems related to whether they will become and remain democracies.

Russian politicians and economists debate among themselves as to how quickly the change to private ownership should be made. Each reform has severe economic consequences, including unemployment and layoffs. Many Russians would like to see the Russian government hold on to large industrial plants and state farms in order to keep more people employed. There has also been inflation, corruption, and increased crime, including racketeering. Russia's economic problems have made it more difficult for Yeltsin to deal with his political opponents.

Meanwhile, the end of Communism in the former Soviet Union brought an end to the cold war and the arms race. Yeltsin and Bush met in 1992 and signed START II, a treaty that calls for deep cuts in the nuclear arsenals of the two countries.

BELARUS, UKRAINE, AND RUSSIA

The capital of Belarus, Minsk, serves as the capital of the C.I.S. Belarus' ties with Russia remain strong, falling into the Russian sphere of influence, and using a common currency; they are reluctantly independent. In fact, Russian troops guard Belarus' border. It is the only former republic to move in this direction.

Ukraine (which means "frontier") is the second biggest nuclear power in Europe. While they have dismantled the intercontinental ballistic missiles (ICBMs) in a joint agreement with Russia and the U.S., they still retain thousands of tactical battlefield nuclear weapons. Ukraine is a key counterbalancing force in Eastern Europe, as it straddles access to Russia's warm water ports and has special status with NATO (as does Russia; Russia and Eastern Europe established a friendly relationship with NATO called the "partnership for peace"). Ukraine had been a major producer of coal and steel and a major exporter of wheat and other crops. But since independence, industrial and agricultural production have declined and the economy has suffered from high rates of inflation and unemployment.

In 1986, the nuclear power plant in Chernobyl, in Belarus, exploded. As a result, much of the soil in the Ukraine was contaminated, and the produce was not safe. So the Soviet Union was dependent on outside sources, especially the United States, for much of its wheat.

Russia and China signed a treaty of friendship in 1997, effectively ending their feud and allowing a scaling back of Russian forces along the Chinese border. With Yeltsin returning to the Russian

Orthodox Church in 1995, the Church has become an ally of Yeltsin's and has a growing influence.

MEANWHILE, IN EASTERN EUROPE...

In 1989, the attitude of change was evident in Czechoslovakia when former dissident playwright Vaclav Havel, who had been arrested earlier that year, won the presidential election. However, different ideas on economic reform caused the people to democratically choose to separate into two countries, and the Czech Republic and Slovakia officially became independent nations in January 1993. Later that month, Havel was elected president of the Czech Republic, which is the most polluted country in Europe.

In December 1989, a violent revolution brought down the Communist regime in Romania. Police fired on a group of protesters, and Romanians became enraged and overthrew their dictator, Nicolae Ceausescu, who was tried and executed. But the new government has been criticized as a disguised continuation of old dictatorship, and they're having trouble changing to democracy. In Bulgaria, Communist leader Todor Zhivkov was forced to resign, and elections were held. In Albania, leader Ramiz Alia saw the rest of Eastern Europe abandoning Communism and was forced to allow thousands to leave the economically devastated country and hold free elections. The Communists were removed in 1992.

THE ARTIST FORMERLY KNOWN AS YUGOSLAVIA

One country that eluded Stalin after World War II was Yugoslavia; it adopted the Communist philosophy, but it didn't become a satellite. Under the leadership of Marshall Josip Broz, known as Tito, Yugoslavian Communists drove out the Nazis and took control of the government without Stalin's help. Tito resisted Stalin's attempt to force Yugoslavia into being a satellite, and followed a policy of nonalignment. After Tito's death in 1980, Yugoslavia began allowing civil liberties, but still there were economic problems and growing nationalism. After the fall of Communism, the nation was torn apart.

In June 1991, the republics of Croatia and Slovenia (which has close ties to Western Europe) declared their independence. This led to conflicts with the Yugoslavian government, which wanted a unified nation and used force to make its point. Slovenia warded it off, but the Croatian government got involved in a civil war against the sizable Serbian minority, which was helped by the Serbian-dominated Yugoslavian army. There were acts of brutality and human rights violations on both sides. The worst example was the "ethnic cleansing," the euphemistic name for a genocide attempt in which Serbs killed or terrorized thousands of Muslim civilians in order to drive them out of the region. There was a truce in 1991, but then war broke out between the Serbians and Muslims of Bosnia-Hercegovina (often called Bosnia). After that republic declared its independence from the Yugoslav federation, it soon became a three-way ethnic war between Bosnia's Serbs, Croats, and Muslims, with the Serbian and Croatian governments arming the Bosnians.

In late 1992, Yugoslavia officially disappeared, as the remaining republics of Montenegro and Yugoslavian Macedonia declared their independence. The killing in Bosnia went on into 1994, and UN involvement couldn't stop it. Finally in 1995, NATO warplanes bombed Serbian positions to try to force a settlement. Later that year in Dayton, Ohio, warring sides finally agreed to a ceasefire. Foreign troops, including Americans, were sent to Bosnia to keep the peace, but tensions remained high.

So, NATO might have announced the end of the Cold War in 1990, but in its place we got old religious and ethnic hatreds. All of these former Communist nations face huge obstacles to freedom.

8

The World Today

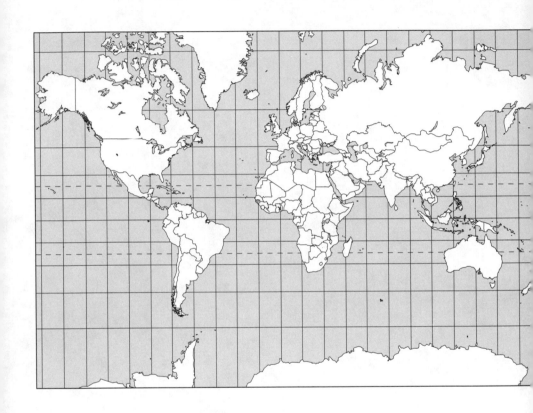

FULL CIRCLE

Remember those eleven Big World Issues we discussed at the beginning of this book? Now that we've reviewed everything, take a look at how those issues apply to Global Studies. Below are examples of each one for you to ponder. Then, try to come up with some of your own.

Issue:	Think About:
War and Peace	Arab-Israeli conflicts
Population	China's population problem
Hunger and Poverty	Hunger in Africa
Political and Economic Refugees	Issues in Cuba
Environmental Concerns	Desertification of the Sahel in Africa
Economic Growth and Development	Latin America's economic development and dependence
Human Rights	Apartheid in South Africa
World Trade and Finance	Oil Politics
Determination of Political and Economic Systems	The Chinese Cultural Revolution
Energy: Resources and Allocations	OPEC
Terrorism	Palestinian Liberation Organization (PLO)

How about those fifteen Big Global Concepts? Take a look at the examples below and connect the concepts with what you've learned in our Global Studies review. Can you think of any other examples?

Concept:	Think About:
Change	The effects of the Crusades
Choice	The former USSR's Communist system of government
Citizenship	Direct democracy under Pericles in Athens
Culture	The Golden Age of Muslim Culture
Diversity	The different ethnic groups amd languages in Northern Eurasia
Empathy	The Spanish missionary priests who spoke out against the mistreatment of Native Americans
Environment	How rainfall shapes South Asian life
Human Rights	The Jews in Nazi Germany
Identity	Islamic fundamentalism
Interdependence	Oil in the Middle East
Justice	Apartheid in South Africa
Political Systems	The Communist Party in China
Power	Japan's expansion prior to World War II
Scarcity	The economic development of the Middle East
Technologies	How India's future is tied to its technological developments, such as the Green Revolution

TODAY'S ISSUES
We've touched on many of the following concerns in previous chapters, but let's review.

Overpopulation
Overpopulation not only has serious implications for the nation or region in which it occurs, but also strains the resources of others trying to meet the resulting increased economic demands. Problems arise when crowded nations seek more territory, or when people migrate to more sparsely populated areas. The resettlement of people uprooted by wars, natural disasters, religious prejudice and industrialization also causes global stress.

There is population growth in both developed and developing nations. Reasons include religious beliefs, like the belief that procreation is essential; cultural factors, like the need to carry on the family name as well as have family around to take care of the old folks; economic factors, like the fact that some families need a lot of kids to help with the work; and lack of knowledge about reproduction and birth control.

Environmental Issues
The devastation of the land and sea by natural and/or human forces has consequences beyond a particular region because the resulting scarcity of resources intensifies the competition for them elsewhere. We're talking about pollution of the water, the earth and the atmosphere. Acid rain is rain that contains a high concentration of acid and pollutants. The burning of fossil fuels, like coal, oil, and natural gas, releases chemical pollutants into the air. They combine with water vapor in the air to form acid rain. Air currents that carry pollution have no boundaries, which makes this a global problem. Fish, animals, and plants are being killed. One solution to the acid rain problem is to restrict the amount of chemical pollutants released into the air by coal-burning industries.

Another kind of pollution is the release of radioactive or toxic particles or chemicals into the atmosphere and water. Nuclear power changed the fundamental nature of warfare, the global balance of power, and the ways to contaminate the planet. In 1986, there was an explosion at the Chernobyl nuclear power plant, and also a fire at a chemical plant in Switzerland that spilled tons of toxic chemicals into the Rhine River. There is so much cyanide in the ocean surrounding the Philippines that the coral reefs there are being harmed. In 1974, scientists found a hole in the ozone layer, the layer of the atmosphere that protects the earth from the harmful ultraviolet rays of the sun. This could lead to an increase in skin cancer and eye disease as well as damage to crops and marine life. There are oil spills, and pollution from cars and industry.

Desertification

Overpopulation leads to desertification, which is caused by the overgrazing of cattle and the overcutting of trees. Widespread grazing eliminates the grass that holds together the soil that prevents erosion; cutting down trees robs the land of another of its natural barriers to soil erosion. As grass and trees are eliminated, the soil loses its nutrients and turns into dry land. It can be fixed by reversing the process, planting trees to act as a barrier against soil erosion, and restricting cattle from overgrazing the land.

Deforestation

In Brazil's Amazon Rain Forest, an area the size of New York State is cleared every year. The plants and animals of the rainforests represent about half of all living species in the world, and deforestation means the loss of food, medicine, and chemical compounds. One possible solution, proposed by the UN, is to reduce Brazil's debt so they don't have to clear the forest to harvest the lumber, grow crops and raise cattle.

The Greenhouse Effect

The Greenhouse Effect is the warming of the earth and its atmosphere caused by the buildup of carbon dioxide. Not all scientists agree that this is happening, but here's how it works. Like the glass in a greenhouse, carbon dioxide traps the heat of the sun and prevents it from escaping. The rising level of carbon dioxide in the atmosphere is due primarily to the burning of fossil fuels. The widespread burning of the rainforests and the use of chlorofluorocarbons (CFCs) in aerosol cans and refrigerators contribute to the problem too. Some solutions include using cleaner forms of energy that are not fossil fuel based, placing stricter controls on automobile emissions, and restricting the use of CFCs.

World Hunger

There is hunger in every nation of the world. Hunger and famine are the result of overpopulation, inadequate natural resources, desertification, political conflicts, and unemployment. The forces of industrialization, urbanization, and environmental depletion cause inadequate food and resource distribution. Governments must balance the population with proper management of natural resources.

Education
Educationally, there is a growing gap between the haves and have-nots. Sometimes social and economic problems in a region take the kids out of schools so they can go to work. Development in the Third World depends on education, but for that, one needs money. Countries that have suffered from civil war for many years have low literacy rates; for example, in Guatemala, only about half the population is literate.

Literacy rates have been rising in developing nations, but the advent of the computer has raised the ceiling of basic literacy. Some students may decide to go to school in developed countries, but then they are likely to stay abroad, bringing about a "brain drain."

International Debt
Latin America, Africa, and Eastern Europe are all experiencing debt. Much of it came from the time when these nations tried to pay for the huge increase in the price of oil during the 1973 oil crisis. There are also huge inflation rates. Dependence on foreign oil makes these regions vulnerable to future price increases.

Human Rights
Human rights are the social, political and economic freedoms that each individual has the right to possess, like the freedoms of speech, religion, press, and assembly, and a decent standard of living. The foundation of the 1948 UN Universal Declaration of Human Rights is the assumption that all people possess those inherent political, social, and economic rights. Unfortunately, the freedoms enjoyed by some societies are not shared by all societies. As international contact broadens and the world becomes "smaller," expectations for human decency and justice rise.

Some of the biggest human rights violations include apartheid, dissidents and forced labor camps in the Soviet Union, genocide in Kampuchea and Uganda, political oppression, pogroms, the Holocaust, the African slave trade, the "death squads" in El Salvador, and the killing of student demonstrators in Tiananmen Square. In 1974, the United States passed the Foreign Assistance Act, which cut aid to any government guilty of human rights violations. Amnesty International monitors human rights violations and pressures governments to release political prisoners.

Technology

Technological progress brings increased contact among people, and it forces the reevaluation of traditional lifestyles. For example, the computer revolution has been compared to the Commercial and Industrial Revolutions before it. The tiny low-cost silicon chip has brought the most important change in human communications since the printing press. The chip makes it possible to perform millions of calculations in a second and store vast amounts of information.

Another technological advance is the Green Revolution, which brings about an increase in the amount of agricultural production from land already under cultivation, and the expansion of farming onto previously nonproductive land. Agricultural scientists called agronomists developed high-yielding plant varieties, and seeds that can produce greater quantities of crops. All of this needs government support in the form of money, of course.

Medicine

Vaccinations and other medical breakthroughs affect life expectancy and the quality of life. They lower death rates, raise birth rates, and make procedures like organ transplants possible. All of this affects a population. There are also ethical considerations, like in genetic engineering and biotechnology (the development of new organisms). The foundation of all this is, of course, money. There's also the nasty ebola virus. Then there's the global epidemic of AIDS: Acquired Immune Deficiency Syndrome is a disease that damages the body's natural immune system, limiting its ability to fight infection. It's caused by a virus for which there is no known cure.

Transportation and Communication

Advances in transportation increase a population's mobility. China manufactures and uses more bicycles than any other nation. More people ride more trains over more miles in India than anywhere else. Television and computers also make the world a "smaller" place. There are also fiber optics and the Internet/World Wide Web. Unfortunately, each technological innovation also creates the possibility of abuse (invasion of privacy) and fraud. The massive oil spill from the Exxon Valdez in 1990 damaged Alaska's coastline and economy. There has been pollution of the North Sea by the USSR dumping radioactive waste from the Soviet North Sea Fleet. There are terrorists hijacking airlines, computer hackers, and smugglers.

Where No One Has Gone Before

The space race began in 1957, when the Soviet Union launched Sputnik, the first manned satellite. Space technology affects the global community and the relationships between nations. For example, electronic communication by satellite links and "spy-in-the-sky" satellites can monitor actions and movements of potential "enemies." On the other hand, international crises can be dealt with more quickly and effectively. Both the former Soviet Union and the United States applied rocket technology from their space programs to develop intercontinental ballistic missiles (ICBMs) for use as carriers of atomic weapons. Meteorology has improved, we use satellites to learn about space, and the medical world may gain knowledge from the opportunity to conduct experiments in the weightless environment of an orbiting space vehicle. There are also issues involving human versus robotic exploration.

Economic and Trade Development

There is a growing gap between the rich and the poor nations. Finding a balance between the traditional and the modern has been an issue in developing nations. Trade relationships must be fair so those nations can develop education and improve their standard of living. There have been many agreements encouraging free trade zones: The European Union, the General Agreement on Tariffs and Trades (GATT), the North American Free Trade Agreement (NAFTA), the Commonwealth of Independent States (CIS), the Organization of African Unity (OAU), and more.

The Impact of Cultures on Each Other

Interaction among different cultures stimulates changes in beliefs, which can create conflicts both between cultures and within them. For example, people in developing nations might see groovy consumer goods on television and want them. Or there can be a linguistic impact, as words for international products become part of the vernacular all over the world. Also, finding out about the possibility of new technologies to increase agricultural and industrial production whets the appetite for a higher standard of living.

It works both ways. For example, beginning in the Sixties, several religious ideas based on Hinduism and Buddhism became popular in the United States. Many Americans are into acupuncture (an ancient Chinese medicine), Yoga and meditation (from India), and Jujitsu, karate and judo (from Japan). Many African Americans have adopted the hairstyles and clothing of Africa, not to mention Islam (such as Muhammed Ali and Malcolm X).

Democracy

What each nation in the Russia/Eastern Europe area has to do now is no less revolutionary than what France and the United States did 200 years ago. And like the French in 1789, Eastern Europeans had high hopes for sudden improvements, hopes, that haven't been met yet. The ethnic strife in the area doesn't help either. Soviet power during the Cold War kept ethnic disputes from erupting, but now there are many brutal civil wars.

War...What is It Good For?

While vocally condemning war, humans have consistently used it as a means of resolving conflicts. Colonialism and imperialism arose from industrial developments, ethnocentrism, and racism, and brought about cultural disruption and in some cases, neocolonialism. With the collapse of the European colonial system, the world has seen the creation of new nations and the expansion of global power systems to a much broader base. Today's second most popular form of war is terrorism, the systematic use of violence such as bombings, assassinations, kidnappings, and chemical and biological terrorism to achieve political goals. There are obvious examples of terrorism in Northern Ireland, the Middle East, Germany, Colombia, and the United States. The most popular form of war today is the civil/ethnic war. Potential areas of major future conflict include Korea, the Persian Gulf, Northern Africa, the Caucasus and Balkan area, India and Pakistan, and China and Taiwan.

Practice Exams

PRACTICE EXAM ONE

Part I (55 credits): Answer all 48 questions in this part.

Directions (1–48): For each statement or question, write on the separate answer sheet the *number* of the word or expression that, of those given, best completes the statement or answers the question.

---

1. Which reference would be used to find the most recent information about the gross domestic product (GDP) of a nation?
    1. historical atlas
    2. thesaurus
    3. world almanac
    4. dictionary

2. Culture is sometimes referred to as "a blueprint for living " because it
    1. flourishes best in traditional societies
    2. includes all the things that contribute to society's development
    3. is determined by genetics
    4. determines the types of jobs offered to the members of a society

3. "We prefer self-government with danger, to servitude in tranquillity."

    The author of this statement would most likely support
    1. imperialism
    2. independence movements
    3. colonial expansion
    4. mercantilism

4. One reason the ancient kingdoms in western Africa prospered was that they
    1. were located along the Tigris and Euphrates rivers
    2. had no contact with the rest of the world
    3. followed the Hindu beliefs of their rulers
    4. developed extensive trade in gold, ivory, and salt

5. In many African nations, a major result of migration from rural to urban areas has been
    1. a strengthening of traditional values
    2. a decline in employment opportunities for educated Africans
    3. a weakening of ancestral lines and kinship bonds
    4. increased agricultural productivity

6. "With the end of the cold war, Africa has lost whatever political luster it may once have had....There is no compelling ...[reason] to catapult it to the top of the global economic agenda. Africa must now take the initiative."

   The New York Times, May 1992

   Which conclusion can be supported by this statement?
   1. Most African nations supported the foreign policies of Communist nations.
   2. African nations no longer control the diamond supply of the world.
   3. Communist and non-Communist nations have contributed large amounts of economic aid to African nations.
   4. African nations can now expect both Western and non-Western nations to invest heavily in Africa.

7. In some African nations today, ethnic rivalries erupt when
   1. political difference are motivated by ancient resentments
   2. trading companies hire nonunion workers
   3. scarce funds halt the exploration for mineral resources
   4. groups share a common heritage

8. Which statement about Japan is a fact rather than an opinion?
   1. Japanese family values have declined with modernization.
   2. Many of Japan's cultural traditions are borrowed from China.
   3. Rapid industrialization has caused few problems for the Japanese people.
   4. Traditional farming techniques in Japan were better than modern ones.

9. Which factor most enabled Japan to rebuild and modernize rapidly after World War II?
   1. vast mineral reserves
   2. large amounts of fertile land
   3. a strong military
   4. a well-trained workforce

10. In China, the building of the Great Wall, the use of he tribute system, and the government's support of the Boxer Rebellion are examples of attempts by different dynasties to limit
   1. foreign influence
   2. nationalism
   3. Communist expansion
   4. industrialization

Base your answer to question 11 on the cartoon below and on your knowledge of social studies.

11. What is the main idea of this 1992 cartoon?
   1. China's government opposes free–trade agreement with Western nations.
   2. Deng Xiaoping personally opposed the introduction of capitalism to China.
   3. The Chinese government is more interested in improving trade than in respecting human rights.
   4. China's economic system is meeting the needs of its people.

12. In China, the Great Leap Forward was an attempt to
    1. promote democratic reform
    2. end the private ownership of land
    3. strengthen economic ties with Europe
    4. increase agricultural and industrial production

13 One similarity between the culture of traditional China under dynastic rule and the culture of modern China under Communism is both stress
    1. a state-supported religion
    2. loyalty to the authority of leaders
    3. the importance of a matriarchal society
    4. limits on population growth

14. Many people in Southeast Asia hope for the timely arrival of the summer monsoons each year because
    1. floods are the only way to water their farmlands
    2. daily temperatures often reach 100°F
    3. little rain has fallen for many months
    4. oases provide water for nomadic herders

15. Which statement about the caste system in present-day India is most accurate?
    1. Most villages are still inhabited by one specific caste.
    2. Although discrimination based on caste is illegal, caste remains an important factor in Indian society.
    3. The caste system is much stronger in India's urban areas than it is in rural areas.
    4. The caste system remains an important part of the Muslim religion.

16. In India today, a major source of conflict has been the
    1. unequal distribution of wealth, between the western and eastern regions of the country
    2. disagreements between national and local governments over control of India's vast petroleum reserves
    3. hostility between the Hindu majority and the Muslim and Sikh minorities
    4. refusal of the Indian Congress Party to hold free elections

Base your answer to question 27 on the map below and on your knowledge of social studies.

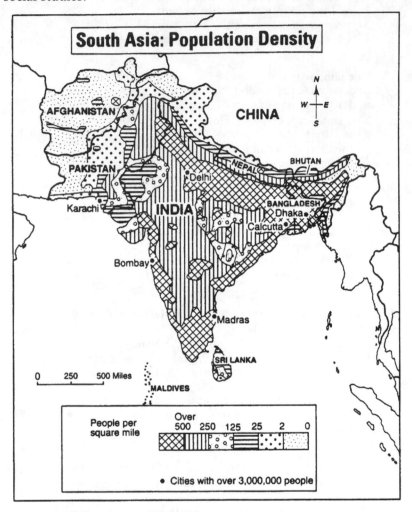

South Asia: Population Density

People per square mile

Over 500 | 250 | 125 | 25 | 2 | 0

• Cities with over 3,000,000 people

17. According to the map, which generalization about the population of India is most accurate?
    1. Most of the nations that border India have population densities greater than India has.
    2. The population density of most of Afghanistan is more than 500 people per square mile.
    3. Most people in India live in or near the city of Bombay.
    4. In India, the southern coasts and the northeastern river valleys support the highest concentration of people.

18. Which statement would be consistent with the views of Fidel Castro?
    1. The spread of Communism is the greatest danger facing Latin America.
    2. An American military presence is the key to the defense of Latin America.
    3. Progress and justice in Latin America can only be achieved through revolutionary socialism.
    4. Introducing a free-market system will improve the economies of Latin American nations.

19. Which of these situations was the direct result of the other three?
    1. Nations of Latin America won independence.
    2. Revolutions occurred in North America and France.
    3. The Napoleonic wars weakened Spain's power.
    4. Creoles and mestizos became discontented with Spanish rule.

Base your answer to question 20 on the statement below and on your knowledge of social studies.

"He once sent fifty horsemen with pikes [spears] to destroy an entire province. Not a single human being survived that massacre, neither women nor children nor aged infirm....This terrible massacre was a punishment for a trifling offense: some Indians had not responded to summons promptly enough when the tyrant had commanded that they bring him a load of maize [corn]...., or else had asked for more Indians to be assigned to serve him or his comrades. And there was no place where the Indians could take refuge...."

20. The purpose of the author was most likely to
    1. encourage the colonial government to change its policies toward native people
    2. explain the problems associated with using native laborers
    3. justify the need for the harsh treatment of the native peoples
    4. show support for the governor's policy toward native peoples

21. A major factor contributing to the destruction of the Amazon rain forests is the
    1. movement of people to end illegal drug traffic
    2. attempt of native peoples to end illegal drug traffic
    3. need for more farmland
    4. spread of Christianity

22. One important effect of the Crusades on Western Europe was that they
    1. led to a decline in the importance of the church in Western Europe
    2. furthered cultural diffusion throughout Western Europe
    3. introduced the Industrial Revolution to Western Europe
    4. ended the Western Europe quest for an overseas empire

23. Which of these events during the Age of Exploration was a case of the other three?
    1. Europeans brought food, animals, and ideas from one continent to another.
    2. European diseases had an adverse effect on the native populations of new territories.
    3. Warfare increased as European nations competed for land and power.
    4. Advances in learning and technology made long ocean voyages possible.

24. During the Scientific Revolution and the Enlightenment, one similarity in the work of many scientists and philosophers was that they
    1. relied heavily on the ideas of medieval thinkers
    2. favored an absolute monarchy as a way of improving economic conditions
    3. received support from the Catholic church
    4. examined natural laws governing the universe

25. The Renaissance and the Protestant Reformation were similar in that both were
    1. stimulated by a spirit of inquiry
    2. supported by the working class
    3. limited to Italy, France, and Germany
    4. encouraged by the successes of the French Revolution

Base your answer to questions 26 and 27 on the statement below and on your knowledge of social studies.

> In the past, European nations have conquered other lands, made them into colonies, and controlled their economies.

26. Which term refers to the situation described in this statement?
    1. socialism
    2. isolationism
    3. imperialism
    4. monotheism

27. This statement describes a situation that resulted from the
    1. industrialization of Europe and the need for raw materials
    2. desire of Europeans to spread Communism throughout the world
    3. Europeans belief in human rights for all people
    4. requests of developing nations for modern machines and technology

Base your answer to question 28 on the diagram below and on your knowledge of social studies.

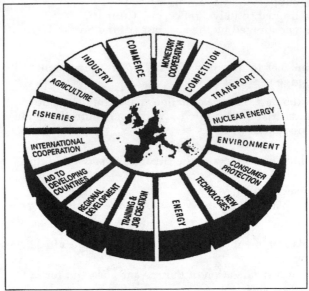

Source: *World Eagle*, June 1993

28. This diagram best represents the activities of the
    1. North Atlantic Treaty Organization (NATO)
    2. Organization of Petroleum Exporting Countries (OPEC)
    3. European Union (European Community)
    4. Warsaw Pact

29. **"The Soviet Union Splits into 15 Republics"**
    "Yugoslavia Experiences Internal Conflict"
    "Germany Reunifies"

    Which conclusion do these three headlines suggest?
    1. Communism remains an important force in Europe.
    2. Many Western European nations are experiencing civil war.
    3. International sanctions strengthen a nation's ability to govern.
    4. The forces of nationalism can either divide or unite a nation.

30. • Lake Baikal is fouled by wastes from factories
     • Plants and wildlife in Siberia are damaged by mining and smelting in the region.
     • Radiation still contaminates 2 million acres near Chernobyl.

Based on these statements about environmental issues in the former Soviet Union, which conclusion would be most valid?

1. The Soviet government spent a large portion of its budget conserving the environment.
2. Communist industrial and agricultural policies resulted in serious environmental problems.
3. Changes in the environment in Russia and Ukraine are largely caused by pollution coming from Western Europe.
4. In Russia today, cleaning up the environment has taken priority over economic development.

Base your answer to questions 31 and 32 on the cartoon below and on your knowledge of social studies.

'Olga! Olga! Is rich nations' clearinghouse sweepstakes! We may have already won 28 billion dollars!'

Pat Oliphant
Universal Press Syndicate

31. The main idea of this cartoon is that Russia has
1. returned to an economy based on agriculture
2. been promised economic aid by Western nations
3. attempted to isolate itself from the West
4. frequently refused economic aid from Western Europe

32. Which event led most directly to the situation referred to in the cartoon?
   1. signing of the Camp David accords
   2. sending of Russian troops to Afghanistan
   3. ending of the Cold War
   4. decision of the United Nations to send troops to Kuwait

   ---

33. As the peace process continues in the Middle East, a major stumbling block to settlement of the Arab-Israeli conflict is the question of
   1. ownership and operation of the Suez Canal
   2. control of the Arabian Peninsula
   3. representation of Palestinian Arabs and Israelis in the United Nations
   4. land and civil rights for Palestinian Arabs and Israelis in the United Nations

34. The Middle Eastern leaders Kemal Atatürk, David Ben-Gurion, and Yasir Arafat are best known for their support of
   1. nationalism   3. colonialism
   2. fascism   4. Communism

35. A topographical map would most likely be used to
   1. identify the major agricultural products of Egypt
   2. determine the population of Beijing, China
   3. estimate the elevation of Bangkok, Thailand
   4. count the number of provinces in India

Base your answer to questions 36 and 37 on the maps below and on your knowledge of social studies.

Distorted World Maps

Oil Reserves
This map represents nations in terms of total oil now known to be available to meet future energy needs.

Oil Consumption
This map shows nations scaled in proportion to their consumption of oil.

36. A comparison of these maps shows that oil reserves are roughly equal to oil consumption in
    1. Japan
    2. Eastern Europe
    3. China
    4. the former USSR

37. Which of these nations would mostly likely achieve the greatest benefit from the development of an efficient alternative energy source?
   1. Japan
   2. Kuwait
   3. Libya
   4. China

Base your answer to questions 38 and 39 on the illustration below and on your knowledge of social studies.

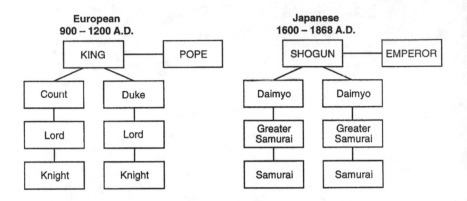

38. Which political system is associated with the social stratification system shown in the illustration?
   1. fascism
   2. feudalism
   3. Communism
   4. socialism

39. In both Europe and Japan, the major reason for the development of the political system shown in the illustration was to
   1. eliminate the need for a legal system
   2. increase trade and manufacturing in the region
   3. consolidate the political power of religious leaders
   4. provide order during a period of weak central governments

40. The ancient Chinese expression "Middle Kingdom" and the European terms "Near East " and "Far East" best reflect
    1. the impact of the enlightenment on global thinking
    2. an improved knowledge of world geography
    3. an objective view of the world's cultures
    4. the influence of ethnocentrism on geographic perspective

41. Economic development in Japan after War II and in Communist China since the 1980s is similar in that both nations have sought to
    1. end foreign investment
    2. develop their vast natural resources to achieve economic growth
    3. utilize the concepts of capitalism to improve their economies
    4. nationalize most major industries and restrict competition

Base your answers to questions 42 and 43 on the passage below and on your knowledge of social studies.

> "From as early as I can remember, the Emperor was an important presence even in our remote home. He was a descendant of the gods from thousands of years before, never to be looked at or listened to by mere mortals, a presence to be revered and protected and obeyed . . . Finally . . . my family and neighbors gathered were heard, saying he was only human after all. Everyone was crying, I was sad and confused. . . "

42. Which event caused the Emperor to announce that he was "only human after all?
    1. his overthrow by communist forces
    2. defeat of the Japanese in World War II
    3. signing of the Versailles Treaty
    4. conclusion of the Russo–Japanese War

43. The attitude toward the Emperor in this passage were based on traditions of
    1. Shintoism   3. Islam
    2. Christianity   4. Judaism

44. Since the late 1940s India, Northern Ireland, and Israel have faced the common problem of
    1. adjusting to a post-Communist political and economic system
    2. continued violent confrontations between different religious groups
    3. economic depression as a result of rapid industrialization
    4. uncertainty of their acceptance by the European Community

Base your answer to question 45 on the graph below and on your knowledge of social studies.

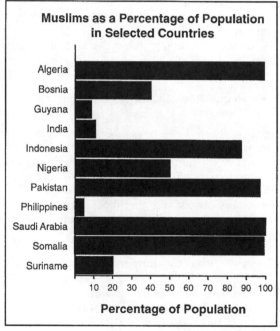

Source: *World Almanac and Book of Facts*, 1995

45. Based on this graph, which statement is a valid conclusion?
    1. Most of the world's Muslims live in Saudi Arabia.
    2. Pakistan is a nation with much religious diversity.
    3. Islam was recently introduced in Indonesia.
    4. Islam is a religion practiced throughout the world.

46. A study of the policy of "ethnic cleansing" in Bosnia and the Holocaust in Europe would suggest that
   1. world opinion is effective in stopping genocide
   2. countries generally use reason and negotiation in dealing with important ethnic issues
   3. anti-Semitism and ethnic hatred remain powerful forces in the 20th century
   4. military leaders cannot be held for acts committed during wartime

Base your answers to questions 47 and 48 on the graphs below and on your knowledge of social studies.

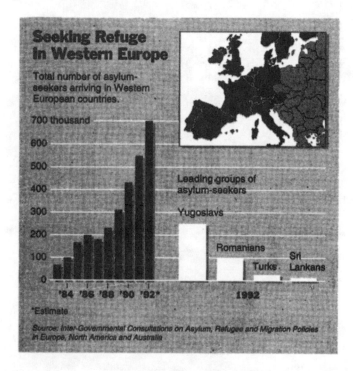

47. The number of people seeking refuge in Western Europe increased by nearly 400,000 between
   1. 1989 and 1992   3. 1986 and 1992
   2. 1984 and 1989   4. 1988 and 1991

48. In 1992, the largest number of people seeking asylum were from
   1. the Middle East   3. Latin America
   2. Asia   4. Eastern Europe

EXAM ONE ANSWER KEY

1.	3	21.	3	41.	3
2.	2	22.	2	42.	2
3.	2	23.	4	43.	1
4.	4	24.	4	44.	2
5.	3	25.	1	45.	4
6.	3	26.	3	46.	3
7.	1	27.	1	47.	1
8.	2	28.	3	48.	4
9.	4	29.	4		
10.	1	30.	2		
11.	3	31.	2		
12.	4	32.	3		
13.	2	33.	4		
14.	3	34.	1		
15.	2	35.	3		
16.	3	36.	4		
17.	4	37.	1		
18.	3	38.	2		
19.	1	39.	4		
20.	1	40.	4		

PRACTICE EXAM TWO

Part I (55 credits): Answer all 48 questions in this part.

Directions (1–48): For each statement or question, write on the separate answer sheet the *number* of the word or expression that, of those given, best completes the statement or answers the question.

1. Social mobility would most likely occur in a society that has a
   1. slow rate of economic growth
   2. low per-capita income
   3. class structure
   4. variety of educational opportunities

2. Which factor is a common characteristic of a subsistence economy?
   1. a barely adequate supply of food
   2 a highly skilled labor force
   3. high levels of capital investment
   4 dependence on the export of goods

3. Which statement can best be supported by the existence of the African kingdom of Songhai, Mali, Kush, and Nubia?
   1. Natural geographic barriers prevented major cultural development in these civilizations.
   2. Africans established thriving civilizations long before European colonization.
   3. These societies were so involved with violent civil wars that there was little time for cultural development.
   4. These African civilizations were entirely self-sufficent and discouraged trade with other areas.

4. A major reason for the recent increase in African urbanization is the
   1. reemphasis on the extended family in many cities in the region
   2. increasing job opportunities in industrial centers
   3. increasing famine relief efforts of the United Nations
   4. growth of political unrest in rural areas

5. Africa's rivers are often of little help in transporting large quantities of goods and people because they
    1. flow toward the mountains
    2. run only north and south
    3. are not long enough
    4. have many falls and rapids

6. A lasting influence of British colonialism on India is most evident in India's
    1. commitment to parliamentary democracy
    2. continuation of the caste system
    3. development of a policy of nonalignment
    4. establishment of a command economy

7. "Your words are wise, Arjuna, but your sorrow is for nothing. The truly wise mourn neither for the living nor for the dead. There never was a time for kings. Nor is there any future in which we shall cease to be...."

    This passage best reflects a belief in
    1. ancestor worship
    2. the Eightfold Path
    3. reincarnation
    4. nirvana

8. In 1947, the subcontinent of India became independent and was divided into India and Pakistan. This division recognized the
    1. rivalries between religious groups
    2. strength of fascism in certain regions
    3. natural geographic boundaries of the region
    4. colonial boundaries established by the British

9. In the late 1980s and early 1990s, the improvement in the economies of most Pacific Rim countries could be attributed to
    1. greater industrialization
    2. a total reliance on cash crops
    3. continuing civil wars
    4. the oil crisis in the Middle East

10. What effect did the Opium War and the Treaty of Nanjing have on China?
    1. Chinese Nationalists increased their influence in rural areas.
    2. The Manchu government expelled the Western powers.
    3. China was divided into spheres of influence.
    4. China adopted a democratic system of government.

11. Which change occurred in China's economy in the 1980s and 1990s under the leadership of Deng Xiaoping?
    1. Economic policies were based on the ideas of the Cultural Revolution.
    2. Collectivization of agriculture was introduced into the economy.
    3. Foreign investment in the economy was encouraged.
    4. Privatization of industry was outlawed.

12. Which action by the Chinese Government since 1949 best reflects the influence of Confucianism?
    1. Dissidents have been allowed to critique the government.
    2. Education has been discouraged at all levels of society.
    3. Democratic policies have been encouraged.
    4. Respect for and allegiance to rulers has been promoted.

13. "...the Japanese people forever renounce war as a sovereign right of the nation and the threat or use of force as a means of settling international disputes...In order to accomplish the aim...land, sea, and air forces...will never be maintained."

    Which event is directly responsible for the inclusion of this statement in Japan's current Constitution?
    1. Japan's defeat in World War II
    2. Japan's involvement in the Persian Gulf War
    3. United Nations sanctions against Japan
    4. Japan's emergence as an economic superpower

Base your answer to question 14 on the diagram below and on your knowledge of social studies.

14. Merchants are shown at the bottom of this social pyramid of feudal Japan because they
    1. comprised the largest percentage of Japan's population at that time
    2. were viewed as having little status in the society
    3. were unable to read or write
    4. did not believe in the Shinto religion

_____

15. The tea ceremony, Kabuki theater, and writing haiku poetry remain important in Japan today. What do these activities suggest about Japanese culture?
    1. Western culture influence contemporary Japanese life.
    2. The ideas of Confucianism continue to dominate Japanese life.
    3. The Japanese continue to value traditional customs and practices.
    4. Social change remains a goal of Japanese society.

16. Which statement provides the best evidence that Spain was the dominant colonial power in Latin America?
    1. Spain and Mexico continue to use the same currency.
    2. Spain continues to provide military support for Latin America.
    3. Spanish is the principal language spoken in most of Latin America.
    4. Argentina elects representatives to the legislature of Spain.

Base your answer to question 17 on the graph below and on your knowledge of social studies.

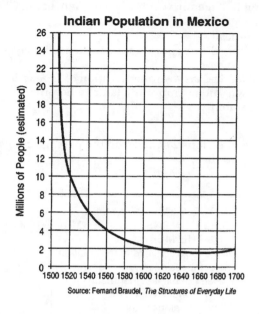

Indian Population in Mexico

Source: Fernand Braudel, *The Structures of Everyday Life*

17. Which statement can best be supported by the information provided by this graph?
    1. The Indian population in Mexico steadily increased between 1500 and 1700.
    2. The effects of the Spanish conquest on the Indian population in Mexico were most severe between 1500 and 1540.
    3. The Spanish conquest of Mexico improved the standard of living for the Indian population in Mexico.
    4. Spanish influence in Mexico had ended by 1700.

_____

18. For many Latin American nations, the reliance on single cash-crop economies has led to
    1. unstable economies as world market prices rise and fall
    2. long-term economic progress as exports continue to increase
    3. an increased standard of living for the majority of farmers
    4. increased agricultural surpluses as production of food exceeds demand.

19. Which conclusion about Latin America political history could be reached after a study of the rise to power of Juan Peron in Argentina and Augusto Pinochet in Chile?
   1. The strongest leaders are those who are elected democratically.
   2. Spain generally supported independence movements in Latin America.
   3. Latin America has a strong tradition of monarchy.
   4. People will often support dictators who promise to restore stability.

Base your answer to questions 20 and 21 on the passage below and on your knowledge of social studies.

> IN THE NAME OF ALLAH
> THE COMPASSIONATE
> THE MERCIFUL
> praise be to Allah, Lord of the creation
> the compassionate, the merciful,
> King of the last judgment!
> You alone we worship,
> and you alone pray for help.

20. People who accept the beliefs stated in this passage believe in
   1. polytheism   3. emperor worship
   2. monotheism   4. papal authority

21. In which book can this passage be found?
   1. Old Testament of the Bible
   2. Analects of Confucius
   3. Talmud
   4. Koran

22. Since 1948, the main disagreement between the Arabs and the Israelis has revolved around
   1. Israel's isolationist policies
   2. the interpretation of monotheism
   3. territorial claims
   4. The possession of oilfields

Base your answer to question 23 on the cartoon below and on your knowledge of social studies.

23. What is the main idea of this 1994 cartoon?
    1. Israelis have become poorer because of their struggle with the Palestinians.
    2. Various economic problems continue despite Palestinian autonomy in the Gaza region.
    3. Israel is willing to invest large amounts of money in the developing of Gaza.
    4. Peace has finally come to the Gaza region.

24. One similarity in the leadership of Mustafa Kemal Ataturk in Turkey and that of Shah Reza Pahlavi in Iran was that both leaders
    1. conquered neighboring countries
    2. began the process of westernization in their nations
    3. promoted traditional Islamic practices
    4. supported the establishment of community

25. The issues of the sale of indulgences and of the worldly lives of the clergy were addressed by
    1. Adam Smith in *The Wealth of Nations*
    2. John Locke in his treatises on government
    3. Martin Luther in his ninety-five theses
    4. Karl Marx in *The Communist Manifesto*

26. The Renaissance, the French Revolution, and the European Industrial Revolution have all contributed to the development of
    1. utopian societies
    2. a powerful Roman Catholic Church
    3. divine right monarchies
    4. a growing and influential middle class

27. "Kings sit upon God's throne and rule according to God's law."
    1. oligarchy   3. democracy
    2. absolutism   4. glasnost

28. Which statement best describes a major reason that the Industrial Revolution began in Great Britain?
    1. Sufficient coal and iron ore reserve and a good transportation system were available.
    2. Industries were owned by the national government.
    3. A strong union movement was able to secure good working conditions and high wages for factory workers.
    4. Cities could easily accommodate the migration of people from rural to urban areas.

29. Which factor contributed most to the rise of totalitarian governments in Europe before World War II?
    1. improved educational systems
    2. expanding democratic reforms
    3. increasing political stability
    4. worsening economic conditions

30. Which term is used to identify the Soviet programs that established production goals for agriculture and industry under the leadership of Joseph Stalin?
    1. Great Leap Forward   3. five-year plans
    2. Four Modernizations   4. perestroika

31. The 1956 invasion of Hungary and the 1968 invasion of Czechoslovakia by the Soviet Union were attempts to
    1. keep Communist governments in power in Eastern Europe
    2. decrease Cold War tensions between Eastern Europe and the United states
    3. prevent German militarism from spreading throughout Europe
    4. provide humanitarian aid to the ethnic minorities of these nations

32. Which concept is best illustrated by the formation of new nations from the areas of the former Soviet Union?
    1. self-determination
    3. imperialism
    2. nonalignment
    4. utopianism

33. In the early 1990s, Czechoslovakia drew the attention of the world when it
    1. expanded its territory south into Bosnia Herzegovina
    2. divided into two independent nations in a peaceful manner
    3. became the first nation to rejoin the Warsaw Pact
    4. resisted a United Nations invasion of Slovakia

Base your answer to question 34 on the cartoon below and on your knowledge of social studies.

34. This 1992 cartoon refers to Russia's
    1. constant fear of invasion from the West
    2. tendency to establish totalitarian rule during a crisis
    3. attempts to settle foreign policy disputes
    4. current difficulty in establishing economic reforms

35. "Let me say that our system of government does not copy the institutions of our neighbors. It is more the case of our being a model to others than of our imitating anyone else. Our constitution is called a democracy because power is in the hands, not of a minority, but of the whole people."

   Which early society is most likely described in this quotation?

   1. Spartan
   2. Babylonian
   3. Athenian
   4. Egyptian

Base your answer to question 36 on the cartoon below and on your knowledge of social studies.

36. The cartoonist is suggesting that forgetting the past has resulted in

   1. tragic consequences for Bosnia's people
   2. an effective solution for Bosnia's problems
   3. independence for Bosnia
   4. fewer Bosnian problems in the 1990s than in previous decades

37. "The relationship between demographic growth and environmental degradation has been clearly established, but reducing birthrates will not, by itself, solve the planet's environmental and human problems. Equally important is lowering consumption rates in industrial countries."

—Alan Durning

Which statement best reflects the meaning of the passage?
1. Industrial societies and developing nations experience different problems.
2. Lifestyles in many nations are depleting the Earth's resources.
3. Technology alone can solve the worlds environmental problems.
4. Consumption rates have little relationship to environmental problems.

38. A major goal of the Green Revolution was to
1. limit environmental pollution
2. prevent global warfare
3. increase agricultural production
4. decrease population growth

39. As global interdependence spreads, it increases the need for
1. trade restrictions between nations
2. the resumption of colonialism
3. economic cooperation between nations
4. a self-sufficient national economy

40. Which environmental problem affects large areas in both the Amazon Basin and Central Africa?
1. deforestation   3. acid rain
2. nuclear waste   4. air pollution

Base your answer to question 41 on the graph below and on your knowledge of social studies.

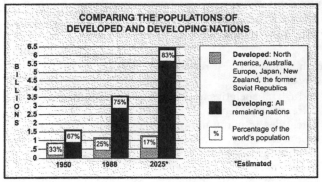

Source: UNESCO

41. Which statement is best supported by the information in the chart?
    1. The population of Kenya is greater than the population of Japan.
    2. The population in developing nations is expected to double by 2025.
    3. The population in developing nations is increasing faster than it is in developed nations.
    4. The percentage of the world's population living in developed nations is increasing.

---

42. **"Asian Tiger Habitat Diminishing by 50%"**
    "Oil Spill Threatens Ecology of the North Sea"
    "Overcropping Limits Agricultural Production in Sudan"

    These three newspaper headlines are most directly concerned with the
    1. lack of pollution controls around the world
    2. effect of humans on the environment
    3. role of science in limiting environmental problems
    4. need for fewer government regulations

43. One similarity in the unification of Italy, the Arab–Israeli conflict, and the breakup of Yugoslavia is that all were fueled by
    1. imperialism   3. Marxism
    2. terrorism   4. nationalism

44. Which factor explains the difficulty of achieving political stability in many of the nations of Southeast Asia?
    1. degree of cultural diversity
    2. rapid economic growth
    3. lack of natural resources
    4. geographic location

45. The divine right theory believed in by several European monarchs is most similar to the concept of
    1. the Mandate of Heaven in imperial China
    2. humanism during the Enlightenment
    3. civil disobedience promoted by Mohandas Gandhi
    4. the White Man's Burden

Base your answer to question 46 on the cartoon below and on your knowledge of social studies.

46. The main idea of this 1992 cartoon is that
    1. communism continues to threaten Western democratic nations
    2. communism is losing its influence throughout the world
    3. communist governments succeed best in nations with high standards of living
    4. most nations in Asia still follow the ideas of Marx and Lenin

47. Which factor has been most important in discouraging economic investment in many Latin American and African nations?
    1. abundance of natural resources
    2. historic dependence on Europe
    3. stable birthrates
    4. political unrest

48. The dominance of Christianity in Latin America and of Buddhism in Southeast Asia is a direct result of
    1. racial intolerance   3. urbanization
    2. cultural diffusion   4. militarism

EXAM TWO ANSWER KEY

1.	4	21.	4	41.	1
2.	1	22.	3	42.	2
3.	2	23.	2	43.	4
4.	2	24.	2	44.	1
5.	4	25.	3	45.	1
6.	1	26.	4	46.	2
7.	3	27.	2	47.	4
8.	1	28.	1	48.	2
9.	1	29.	4		
10.	3	30.	3		
11.	3	31.	1		
12.	4	32.	1		
13.	1	33.	2		
14.	2	34.	4		
15.	3	35.	3		
16.	3	36.	1		
17.	2	37.	2		
18.	1	38.	3		
19.	4	39.	3		
20.	2	40.	1		

Index

Dutch East Indies Company   10

E

Edict of Milan   117, 141
Edict of Nantes   164
Eisenhower, Dwight   217
El Greco   155
El Salvador   97
Emperor Constantine   117
Emperor Hirohito   72
Enclosure Acts   172
Encomienda System   87
Endara, Guillermo   99
Engels, Friedrich   174
England   161
English Bill of Rights   163, 167
Enlai, Zhou   58
Epicurus   147
Eratosthenes   147
Ershad, Hussein Mohammed   37
Ethiopia   18
Euclid   146, 147
European Economic Community
      (EEC)   16, 189
European Parliament   190
European Recovery Act   185
European Union   190

F

Factory Act   172
Faraday, Michael   172
Father Jean-Bertrand   99
Federation of Central America   90
Feudalism   67, 151
Fillmore, Millard   69
Five Pillars   113
Five-year Plan   56
Five-Year Plans   212
Four Noble Truths   28
four tigers   41, 60, 63
Fourier, Charles   173
Fourteen Points   177
France   164
Franco, Francisco   188
Franco, Hamar   98
Franco-Prussian War   170
French and Indian War   159
French East India Company   10

French Revolution   167
French-Indochina   187
Fulton, Robert   172

G

Galileo, Galilei   156
Galtieri, General   95
Gandhi   34, 36
Gandhi, Indira   35
Gandhi, Rajiv   35
Gang of Four   58
Gantama, Siddhartha   28
Garibaldi, Giuseppe   170
Gaza Strip   125, 126, 127
George, David Lloyd   177
Ghana   9
Glasnost   219
Glorious Revolution   163
Gobi Desert   45
Godzilla   66
Golan Heights   126
Golden Age of Greece   145
Golden Age of Islam   120, 154
Good Neighbor Policy   93
Gorbachev   56, 219
Government of India Act   33
Great Leap Forward   57
Great Rift Valley   5
Greater East Asia Co-Prosperity
      Sphere   71
Green Revolution   35, 234
Greenhouse Effect   232
Guatemala   98
Guerero, Vincente   90
guilds   153
Gulf of Tonkin Resolution   39
Gupta Empire   31
Gutenberg, Johannes   155

H

Haiti   89
Hapsburgs   207
Harappan civilization   30
Harvey   156
Havel, Vaclav   224
Hay-Bunau-Varilla Treaty   93
Helsinki Accords of 1975   218
Henrique Cardoso, Fernando   98

Locke, John 164
Long March 54
Long Parliament 163
Lopez, Antonio 91
Lorenzo de' Medici 154
Louis XI 164
Louis XIII 164
Louis XIV 164
Louis XVI 165, 167
L'Ouverture, Toussaint 89
Loyola, Ignatius 158
Luther, Martin 156

M

Maastricht Treaty 190
MacArthur, Douglas 72
Machiavelli, Niccolo 155
Magellan, Ferdinand 159
Magna Carta 162
Magyars 150
Major, John 188, 190
Mandate of Heaven 50
Mandela, Nelson 14
manorialism 151
Mansei Uprising 61
Mansur 120
Marat, Jean 167
March Revolution 208
Marco Polo 154, 158
Marcos, Ferdinand 40
market economy 173
Marshall, George C. 185
Marshall Plan 185
Marx, Karl 174, 209
Marxism 174
Maurya Empire 30
Mayans 84
Mazzini, Guiseppe 170
Meiji Restoration 69
Menachem Begin 126
Menem, Carlos 95
mercantilism 10, 32, 160
mercantilist system 87
Methodius 202
Michelangelo 155
Middle Ages 142, 150
Mines Act 172
Minh, Ho Chi 38
Mobutu, Joseph 17

Mongols 202
Mongul Empire 31
monsoons 25, 45, 64
Montagu-Chelmsford Reforms 33
Morelos, Jose 89
Mubarak, Hosni 126
Muhammad 113, 118
Munich Pact 182
Muscovy 203
Muslim League 33
Mussolini, Benito 181
Muswiyah 119

N

Nagasaki 72, 183
Napoleonic Code 168
Nasser, Gamel Abdel 125, 134
nation-states 154, 161
National Congress 33
NATO 186
Nazi 179
Nazi-Soviet Nonaggression 182
Nazi-Soviet Nonaggression Pact 213
Nehru 34, 36
neocolonialism 14
New Economic Policy (NEP) 210
Newton 156
Nicaragua 96
Nicholas I 205
Nicholas II 206
Nigeria 13
Nile River 108
Ninety-Five Theses 156
Nixon, Richard 59, 93
NKrumah, Kwame 12
nomads 4, 110
nonalignment 17, 41
Noriega, Manuel 99
North American Free Trade Agreement
   (NAFTA) 94
North Atlantic Treaty
   Organization 186
North Atlantic Treaty Organization
   (NATO) 215
North Korea 62
November Revolution 209
Nuremberg Laws of 1935 181
Nuremberg War Crimes Trials 183
Nyerere, Julius K. 12, 15

O

Octavian 148
O'Higgins, Bernardo 89
oil politics 126, 134
Olmec 84
OPEC 133
Opium War 52
Organization of African Unity 12
Organization of American States 100
Organization of Petroleum 133
Organization of Petroleum Exporting
    Countries (OPEC) 16
Orlando, Vittorio 177
Ortega, Daniel 97
Ostrogoths 149
Ottoman Empire 121
Ottoman Turks 207
Owen, Robert 173

P

P.V. 35
Pahlevi, Muhammad Riza 130
Paine, Thomas 164
Palestine 117
Palestine Liberation Organization
    (PLO) 126
Pan-Africanism 12
Paris Peace Treaty 39
Parliament 162
Pasternak, Boris 200
Pax Romana 148
Pearl Harbor 71, 183
Pedro I 90
Peloponnesian Wars 146
Perestroika 220
Peron, Juan 95
Persian Gulf 109, 129
Persian Gulf War 131
Persian Wars 145
Peter I 204
Peter III 204
Peter the Great 198
Petrarch, Francesco 155
Picasso, Pablo 144
Pinochet, Augusto 99
Plato 146
Platt Amendment 92

pogroms 124, 207
Pol Pot 39
Politburo 212
Pope Urban II 153
Prague Spring 217
Prince Henry the Navigator 159
Prince Klemens 169
Prince Vladimir 198
Protestant Reformation 156
Punic Wars 147
Puritan Revolution 163
Pushkin, Alexander 200
Pythagoras 146

Q

Qaddafi, Muammar 132
Qing, Jiang 58
Queen Elizabeth 158
Queen Elizabeth I 162
Queen Isabella 159

R

Rabin, Yitzhak
Rachmaninov, Sergei 200
Rahman, Sheik Mujibur 37
Ramo, Fidel V. 40
Rasputin, Grigory Efimovich 208
Reagan, Ronald 131, 218
Reform Bill of 1832 173
Rembrandt 155
Renaissance 142, 154
Revolution of 1905 206
Reynolds, Albert 188
Richelieu 164
Rimsky-Korsakov, Nikolai 200
Robespierre, Maximilien 167
Romanov, Michael 204
Rome 147
Roosevelt, Franklin 12
Rouge Khmer 39
Rousseau, Jean Jacques 166
Russian Revolution 177
Russo-Japanese War 61, 70, 206
Rwanda 19

S

Sahara 4, 107
Sahel 4

ABOUT THE AUTHOR

Karen Lurie was educated by the state of New York. She is a professional writer who has worked in the field of education for over nine years. She lives in New York City.

NOTES:

NOTES:

NOTES:

NOTES:

FIND US...

International

Hong Kong
4/F Sun Hung Kai Centre
30 Harbour Road, Wan Chai,
Hong Kong
Tel: (011)85-2-517-3016

Japan
Fuji Building 40, 15-14
Sakuragaokacho, Shibuya Ku,
Tokyo 150, Japan
Tel: (011)81-3-3463-1343

Korea
Tae Young Bldg, 944-24,
Daechi- Dong, Kangnam-Ku
The Princeton Review- ANC
Seoul, Korea 135-280,
South Korea
Tel: (011)82-2-554-7763

Mexico City
PR Mex S De RL De Cv
Guanajuato 228 Col. Roma
06700 Mexico D.F., Mexico
Tel: 525-564-9468

Montreal
666 Sherbrooke St.
West, Suite 202
Montreal, QC H3A 1E7 Canada
Tel: (514) 499-0870

Pakistan
1 Bawa Park - 90 Upper Mall
Lahore, Pakistan
Tel: (011)92-42-571-2315

Spain
Pza. Castilla, 3 - 5° A, 28046
Madrid, Spain
Tel: (011)341-323-4212

Taiwan
155 Chung Hsiao East Road
Section 4 - 4th Floor,
Taipei R.O.C., Taiwan
Tel: (011)886-2-751-1243

Thailand
Building One, 99 Wireless Road
Bangkok, Thailand 10330
Tel: (662) 256-7080

Toronto
1240 Bay Street, Suite 300
Toronto M5R 2A7 Canada
Tel: (800) 495-7737
Tel: (716) 839-4391

Vancouver
4212 University Way NE,
Suite 204
Seattle, WA 98105
Tel: (206) 548-1100

National (U.S.)

We have over 60 offices around the U.S. and
run courses in over 400 sites. For courses and locations
within the U.S. call 1 (800) 2/Review and you will be
routed to the nearest office.

Free!

Did you know that The Microsoft Network gives you one free month?

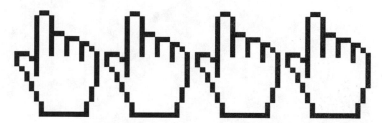

Call us at 1-800-FREE MSN. We'll send you a free CD to get you going.

Then, you can explore the World Wide Web for one month, free. Exchange e-mail with your family and friends. Play games, book airline tickets, handle finances, go car shopping, explore old hobbies and discover new ones. There's one big, useful online world out there. And for one month, it's a free world.

Call **1-800-FREE MSN,** Dept. 3197, for offer details or visit us at **www.msn.com**. Some restrictions apply.

Microsoft Where do you want to go today?® The Microsoft Network